MEDIEVAL
LITERATURE

Also by David Aers:

Chaucer, Harvester Press, 1986

MEDIEVAL LITERATURE
CRITICISM, IDEOLOGY & HISTORY

edited by
DAVID AERS

Reader in English Literature
University of East Anglia

THE HARVESTER PRESS

First published in Great Britain in 1986 by
HARVESTER PRESS LIMITED
Publisher: John Spiers
16 Ship Street, Brighton, Sussex

© David Aers, 1986

British Library Cataloguing in Publication Data

Medieval literature.
  1. English literature—Middle English,
  1100-1500—History and criticism
  I. Aers, David
  820.9′001   PR281

ISBN 0-7108-1021-0

Typeset in 11 on 12 point Garamond by Witwell Ltd, Liverpool
Printed and bound in Great Britain at
The Camelot Press Ltd, Southampton

THE HARVESTER PRESS GROUP
The Harvester Group comprises Harvester Press Ltd (chiefly publishing
literature, fiction, philosophy, psychology, and science and trade books);
Harvester Press Microform Publications Ltd (publishing in microform
previously unpublished archives, scarce printed sources, and indexes to
these collections); Wheatsheaf Books Ltd (chiefly publishing in economics,
international politics, sociology, women's studies and related social
sciences); Certain Records Ltd and John Spiers Music Ltd (music
publishing).

Contents

The Contributors

David Aers is a Reader in English Literature at the University of East Anglia.

Toril Moi is Director of the Centre for Feminist Research in the Humanities, University of Bergen, Norway.

Sarah Beckwith is a Lecturer in English Studies at the University of East Anglia.

Anthony Gash is a Lecturer in English Studies at the University of East Anglia.

Stephen Knight is a Reader in English Literature at the University of Sydney.

Derek Pearsall is a Professor of English Literature at Harvard University.

Judith Ferster is an Associate Professor of English Literature at North Carolina State University.

Jon Cook is a Lecturer in English Studies at the University of East Anglia.

Bernard Sharrett is a Reader in English and American Studies at the University of Kent.

1

Introduction

David Aers

This collection of essays addresses a variety of medieval works, some much debated topics, such as courtly love, and some fundamental issues in reading medieval people's writings. The authors are concerned, in different ways, with the intimate relations between (mainly) late medieval texts, a heterogeneous culture and an increasingly diversified society, one marked in fourteenth-century Europe by sustained social struggles which moved into open violence with astonishing frequency.[1] They study how medieval texts mediate the world which both produced them and which they helped to produce; how conflicts and problems are figured forth, worked over. Often they return to consider the modes in which the generation of meaning is bound up with the material and ideological structures of power, control and resistance.

They acknowledge that the present readings of texts and history, like all others, are conditioned by specific social and institutional circumstances, as they are by the readers' preoccupations, critical theory and overall ideology. As Hans Jauss warns, weaving in a quotation from his former teacher, Hans-Georg Gadamer:

> Whoever believes that the 'timelessly true' meaning of a literary work must immediately, and simply through one's mere absorption in the text, disclose itself to the interpreter as if he had a standpoint outside of history and beyond all 'errors' of his predecessors and of the historical reception—whoever believes this 'conceals the involvement of the historical consciousness itself in the history of influence.' He denies 'those presuppositions—certainly not arbitrary but rather fundamental—that govern his own understanding', and can only feign an objectivity... (Jauss, 1982, p. 29)

Throughout this volume we have been especially interested in the particular theoretical and politcal 'presuppositions'—including those concerning the politics of gender and sexuality—informing all texts, whether past or present. Texts written by scholars and critics too. Indeed, we hope to encourage discussion about the choices everyone makes in doing criticism, in interpreting what they read. If we fail to recognise such choices it is because they have simply been made for us—behind our backs, as it were—by the dominant paradigms within the communities where we are taught to read and write 'competent' essays. The will to gain historical knowledge of the text in its otherness, in its own moment of production, needs to be combined with an active consciousness of our own rootedness in a present which shapes our 'presuppositions—certainly not arbitrary but rather fundamental'. To acknowledge this is to acknowledge severe problems. But these are simply unavoidable, and they are best confronted openly. As Frank Lentricchia observed during his recent exposition and evaluation of critical theory in the USA, 'a perfectly objective interpretation is possible only if the interpreter is a transcendental being—that is, if he is not human': humans have to undertake the rigours of historical self-examination with 'a situated human consciousness that has spatiotemporal location, idiosyncratic colorations, and philosophical prejudices' (Lentricchia, 1980, p. 207).

And so it is unavoidable that our 'situated' criticism, our teaching, is inextricably bound up with current attempts to preserve our society in its present form, with its legitimating ideologies, organisations of power and distribution of resources; or it is bound up with efforts to change it. Our cultural activity as teachers and intellectuals cannot be without political dimensions. In *Criticism and Social Change*, Frank Lentricchia expresses and elaborates this view:

> Neither the literary object nor its receiver exists in that transhistorical community that putatively defines Western civilization (a 'general nature' that demands 'general readers'). The contemporaneity of the tradition-receiver must be viewed, rather, as the vital site of tradition-making, a ground on which the so-called ideal object is not only received but reconstituted in an active reception which *makes* relevant, *makes* contemporary…. The contemporaneity of the tradition-maker, in the most active sense of 'maker', is the site of historical struggle; active reception is the site… where, for better or for worse, the cultural

future is decided, where differences (and not only linguistic ones) are made. The purpose of the traditionalists account of tradition, however, is to promote its own inevitability, by covering up the struggle. (Lentricchia, 1984, p. 141)

Because it is normally helpful to have concrete examples of what is being described rather generally, it seemed worth completing this introduction with one of these. Hardly momentous, but immediately relevant, it is taken from the production of this book and illustrates some of the critical issues just outlined.

When the publisher's editors received the almost complete collection of essays they had commissioned, they sent it to a university teacher of English Literature to act as 'reader'. Such readers remain anonymous, doubtless to enhance the appearance of impersonality, of 'objectivism', of authority. That they are customarily described as 'readers' is not without interest; here those 'reading' are paid by the publisher to act as examiners and judges of the manuscript. The publisher uses their evaluations in deciding whether the manuscript will receive a voice in the public domain, or whether it will be consigned to silence, at once. So here (as in teaching and examining), 'reading' involves power, an act in decisions about cultural production, an expression of the political work of culture-making. Of course, as with even the most powerful people, these readers' social power is related to their position in the relations of production, the economic structure of society. They do not control the means of production: their employers, the publishers, do that. And because publishers' existence in a capitalist society depends on the production of *commodities* for exchange-value on the market, their goals are not identical with those of the academic readers they employ. So in certain cases they will overrule the views of those they pay. Nevertheless, the chief *market* for academic books is the community in which their readers are examiners, the people who design students' courses, who recommend, or choose not to recommend, books to students and librarians. For this reason, publishers tend to take readers' advice seriously: hence the readers' real, though circumscribed, power.

Let us now turn to the first reader of the manuscript that became this book. Because the report is uninformed by any evidence of the slightest knowledge of feminist critical theory or preoccupations its author receives the male pronoun, which seems at least symbolically appropriate. Nowhere in the report does the reader acknowledge that he has *any* ideological presuppositions whatsoever. Nor does he acknowledge that his critical practice is shaped by a particular theoretical framework. Not surprisingly then, there is no hint that his theory and practice might be the occasion for political work that not all would wish to join him in. Yet his reading is part of a quite easily identifiable ideological tradition, one that is loaded with 'presuppositions' about correct politics, morality and cultural work. In the first paragraph of his reading, for instance, he observes that this volume, one that 'does not feel very unified' (why should it be very unified?), 'bears out Eliot's dictum that the only thing for the critic is to be very intelligent'. This seems a neutral enough banality. After all, whoever would recommend that a critic should be un-'intelligent'— or anyone else for that matter. But then why introduce such an uncontentious truism under the sign of Eliot? The answer is probably the following: the concept of intelligence is neither simple, obvious nor unproblematic. On the contrary, it is a concept which as *used* in our culture has long been, like the word 'reason', loaded with unexamined and unacknowledged ideological and social dimensions. Indeed, it has often served to claim universal validity for positions, for modes of thinking, talking and writing which represent class interests in a specific social order.

A fairly recent example of this emerged in the debates around the placing of children into a 'higher' or 'lower' type of school (funded with very different resources and ideologies), allegedly according to the objective criterion of 'intelligence', measured in tests designed by the state's intellectuals when the children reached the age of eleven. Under careful scrutiny, it became clear that what was being identified was not some quintessential 'intelligence' but a particular set of linguistic and perceptual features which were characteristic of white middle-class culture and interests. The test of 'intelligence', legitimising (in conservative people's eyes) the separation of the population into higher schools (about 20 per cent) and lower (the rest) was simply part of the maintenance of the existing class structure under the guise of 'objective' and meritocratic selection. (Ramin, 1974).

The reader's rather reverential appeal to Eliot suggests his suspicion that he needs more than argument to sustain his position: he needs *authority*. But Eliot's name will only sound authoritative to those with a particular set of ideological presuppositions. This is not the place to rehearse Eliot's (hardly consistent) cultural views: readily accessible in *After Strange Gods* and *Christianity and Culture* (including 'Notes towards the definition of culture') their composition and their reception in the Anglo-American critical community has been recently described by Christopher Baldick in *The Social Mission of English Criticism* (see too, Lentricchia, 1984, pp. 127–32; Craig, 1973, Chapter 9; and Eagleton, 1983, pp. 39–42). Here it must suffice to recall that the Eliotic 'intelligence' our reader invokes converged with the politics of the Right, indeed the far Right—a denial of the politics of culture while practising a thoroughly political and material culturalism (one also pervaded by sexism). Why should the reader simply *assume* that all critics should write under the sign of such a guru? The answer, of course, lies in his failure to unpack his own ideological stance, and the existence of a community where such views are held by enough teachers for them to seem 'natural', free from 'ideology': views that could, by definition, only be contested by unnatural or at least distinctively *un*-'intelligent' people.

The reader does, however, gloss Eliot briefly: 'I think he meant that the good critic will always be aware of context, implications, etc., and the bad critic, no matter how noble his motives, will always be narrowed and blinkered.' This is hardly contentious, but pretty tame stuff when set against the master's voice in, say, *After Strange Gods*: and it leaves a great deal to 'etc.'. A psychoanalytic and feminist critic would specify that 'etc.' on very different and antagonistic lines from those chosen by a conservative critic (whether a medievalist or not); so would a 'poststructuralist' critic; so would... one could go on. But then a conservative 'Leavisite' critic would proceed very differently from a conservative structuralist, or Jungian critic. And each might find the other as 'narrowed and blinkered' as some find Eliot. The reader's gloss turns out to be vapid. But that does not mean it is without rhetorical effect. It assures the publisher that critical sheep and goats can be easily separated by this judge: 'the good' and 'the bad' stand disclosed and the publisher only has to execute the judge's verdict... on the manuscript. And a judgement that will have been charged with contestable political, religious, sexual and critical pre-suppositions will have been presented as unproblematically objective, impersonal, value-free, a-politcal. What could the critical goats do in the face of this but respond like Angelo before the Duke:

> 'I perceive your Grace, like power divine,
> Hath look'd upon my passes. Then good prince,
> No longer session hold upon my shames
> But let my trial be mine own confession'
> *(Measure for Measure*, V.1)

In fact these critical goats were called before other readers from the academic community because the publisher's editor had noticed one of the factors the first reader overlooked. She understood that he *did* have undeclared presuppositions, that they were in fact deeply conservative and that the potential readership (market) for such a collection was not as homogeneously conservative as the reader's rhetoric assumed. She knew that as Jonathan Dollimore and Alan Sinfield recently wrote, the 'break-up of consensus in British political life during the 1970s was accompanied by the break-up of traditional assumptions about the values and goals of literary criticism' (Dollimore and Sinfield, 1985, p. vii). For many teachers and students the invocation of Eliotic 'intelligence', politics and cultural choices has little to commend it. So she hired a second reader. This one wrote a report which began with a statement about its own theoretical grounds. There was no attempt to posture as a transcendental intelligence and the judgements the same essays elicited were often hilariously different. Two essays the first reader selected as especially bad, 'very bad'. One, in magisterial idiom, he judged as 'very boring, and wrong both in detail and overall': indeed, it 'leaves us [sic!] with ashes in our mouth'. Having said that, he found it unnecessary to offer any specific criticism. Of course, while he might have been just ignorant concerning the texts and topics addressed by the essay in question, his failure is more likely to be the consequence of animosity towards the writer's critical paradigms. If one is unwilling to acknowledge that one works within a paradigm (entailing, as all paradigms do, blindness as well as insight), one cannot engage in debate at that level; yet specification of detail will also seem rather irrelevant, 'very boring', when one simply wants to silence the speaker! The second reader, however, responded with some detailed criticism of textual and historical inter-pretation, of some signs of 'cultural imperialism', of what s/he took to be some local incoherences in the arguments: this response was framed by the following comment: 'Very interesting and often inspiring; I like it very much'. A judgement more antithetical to the first reader's is hard to imagine. Yet both readers are employed within the institutions of higher education, both officially deemed to be 'intelligent'. The decisive difference in their reading is a consequence of different critical models carrying very different historical, political, sociological and ethical orientations. This would be no news to the second reader; the first would doubtless assert that his colleague was just another *un-*'intelligent', 'bad critic'.

Similar conflict was illustrated over another essay which the first reader judged a 'disaster', complaining that the critic was 'very angry and very sure that he is right' (unlike the reader). He also claimed that the author 'doesn't like most things about medieval culture and is therefore the last person to talk about it'. In fact, by 'culture' the reader seems to mean the *official* culture of the dominant clerical élite which, as conservatives often do, he mistakes for all 'culture'. Through this (ideologically-determined) mistake, the critic blots out heterogeneity and conflict in medieval society. While some version of this conservative view is frequently assumed in medieval criticism its statement here is exceptionally bizarre, for it would mean, for instance, that only those who 'like most things' about the Nazi state and its culture should write about it. But the reader does not pursue such problems. Instead of substantiating his unequivocal judgement, he invokes V.A. Kolve's recent book on the *Canterbury Tales* as an example of what criticism *should* be. This act of uniformity is once again passed under the seal of Eliot: for Kolve is praised for 'picking up and expanding the insights of Eliot'—a view which does less than credit to Kolve. The second reader, however, judged this essay rather differently: 'Very nicely done: I liked this very much. Clear, cogent, and stimulating; I look forward to getting my students to read this.' (Well, the first reader's students won't find it on their reading lists!) Once more, it is clear that the difference in readers' reading and judgements is *inextricably* bound up with their ideological and political presuppositions.

To cut this story short, for its point has been made, the publisher's editor employed a third reader. This one wrote from a position marked by an acknowledgement and ironic tolerance of conflicting models, combined with a scrupulous attempt to summarise for the publisher the arguments of the essays. S/he concluded that the essays should be published, and observed:

> Traditional readers and reviewers will find plenty to raise their hackles and to disagree with, but they will not find much in the readings of the texts to scorn or patronize. The emphasis throughout on reading the text ... is vital, since those who do not want to change or examine their minds can always fortify themselves inside their prejudices if they find odd misreadings (there are such things) they can castigate.

This situates the collection of essays in a community of interpreters whose conflicting readings are grounded in presuppositions some teachers are reluctant even to examine. The publisher decided to follow the judgements of the second and third readers, while acknowledging that the conservative invoker of Eliot represented a powerful and vociferous bloc in our departments of English Literature and the reviewing organs they pump up. We hope that the volume as a whole will enhance students' enjoyment of late medieval literature, disclosing how, without cultural imperialism or avoidable anachronism, it can be related to issues that concern many readers today. We hope this has been done, and that while we have sought to encourage greater attention to the ideological framework of critical studies, we have appreciated the literary text's 'otherness', acknowledging, where this is appropriate, its excess of significance, its resistance to the interpreters' strategies, its ability to teach.

Notes

1. The evidence for this is now massive and still accumulating as more attention is paid to fourteenth-century culture and society: traditional myths and clichés about the Middle Ages as a period of harmonious order, unrecognisably and so relievingly different in this respect from our own conflict-riven era, can today only be asserted out of ignorance and rather desperate nostalgia.

   For an introduction to the society and culture of the later Middle Ages, see the works in the Bibliography below by Brenner, Dobson,

Hilton, Ladurie, Lambert, Leff, LeGoff, Lerner, Little, Miskimin, Postan, Thrupp, Toussaert and Tuck. Toussaert's fascinating and detailed work is especially worth drawing attention to since it seems rarely noticed today, but should be of immense importance to those interested in late medieval culture, especially the beliefs and practices of the majority of women and men who were not part of the tiny élite of male clerics producing the texts of 'official' ideology.

Bibliography

Baldick, C. (1983) *The Social Mission of English Criticism* (London: Oxford University Press).

Brenner, R. (1976) 'Agrarian Class Structure and Economic Development in Pre-industrial Europe', *Past and Present*, 70, 30–75.

Brenner, R. (1982) 'The Agrarian Roots of European Capitalism', *Past and Present*, 97, 16–113.

Craig, D. (1973) *The Real Foundations* (London: Chatto & Windus).

Dobson, R. B. (ed.) (1970) *The Peasants' Revolt* (London: Macmillan).

Dollimore, J. and Sinfield, A. (eds) (1985) *Political Shakespeare* (Manchester: Manchester University Press).

Eagleton, T. (1983) *Literary Theory* (Oxford: Basil Blackwell.)

Hilton, R. (1973) *Bond Men Made Free. Medieval Peasant Movements and the English Uprising of 1381* (London: Temple Smith).

Hilton, R. (1975) *The English Peasantry in the Later Middle Ages* (London: Oxford University Press).

Hilton, R. (1976) 'Feudalism and the Origins of Capitalism', *History Workshop*, 1, 9–25.

Hilton, R. (1982) 'Lords, Burgesses and Hucksters', *Past and Present*, 97, 3–15.

Jauss, H.R. (1982) *Towards an Aesthetic of Reception* (Brighton: Harvester).

Ladurie, E. Le Roy (1978) *Montaillou: Catholics and Cathars in a French Village* (London: Scholar Press).

Lambert, M. D. (1977) *Medieval Heresy* (London: Edward Arnold).

Leff, G. (1967) *Heresy in the Later Middle Ages*, 2 vols (Manchester: Manchester University Press)

Leff, G. (1976) *The Dissolution of the Medieval Outlook* (New York: Harper & Row).

LeGoff, J. (1980) *Time, Work and Culture in the Middle Ages* (Chicago: University of Chicago Press).

Lentricchia, F. (1983) *After the New Criticism*, (London: Methuen).

Lentricchia, F. (1984) *Criticism and Social Change* (Chicago: University of Chicago Press).

Lerner, R. E. (1968) *The Age of Adversity* (Ithaca, N.Y.: Cornell University Press).

Little, L. K. (1978) *Religious Poverty and the Profit Economy in Medieval Europe* (London: Elek).

Miskimin, H. A. (1969) *The Economy of Early Renaissance Europe* (Englewood Cliffs, N.J.: Prentice-Hall).

Postan, M. (1973) *Essays on Medieval Agriculture and General Problems of the Medieval Economy* (Cambridge: Cambridge University Press).

Thrupp, S. L. (1962) *The Merchant Class of Medieval London* (Michigan: Michigan University Press).

Toussaert, J. (1963) *Le Sentiment Religieux en Flandre à la fin du Moyen Age* (Paris: Plon).

Tuck, A. (1973) *Richard II and the English Nobility* (London: Edward Arnold).

2

Desire in Language: Andreas Capellanus and the Controversy of Courtly Love

Toril Moi

'Love is a thing of jealousy and dread.'

(*Troilus and Criseyde*, IV.235)

Composed in France in the 1180s, Andreas's treatise on love, the *De amore*,[1] is celebrated as the first comprehensive discussion of the theory of courtly love. Often hailed as the key to the understanding of a whole range of medieval texts on love from Chrétien de Troyes's *Lancelot* to Chaucer's *Troilus and Criseyde*, the *De amore* is situated at the centre of the modern debate on the nature of courtly love. Indeed, it would seem that much of this debate is little more than a conflict over the 'correct' interpretation of Andreas's text. The first part of this essay, 'Text and History: the Controversy of Courtly Love', relates the different readings of Andreas to the debate over the historical reality of the institution of courtly love in the Middle Ages, showing how this debate raises the wider question of the relations between texts and reality. Focusing on the interlocking structures of desire, knowledge and rhetoric, the second part, 'Love, Jealousy and Epistemology in the *De amore*', presents a new, feminist reading of Andreas's essay. Given the importance of the *De amore* for our understanding of the ideology of courtly love, a re-reading of Andreas would naturally lead to the reconsideration of a series of other medieval love-texts as well. Such a project, however, would far exceed the scope of a single paper, and the task of re-reading Chrétien or Chaucer will have to be left to others.

11

Text and History: the Controversy of Courtly Love

To English-speaking readers, C. S. Lewis's study, *The Allegory of Love*, is the book which first presented courtly love, defined as an idealisation of women in the name of romantic passion, as a fundamental aspect of medieval culture. Inspired by Gaston Paris's original essay on Chrétien's *Lancelot (Le Chevalier de la Charrette)* (Paris, 1883), Lewis gives a short and succinct summary of the main features of what he sees as a cult of love:

> Every one has heard of courtly love, and every one knows that it appears quite suddenly at the end of the eleventh century in Languedoc.... The sentiment, of course, is love, but love of a highly specialised sort, whose characteristics may be enumerated as Humility, Courtesy, Adultery, and the Religion of Love. The lover is always abject. Obedience to his lady's slightest wish, however whimsical, and silent acquiescence in her rebukes, however unjust, are the only virtues he dares to claim. There is a service of love closely modelled on the service which a feudal vassal owes to his lord. The lover is the lady's 'man'. ... The poet normally addresses another man's wife, and the situation is so carelessly accepted that he seldom concerns himself much with her husband: his real enemy is the rival. (Lewis, 1936, pp.2–3)

Perhaps even more influential than *The Allegory of Love*, Denis de Rougemont's *L'Amour et l'Occident* (1939: translated as *Passion and Society* or *Love in the Western World*) has shaped western belief in the existence of unpunished adulterous passion in the Middle Ages. For Rougemont, the 'great European myth of adultery', *Tristan et Yseut*, enacts the courtly code much as described by C. S. Lewis; however, far from sharing Lewis's romanticising vision of courtly love, Rougemont deplores its idealisation of the destructive and narcissistic form of desire which he labels 'Eros'. For Rougemont, only *agape*, or disinterested love in God, can elevate and purify mankind.[2] However, in spite of their otherwise opposing views, Lewis and Rougemont, both writing in the 1930s, shared the belief that 'courtly love' was an actual medieval institution which flourished in the Provence of the troubadours, and then, in the 1170s, came to dominate the love practices of the Court of Champagne, ruled at the time by the Countess Marie and her spouse, Count Henri of Champagne.

It was not until the 1960s that scholars unleased a veritable campaign against this eroticised vision of medieval life.[3] Thus John F. Benton's minutely researched account of life at the Court of Champagne in the 1170s dealt a considerable blow to the devotees of courtly love. He concluded that there is absolutely no historical evidence that 'courtly' love was practised there at that time, nor that the famous 'courts of love', where beautiful and noble ladies gave judgements on points of erotic etiquette, ever existed (Benton, 1961). Later, he also came categorically to reject the value of the term 'courtly love' itself, and in doing so he focused precisely on the problem of reading Andreas's *De amore*:

> I have found the term 'courtly love' no advantage in trying to understand the theory and practice of love in medieval Europe. It is not a medieval technical term. It has no specific content. A reference to 'the rules of courtly love' is almost invariably a citation of Andreas's *De amore*, a work which I think is intentionally and humourously ambiguous about love. The study of love in the Middle Ages would be far easier if we were not impeded by a term which now inevitably confuses the issue. (Benton, 1968, pp.36–7)

According to Benton, then, some people's misguided ideas about courtly love stem directly from their misreading of Andreas: they have committed the cardinal sin of taking seriously a work which should be seen as no more than light-hearted fun. In other words, the ambiguous status of the concept of courtly love reflects the ambiguous nature of the *De amore* itself. But how does Benton know that his own reading of Andreas is superior? And how is it that the text of the *De amore* supports such seemingly contradictory interpretations?

The *De amore* consists of three Books addressed to a young man called Walter. The first two Books instruct Walter in the art of courtly love, and seem at first glance wholly to justify C. S. Lewis's description of its conventions. The third, however, is entitled 'The Repudiation of Love', and not only contains a vehement rejection of secular love, but also reels off a list of the vices of womankind in the misogynist tradition of the Church Fathers. According to Book III, far from ennobling man, as claimed in Books I and II, his love for woman can only pollute and destroy him. Given this apparent contradiction, it is hardly surprising that critics have presented divergent readings of

Andreas's treatise. Most of these readings, however, can be summarised under four main headings:

1: Andreas defends courtly love. Books I and II are serious; Book III must be seen as a conventional piece of retraction only meant to save the author, a priest, from getting into trouble with the Church.

2: Andreas holds that both the Church and the adherents of courtly love are right. All three books are serious; Andreas is an exponent of the doctrine of 'double truth'.

3: Andreas defends the Church and condemns courtly love. Books I and II are ironic; Book III is serious and contains Andreas's real opinion.

4: All three books are ironic. Andreas has provided an entertaining, but not necessarily subversive, pastiche of scholasticism and courtly love alike.

The most famous representatives of Reading 1 are, as already mentioned, C. S. Lewis and Denis de Rougemont. Reading 2 can be found in A. J. Denomy's *The Heresy of Courtly Love*. Denomy argues that Andreas held the so-called doctrine of 'double truth', which implied that 'what Andreas teaches to be true according to nature and reason, he teaches to be false according to grace and divine authority' (Denomy, 1947, p. 39). In other words, Andreas believed that according to reason and nature, secular love is the source of all virtue, but also that according to revelation the highest good originates in God; revelation, moreover, always takes precedence over the insights provided by reason. For Denomy there is therefore no doubt that Andreas ultimately was a good Christian.[4]

The major exponent of Reading 3 is D. W. Robertson who, in his *A Preface to Chaucer*, reveals himself as a formidable opponent of courtly love. His thesis is that the 'discouragement of the pursuit of love is ... something that runs through the whole work *De Amore*, not something confined to the last book' (Robertson, 1962, p. 395). Stressing Andreas's equation of love with fear and jealousy in the first two Books, Robertson argues that Book III only makes explicit the implications of the first two. As a whole, then, the *De amore* should show that the 'fear and jealousy of love constitute a miserable servitude' (ibid., p. 447). He thus sees Andreas's treatise as a coherent attack on profane love, made in order to advocate St Augustine's doctrine of charity as the only ennobling form of love; a doctrine which also constitutes the true meaning of works as different as Chrétien de Troyes's *Lancelot* (*Le Chevalier de la Charrette*), *Tristan et Yseut*, and Chaucer's *Troilus and Criseyde*. Argued in relation to Andreas, the case may seem plausible enough. Repeated in relation to a whole series of medieval works, Robertson's plea for Augustinian theology sounds rather less convincing. Thus other critics have seriously questioned Robertson's readings. E. Talbot Donaldson, for instance, argues that Andreas cannot by any stretch of the imagination be turned into a devotee of St Augustine's:

> I do not agree with Robertson's oft-stated premise that any serious work written in the Middle Ages that does not overtly promote St Augustine's doctrine of charity will be found, on close examination, to be doing so allegorically or ironically, nor do I agree that Andreas can be made to read as a good disciple of St. Augustine. Yet I agree with Robertson that Andreas is not to be understood as seriously promulgating immoral doctrine. (Donaldson, 1970, pp. 159–60)

According to Donaldson, Andreas has 'merely adopted Ovid's theme of adulterous love and medievalized it by subjecting it to scholastic analysis, and by infusing it with that spiritualization of the erotic that the troubadours show' (Donaldson, 1970, p. 160). Andreas simply wanted to be outrageous, Donaldson claims, and therefore also grossly exaggerated the anti-eroticism and anti-feminism of Book III: Book III, in other words, is as ironic as Books I and II (Reading 4).[5]

When it comes to the question of the historical reality of courtly love, the different readers of Andreas split neatly down the middle: critics adopting Readings 1 or 2 (that Andreas in some way can be said to be positive about the practice of courtly love) believe that courtly love was a real, historical practice, whereas critics who adopt Readings 3 or 4 (that Andreas condemns courtly love in some way) believe equally firmly that it was not. Thus Donaldson holds that 'at least a part of what is called courtly love was no more real in the Middle Ages than it had been before and has been since' (Donaldson, 1970, p. 163). And Robertson, like Benton, rejects the concept entirely:

The study of courtly love, if it belongs anywhere, should be conducted only as the subject is an aspect of nineteenth- and twentieth-century cultural history. The subject has nothing to do with the Middle Ages, and its use as a governing concept can only be an impediment to our understanding of medieval texts. (Robertson, 1968, p. 17)

Robertson is, of course, quite right in stressing the historically determined nature of this kind of research: if 'courtly love' became a focal point of interest first in the 1930s and then again in the 1960s, this is surely not unrelated to the fact that these two decades witnessed a crisis of conventional sexual ideology and values. Similarly, my own interest in Andreas and courtly love is inspired by contemporary feminist debate on love and sexuality. The point is, surely, that there is nothing particularly unusual about this: to a careful observer all research will bear the mark of its own historical situation. But if Robertson's point can be shown to be generally true, it loses its force as a specific argument against certain readings of Andreas. The question of the historical reality of courtly practices cannot, in other words, be decided as easily as Robertson seems to believe, nor can it, *pace* Benton, be decided simply through empirical research of the Court of Champagne in the twelfth century. For Benton has taken for granted that the relationship between text and history is static and one-sided: his painstaking work is based on the implicit assumption that texts (in this case Andreas's treatise) are no more than reflections of a given reality.

Since the 1960s this kind of naive reflectionism has come in for an increasing amount of criticism, particularly from Marxist theorists (for further discussion of this problem, see Macherey, 1966; Eagleton, 1976; Jameson, 1981; and Pearsall in this volume), and it is now quite possible to argue that Benton's efforts do not really tell us very much at all about the meaning of Andreas's text. But before we return to this point it may be useful to take a closer look at the function of courtly ideology in France, since this will provide us with a concrete example of the difficulty of arguing, as Benton does, a simple reflectionist case about the relations between the literary text and society.

The function of chivalry and courtliness seems to have been to provide the ruling feudal aristocracy with a legitimising ideology. According to Marc Bloch (1940), the twelfth century witnessed the apotheosis of feudal power in France, a power as yet unthreatened by the bourgeoisie. This stabilisation of power produced a culture designed to display aristocratic superiority; the codes of courtly and chivalric behaviour seem selected precisely by virtue of their inaccessibility to the lower classes. The fundamental requirements for any exercise of courtliness were leisure and money: the time and resources necessary to woo the fair lady according to the courtly canon would only have been available to an aristocratic minority. The stress put on cleanliness (frequent use of baths, perfumed oils, etc.) as well as the need to wear beautiful and well-kept clothes also made it impossible for poor and working people to be courtly, had they wanted to be. The necessity of being generous on a large scale (giving banquets, holding tournaments, giving away precious objects) made *courtoisie* the exclusive domain of the rich; the whole chivalric code (the knight proving his worth and his love for the lady by his prowess in armed combat) would seem to be tailor-made for the feudal nobility who perceived themselves as a warrior class. Although the insistence on culture as a necessary part of the accomplishments of the courtly hero and lover (he had to be able to compose and recite poems and songs, write letters to the lady, and read suitable books with her) gave some scope for the special talents of the clergy, it also catered specifically for the other reading and writing class at the time: the aristocracy. In this context it is interesting to note that Andreas takes great care to define all clergy as belonging to the highest class of all on the grounds of their noble occupation (p. 36). As far as class is concerned, this code is almost watertight: a wealthy and educated bourgeois man might have fulfilled all these requirements only to fall foul of the demand for knightly deeds. The weak link in the chain is the bourgeois woman: since a lady was not supposed to fight in heroic battle, nothing would prevent a rich and graceful bourgeoise from winning the favours of a man of the highest nobility. Andreas neatly solves this problem by making his two bourgeois ladies stalwart defenders of the status quo: refusing all hope of their love to their noble suitors, their discourse eloquently demonstrates the dangers of upsetting the social order, thus obligingly helping Andreas to fend off his obvious anxiety about the potentially subversive nature of passion.

In addition to its evident appeal to aristocratic exclusivity, the code of courtly love and chivalry also mobilises a more subtle

17

interpretation of the categories of nature and culture in order to produce its ideological impact. Fundamentally unnatural, courtly love emphasises the cultural and spiritual values of love. Love ennobles the (male) lover, Andreas claims, it refines and reforms him through the influence of the beloved lady, presumably already a fairly ethereal being herself. Dante's Beatrice is only the most sublime in a series of spiritualised ladies in courtly literature. In Andreas's text, as in the *Chevalier de la Charrette*, the spiritualising power of love nevertheless remains at odds with its crudely physical manifestations. Andreas seems to be uneasily aware that there is something illogical about a spiritual desire for the good and virtuous which in the end posits the same tediously physical act as the lover's highest bliss. He thus goes to great lengths to imply that there is a difference between courtly love, even if this is of a 'mixed' (i.e. sexual) kind, and straightforward, 'natural' sex: 'We say it rarely happens that we find farmers serving in Love's court,' Andreas writes, 'but, naturally, like a horse or a mule, they give themselves up to the work of Venus, as nature's urgings teaches them to do' (p. 149). Natural desire has nothing, or very little, to do with love in the courtly sense, at least according to Andreas's commentary at this stage. This, incidentally, leads him to conclude that a courtly lover (clearly not a farmer) ought simply to rape peasant women at will:

> If you should, by some chance, fall in love with some of their [peasants'] women, be careful to puff them up with praise and then, when you find a convenient place, do not hesitate to take what you seek and to embrace them by force. For you can hardly soften their outward inflexibility so far that they will grant you their embraces quietly or permit you to have the solaces you desire unless first you use a little compulsion as a convenient cure for their shyness. (p. 150)

Though there is some ambiguity in Andreas's use of the word love in this passage, it would seem that the message is clear: peasants are natural creatures and must be treated as such. Intercourse with peasant women can neither refine nor ennoble the courtly lover; in fact, Andreas advises Walter to restrain his dealings with them to the utmost, presumably because such *natural* relations could seriously undermine his claim to possess a sophisticated, cultured courtliness.

This aversion to the natural life of peasants reveals the real function of courtly ideology. If, as Bloch (1940) has argued, courtly ideology can be seen as an effort to impose the more refined habits of the aristocratic ladies on the boorish feudal lords, the cultured noble lady becomes the arbiter of taste in courtly society; no wonder then that peasant women were considered their absolute antithesis. The whole point of the various courtly and chivalric exercises described in Andreas's and Chrétien's texts was to escape all comparison with villeins. Signalling their cultural superiority, the 'effeminisation' of the aristocracy paradoxically enough comes to signify their 'natural' right to power. It is precisely in its insistence on the 'natural' differences between rulers and ruled that courtly ideology achieved its legitimising function, a function which operates long after the feudal aristocracy has lost its central position in society.

In his influential study of the fourteenth and fifteenth centuries, *The Waning of the Middle Ages*, J. Huizinga emphasises the lasting influence of courtly and chivalric codes of behaviour on the aristocracy: 'Long after nobility and feudalism had ceased to be really essential factors in the state and in society,' Huizinga writes, 'they continued to impress the mind as the dominant form of life' (1924, p. 54). This society was obsessed with courtly love:

> In no other epoch did the ideal of civilisation amalgamate to such a degree with that of love. Just as scholasticism represents the grand effort of the medieval spirit to unite all philosophic thought in a single centre, so the theory of courtly love, in a less elevated sphere, tends to embrace all that appertains to the noble life. (ibid., p. 105)

In this period the courtly texts seem to precede reality, not vice versa: the courts of love which Benton could not find in the twelfth century are enacted now as an imitation of the courtly ideals of Andreas's and Chrétien's time by an aristocracy whose 'whole system of ideas was permeated by the fiction that chivalry ruled the world,' as Huizinga put it (p. 65).

At this point it is tempting to argue, *pace* Benton and Robertson, that *no* reading of the *De amore* (or any other courtly text) will tell us anything at all about 'reality' in the twelfth century. But this case is not altogether convincing. If, after our study of courtly ideology in the Middle Ages, we feel obliged to drop the idea that literature should be no more than a pale reflection of reality, we might want to consider the view that texts produce a reality of their own. But it does not follow that this textual reality is entirely cut off from its own historical moment of production. Rejecting the fashionable view that history is just another text and therefore cannot constitute a 'ground' of truth for other texts, Fredric Jameson suggests that: 'History is not so much a text as rather a text-to-be-(re)-constructed. Better still, it is an obligation to do so, whose means and techniques are themselves historically irreversible, so that we are not at liberty to construct any historical narrative at all' (Jameson, 1977, p. 388). For Jameson, history is the Real in the Lacanian sense, that is to say, 'that which resists symbolisation'. The Real is only available to us through language, and language can never coincide with reality; the text stands in an asymptotic relationship to history.

One of the reasons why it is extremely difficult to say just where on the asymptote a particular text is situated is that all texts, among other things are manifestations of ideology. Ideology, of course, represents social relations, but nothing guarantees the veracity of the ideological representation: it may very well be mistaken about the real nature of its own society. In this sense, it is the very nature of the text's mistakes and omissions which most tellingly reveals its ideological preoccupations (for a full discussion of this view, see Macherey, 1966). It is thus paradoxically only through the study of the text's 'misrepresentation' of reality that we can seize its ideological dimension as that 'indispensable mapping fantasy or narrative by which the individual subject invents a "lived" relationship with collective systems', as Jameson puts it (Jameson, 1977, p. 394). In this way we can construct the text as a map of its own ideological and psychological investments, its fears, hopes and desires. The fact that the map never coincides with the terrain does not mean that there never was a terrain at all.

Love, Jealousy and Epistemology in the De amore

In his admirable study of Proust, Leo Bersani claims that the hopelessly jealous and insecure love of a Swann or a Marcel has little in common with the nobler forms of passion represented in courtly literature:

In the medieval courtly epics and lyrics, for example, as well as in Corneille, Rousseau and Claudel, love includes moral admiration; the lover's personality is ennobled by his passion for someone worthy of being loved. Love thus realizes and intensifies a profound harmony between the self and the world: the lover *knows* the object of his love, and his responses are governed by moral qualities he rightly perceives. (Bersani, 1965, pp. 98–9)

One of the purposes of this essay is to show that, at least as far as the *De amore* is concerned, such an idyllic vision of medieval passions is simply mistaken. Already in the introductory passages (Chapters 1–5 of Book I) where Andreas sets out, in his best scholastic manner, to define his topic, love is the object of considerable ambivalence and hesitation:

Love is a certain inborn suffering derived from the sight of and excessive meditation upon the beauty of the opposite sex, which causes each one to wish above all things the embraces of the other and by common desire to carry out all of love's precepts in the other's embrace. (p. 28)

Here *suffering* is presented as the essence of love: unfulfilled sexual desire never ceases to torment the (male) lover. This suffering, moreover, is 'inborn', or in other words, *natural*. In this way Andreas's treatise can be read as an effort to conceal or displace the painful naturalness of love by dressing it up in the necessary courtly trappings. This process is, however, never entirely successful: the 'inborn' suffering never disappears; love for Andreas, like desire for Freud or Lacan, is doomed to remain unsatisfied.

The sexual frustration suffered by the lover is aggravated by his constant anxiety: in one paragraph the word 'fear' occurs no less than eleven times. Or as Andreas himself puts it: 'To tell the truth, no one can number the fears of one single lover' (p. 28). The lover's main fear is that his chosen lady will reject him, either because of rumours about their illicit love, or because she finds him insufficient or unworthy in character, behaviour or social status. There is no 'safe' position here: if the lover is poor, he fears that the lady will scorn his poverty; if he is rich, he trembles that she may despise his past parsimony. By far the greatest threat to the lover's project of conquering the lady's favours, however, is posed by his rivals: constantly agonising in his neurotic fear of being rejected for another suitor, the lover is driven to despair by extreme jealousy.

It is always the lady who is invested with the power to make judgements of a social nature: *her* desire seems either to be non-existent or entirely cultural, inextricably caught up, as it must be, in a series of mundane considerations of wealth and social prestige. Perhaps it is from her very unnaturalness, the fact that she incarnates the cultural standards of her society, that she derives the power to ennoble and civilise her lustful lover. 'Every attempt of a lover tends towards the enjoyment of the embraces of her whom he loves,' Andreas writes, 'he thinks about it continually, for he hopes that with her he may fulfill all the mandates of love... in the sight of a lover nothing can be compared to the act of love' (p. 30). It is strange that this very basic drive for sexual satisfaction should have such ennobling consequences: 'O what a wonderful thing is love,' enthuses Andreas, 'which makes a man shine with so many virtues and teaches everyone, no matter who he is, so many good traits of character!' (p. 31). The paradox is that if the lover were to become as refined as his lady, he might lose the very natural desire which led him to seek her 'solaces' in the first place.

Andreas extends his definition of love by providing it with an etymological origin, apparently derived from Isidore of Seville's (false) etymology for the word *amicus*, friend:

> Love gets its name (*amor*) from the word for hook (*amus*), which means 'to capture' or 'to be captured', for he who is in love is captured in the chains of desire and wishes to capture someone else with his hook. Just as a skilful fisherman tries to attract fishes by his bait and to capture them on his crooked hook, so the man who is a captive of love tries to attract another person by his allurements and exerts all his efforts to unite two different hearts with an intangible bond, or if they are already united he tries to keep them so forever. (p. 31)

The lover here is both beast and prey; a slave bound by the chains of desire, he is at the same time a skilful fisherman trying to trick the lady into swallowing his bait. The ambiguity of the image of the lover as simultaneously fish, bait and fisherman signals the same hesitations as in Andreas's uneasy definition of love as an inborn suffering which relentlessly forces men to seek bliss. No wonder, perhaps, that the lover's 'crooked hook' seems curiously unsuited to the delicate task of creating an 'intangible bond' between two hearts.

In spite of his expressions of admiration for the ennobling force of love, Andreas finishes off this introductory section by warning Walter that 'love, at times, does not use fair weights' (p. 32). In fact, Andreas believes that desire is both deceitful and untrustworthy: 'Because [love] is in the habit of carrying an unjust weight in his hand, I do not have full confidence in him any more than I do in a judge whom men suspect' (p. 32). Living then as he does in a universe filled with jealousy, fear and deceit, Andreas's lover apparently has little choice. Since love's sufferings are inborn, he cannot escape the yoke of desire; his only option is to make the best of a bad job. Andreas therefore reluctantly agrees to instruct Walter in the art of courtly love since, as he puts it in his prefatory note, 'I know clearer than day that after you have learned the art of love your progress in it will be more cautious' (p. 28). On the surface then, Andreas presents the *De amore* more as an emergency kit for wounded (male) lovers than as an introduction to the delights of love.

After this introduction to love, Andreas gets down to his main task, which is to teach Walter 'in what manner love may be acquired, and in how many ways' (p. 33), and launches into eight sample dialogues organised according to the participants' class-background ('A man of the middle class speaks with a woman of the same class'; 'A man of the higher nobility speaks with a woman of the simple nobility', etc.). These dialogues are, not surprisingly, obsessed with class, and particularly with the threat that desire poses to stable social structures. And, as in the introductory sections, it is the man who is tempted towards subversive action by his unruly passions, whereas the woman defends the social status quo.

The dialogues of Book I alone take up over half of Andreas's treatise, and constitute the bulk of the two Books dealing with the art of love, whereas the rejection of love (Book III) apparently requires no such linguistic patterns. In fact, language is so prominent in Andreas's model of courtship that the reader, like the lady, occasionally feels submerged by the endless flow of the lover's discourse. For it is the lover who does most of the talking: the lady, although obviously capable of a quick repartee, limits her remarks to shrewd criticism of the lover's points, and hardly ever instigates a new topic of her own. The lover's lust makes him speak, and when he does so his style is rational in the extreme: every single one of Andreas's lovers attempts to *prove* to the woman that she ought to love him. However discouraging her response, the lover is prepared to go on talking until dismissed by her. It is as if this veritable deluge of passionate, scholastic argumentation could go on forever: the lover's eloquence seems to give him pleasure for its own sake. And it is, of course, true that by the very act of speaking the lover has already achieved an important courtly aim, the elegant use of language being precisely one of the distinctions which set the upper classes apart from the common crowd. A courtly lover cannot speak like a country yokel; the lover's untiringly intellectual discourse validates his claim to *be* a lover in the first place. In spite of appearances then, desire does not necessarily precede language in Andreas's text; on the contrary, if the man's linguistic performance establishes him *as* a lover, his desire is produced *by* language and seeks its satisfaction *in* it. (It is, for instance, remarkable how little sexual success the lovers in these dialogues have in proportion to their verbal efforts: the prowess is linguistic, not erotic.)

The language which thus constitutes the lover's passion is curiously aggressive. His pleasure lies in his *mastery* of language, obtained through his neurotic ordering and scholastic subdivision of his discourse. In this sense, of course, the dramatised lovers in Andreas's dialogues give but a shadow of Andreas's own performance in the De amore as a whole. The lover is in love with his own eloquent lucidity: by dominating the word, he gains a phallic power that contradicts his seemingly humble stance towards his lady. This mastery is only achieved, however, by the most humble submission to the inflexible rules of scholastic rhetoric. Chained and fettered, the lover's discourse enacts his own lack of freedom, which is bearable only because it procures him at the same time the satisfaction of a certain sadistic dominance. As in Andreas's etymology of love, the lover is both master of and slave to his own discourse of desire. The effect of his aggressive verbal onslaught is that the lady in these dialogues, in spite of her vigorous replies to the lover, remains a curiously cold, distant and enigmatic creature whose love is perceived as a capricious and unreliable entity precisely because we, as well as the lover, suspect her of having no passion at all, deprived as she is of a discursive initiative of her own.

It is perhaps for this reason that Andreas's lovers often recur to scarcely veiled threats in order to make her succumb. In the fifth dialogue the lover launches into an elaborate allegory which is supposed to prove that women who refuse to take lovers suffer horrible torments after death. The courtly lover's strategy is thus one of intimidation and verbal sadism: his language enacts his aggression (which becomes all the more menacing precisely because of its dependence on an abject surrender to the rules of discourse), and the fact that the courtly lady, unlike the peasant woman, escapes outright rape ought not to be interpreted as conclusive evidence of his respect for her.[6] In the end, the lover is not interested in the woman; his narcissistic self-display centres on his own desire, his own discursive performance.

The *De amore* does, of course, also present language as the 'hook of love' which allows the lover to attract the lady by his 'allurements' in order to create an 'intangible bond' between their hearts. There is in Andreas's treatise a deep desire for a trusting union with the other, a union which, if successful, would infinitely improve the man's character and behaviour. But as the original image of the 'hook of love' is double-edged (to be caught on the fisherman's hook is a painful and ultimately deadly business), the intermittently expressed desire for full knowledge of the partner is undercut by a whole series of rhetorical and thematic moves which indicate that true love, the blissful union of two different hearts, is an unrealisable fantasy. It is the misfortune of (male) lovers that they have to spend their lives in pursuit of such a chimera.

The fundamental scepticism of Andreas's vision emerges in his treatment of jealousy. For Andreas, jealousy is the 'mother and nurse of love' (p. 101). True jealousy, not to be confused with the possessive tyranny of a husband, consists of a triple fear:

> Now jealousy is a true emotion whereby we greatly fear that the substance of our love may be weakened by some defect in serving the desires of our beloved, and it is an anxiety lest our love may not be returned, and it is a suspicion of the beloved, but without any shameful thought. (p. 102)

In this passage we recognise the endless fears of the lover described as an essential part of love at the very outset of Andreas's treatise. The puzzling part of this passage is the reference to jealousy as an *unshameful* suspicion of the beloved. *Shameful* suspicion, according to Andreas, is that nourished by possessive husbands only interested in protecting their own dynastic interests.[7] The lover's jealous suspicion seems entirely different: perhaps it is not shameful simply because it is an integral part of love. 'He who is not jealous cannot love', Andreas comments (p. 107). From the context, it seems clear that his jealousy is a form of fear, a generalised worry about the lady's activities and thoughts, clearly not limited (as in the case of the husband) to straightforward sexual jealousy (it is not 'shameful'). His jealousy, then, seems caused by the feeling that the lady remains *other*: however hard he tries to master her by his discourse, he will always suffer in the knowledge that her consciousness is not his. In this respect, Andreas is no different from a Marcel or a Swann. As with the Proustian lover, the beloved becomes enigmatic precisely in so far as the lover perceives her as a secretive space which at all costs must be penetrated.

Desire, in the *De amore*, is not only a discursive enterprise but a hermeneutical challenge. The lover's happiness depends on his ability to decipher the lady's words and uncover their hidden meaning. This is surely why Andreas insists on the dialogue form: the lover is in desperate need of an introduction to the art of rhetoric which might make him a more proficient hermeneuticist, a better reader of the lady's text. But in this case it is *love* (desire) itself which requires the lover to become an expert reader. The necessity of deciphering the beloved's discourse would of course not be particularly painful if the lover could be reasonably sure of reaching the correct interpretation. If the torments of jealousy constitute, as Andreas claims, the 'very substance of love' (p. 101), it is because they reveal the most unspeakable secret of all: that the lover *never* knows whether he has hit upon the true reading. For the jealous lover, the world is transformed into a treacherous text full of traps; since every utterance, every event, is susceptible to different, often contradictory readings, he must suspect every single word or phrase. There is no refuge from this vertiginous multiplicity of meanings; the jealous lover must live in a universe deprived of a firm ground upon which truth can rest. His raging desire for knowledge ('epistemophilia', as Freud would call it; Othello's need for the 'ocular proof') is pathetic and painful precisely because this desire can never be satisfied. The paradox is that it is the nature of jealousy itself which ensures that the jealous lover (and for Andreas all lovers are jealous) will never find a transcendental signified, a point at which his interpretations can come to rest.[8]

If we are to believe Andreas's claim that 'jealousy is the substance of love', this epistemophiliac drive also constitutes the essential movement of desire. The lover's need for union with the beloved represents a need for absolute insight into the innermost recesses of her mind, but her very otherness, the fact that her consciousness is not his, means that she will always escape his hermeneutical probings. The logic of his desire may thus lead him to conclude that the best way of preventing her consciousness from escaping him yet again is simply by annihilating it: however counter-productive, Othello's murder of Desdemona at least put an end to his anxiety about her behaviour. The endless fears of the jealous lover is thus accompanied by the temptation to put an end to it all by an act of sadistic violence.

Andreas's treatise is not only candidly open about the lover's jealous dilemma; it also focuses on the problem of the amorous language in this context. The problem, as Andreas sees it, is how the man can interpret the woman's words correctly (in keeping with his insistence on male lust and female impassivity, the man is of course always the reader, the woman the text to be read).

A particularly graphic example of this can be found towards the end of Book I, in the chapter entitled 'Love got with Money'. Here Andreas discusses the dangers of dealing with women who only pretend to be in love in order to 'draw money' out of the lover. These women conceal their desire for money behind a mask of love, and Andreas mobilises his most aggressive language in his description of their deceit: 'A woman who you know desires money in return for her love should be looked upon as a deadly enemy, and you should be careful to avoid her like a venomous animal that strikes with its tail and fawns with its mouth' (p. 145). In an extraordinarily violent passage, Andreas seeks to persuade himself and Walter that if the lover just acts early enough it is not impossible to capture the sordid truth behind the lady's loving appearance:

Therefore, my friend, you should always follow this maxim: whenever you have reason to believe that a woman is interested in piling up the coin, be careful to avoid her in the very beginning and not to involve yourself at all in her snares. For if you try to fall in with what she says in order to find out what her real intention is, you will find yourself foiled by your own plan, because no amount of searching will reveal how she feels and what she means to do until the leech is full of blood and leaves you only half alive with all the blood of your wealth drained off. A wise man's best efforts can hardly find out what is beneath the guile of a deceitful lady-love, for she knows how to colour her frauds by so many arts and with so much cleverness that the faithful lover is rarely clever enough to see through them. The ability of a greedy woman is greater than that of the Ancient Enemy was when by his shrewdness he cleverly perverted the mind of our first parent. Therefore you should use all your cleverness to see that you are not tripped up by the snares of such a woman, because a woman of that kind does not want to love, but to revel in your wealth. (p. 147)

The grisly imagery of the woman as a venomous animal (a scorpion?), a blood-sucking leech, as more cunning than the devil, is, if anything, even more sadistic than the openly misogynistic passages of Book III. The difference is that here Andreas claims that 'We do not say these things with the desire of running down honourable women' (p. 147), whereas in Book III he allows no such distinction between good and bad women: '*no* woman ever loved a man' (p. 200) he asserts, '*no* woman ever has enough money' (p. 201), and so on. In Book III there are no exceptions from the rule:

> Furthermore, not only is every woman by nature a miser, but she is also envious and a slanderer of other women, greedy, a slave to her belly, inconstant, fickle in her speech, disobedient and impatient of restraint, spotted with the sin of pride and desirous of vainglory, a liar, a drunkard, a babbler, no keeper of secrets, too much given to wantonness, prone to every evil, and never loving any man in her heart. (p. 201)

The blood-sucking leech never ceases to 'drain away' her unsuspecting lover's property, an action which leaves him without any 'substance' (p. 144). But this 'substance' is clearly more than just property: 'There is nothing so contemptible as for a man to waste his substance on the work of the flesh and the solace of Venus' (p. 147), Andreas claims. This substance/semen also appears disguised as the man's life-blood: 'No amount of searching will reveal how she feels and what she means to do until the leech is full of blood and leaves you only half alive with all the blood of your wealth drained off' (p. 147). When the greedy and deceitful female vampire is done she will leave the man drained of all substance/semen/property/blood.[9]

But is Andreas's distinction between deceitful and honourable women really tenable? If we return to the passage quoted above, it is easy to see that the text is caught here in a particularly unpleasant paradox. If it is true that the greedy woman's cunning pretence of love is so convincing that even a 'wise man's best efforts' cannot find the truth located 'beneath the guile of a deceitful lady-love', the lover clearly has a problem. The deceitful woman's duplicity is even greater than the devil's, and so it follows that no amount of conversation will uncover the unpalatable truth. Andreas's only advice to Walter is therefore to avoid such women altogether. But this is far too easy a way out. If the deceitful woman's language is indistinguishable from an honest woman's, the lover will never know whether he is listening to truth or deceit. He thus finds himself caught in exactly the same trap as the jealous lover: they are both in a situation where no amount of subtle interpretation will reveal the lady's true intention. Jealousy is indeed the essence of love; and Andreas's advice to Walter really amounts to saying that he ought to avoid *all* women, given the impossibility of distinguishing between them.

Andreas conveniently represses the fact that he has unmasked a problem of general linguistic and epistemological importance (how can language convey truth?), and blames it all on the deviousness of women instead. If the deceit of language only presents us with appearances, the distinction between good and evil women necessarily collapses, and Andreas's Book III logically enough explicitly recommends a total rejection of all women. The fact that by his own analysis men's language would be equally devious and impossible to pin down to an essential truth apparently does not occur to him. Irksome as this may be to feminists, it is interesting to observe that in the modern debate over the 'true' meaning of the *De amore*, the critics accurately enact the problematics of the text: like hermeneutically distraught lovers, they untiringly try to decipher the sibylline utterances of the lady, who now, in a final twist of the plot, turns out to be Andreas himself. There is much consolation for feminists in the thought that in the end the old misogynist has been forced to play the female lead himself.

If desire is constituted by and conducted in language, the lover is helplessly thrown from one set of deceitful appearances to another. Andreas's final solution is again rigourously logical: reject earthly love altogether and turn to God, who is Alpha and Omega, the beginning and the end, the only self-sufficient cause in the universe; in short, the transcendental signifier and signified *par excellence*. In the end, then, the courtly lover's constant search for the essence beneath the multiple, treacherous appearances of language is resolved: God for Andreas, like death for Lacan, is the only instance which can put a final end to the discourse of desire.

Notes

1. My quotations are from John Jay Parry's elegant translation *The Art of Courtly Love* (New York: Columbia University Press, 1941; rpt. 1969). Readers interested in studying the Latin original should consult the bilingual Latin/English edition, edited and translated by P.G. Walsh, entitled *Andreas Capellanus on Love*, (London: Duckworth, 1982). I chose Parry's translation in the knowledge that as far as my selected quotations are concerned, there are no important disagreements between Parry and Walsh. All page references to Parry's translation are put in brackets in the text without any preceding identification.

2. In his *The Mind and Heart of Love*, Martin d'Arcy argues against Rougemont's definitions of Eros and *agape* as entirely separate and opposed concepts (d'Arcy, 1945).

3. Henry Ansgar Kelly, in his *Love and Marriage in the Age of Chaucer*, states that the first full attack on this idealising view of courtly love was presented as early as in 1938 in an unpublished thesis by Donnel van de Voort at Vanderbilt University (Kelly, 1975, p. 21).

4. Denomy's reading is heavily dependent on a late dating of the *De amore*. The doctrine of 'double truth' was not widely known until the Latin translation of Averroes appeared in 1179. If the *De amore*, as Denomy argues, was composed in the 1170s, the 'double truth' claim becomes dubious. Peter Dronke has pointed out this inconsistency, but has also argued that Andreas's treatise could have been written at any time between 1174 and 1238 (Dronke, 1976).

5. Donald R. Howard shares Donaldson's view. In his *The Three*

Desire in Language

Temptations: Medieval Man in Search of the World, he writes about
the *De amore:* 'I should be inclined to ... say that while the first two
books are ironic and game-like, the last is no less so' (Howard, 1966,
p. 96). Jean Leclercq's *Monks and Love in Twelfth-Century France*
(1979) takes a similar view.

6. Andrée Kahn Blumstein, in her study of German courtly romances
in the twelfth and thirteenth centuries, has also criticised the implicit
patriarchal assumptions of the courtly code: 'The courtly code' of
love and most especially the idealization of women in the romance
are in many respects a *covert* form of misogyny; chivalry is but one
more method by which what has been called the 'great patriarchal
conspiracy' is perpetrated and perpetuated in our culture (Blumstein,
1977, p. 2).

7. In an illuminating article, Erich Köhler (1970) compares the attitude
towards jealousy in troubadour lyrics with Andreas's views, and
shows that the seemingly opposed ideas in the two kinds of text
really cover the same jealous mechanisms. According to Köhler, the
troubadours are not particularly jealous of the husband since he
represents an established attitude towards property and social class,
which they as an upwardly mobile group (the *chevalerie*) despise.
Their jealousy is directed towards the whole of their peer group, all
of whom are seeking social promotion through the favours of the
lady. This generalised, competitive form of jealousy is then often
projected onto one figure, representative of the whole group, the
much despised 'lauzengier', the *slanderer* or *flatterer,* who by
divulging the secret of the poet's love destroys all possibility of
exclusive communication between him and the lady.

8. A modern psychiatrist has described the same phenomenon in cases
of pathological jealousy: 'The desire to obtain proof of the offence is
often overwhelmingly strong; it appears to be related to a need to
resolve a tormenting doubt which in some cases leads to repeated
attempts to extort a confession from the partner. Such patients
declare this to be the only satisfaction that they demand, but the
irrational nature of their request is strikingly demonstrated by the
futility of the confession which is occasionally feigned by a blameless
but desperate spouse' (Shepherd, 1961, p. 690).

9. Several authors have discussed the psychological structures of courtly
love from a psychoanalytical perspective. Richard A. Koenigsberg
reads the *De amore* as a straightforward case of Oedipal desire for a
mother figure (Koenigsberg, 1967); whereas Herbert Moller, in a
thoughtful article, explains the love-lyrics of the troubadours as a
case of infantile desire for the pre-Oedipal mother (Moller, 1960).
Melvin Askew's 'Courtly Love: Neurosis as Institution' is a more

31

superficial approach to the topic (Askew, 1965). Lack of space prevents me from discussing this type of reading more fully.

References

Editions of the De amore
The Art of Courtly Love (1941) tr. John Jay Parry (New York: Columbia University Press, rpt. 1969).
Andreas Capellanus on Love (1982) ed. and tr. P.G. Walsh (London: Duckworth).

Other Sources
Askew, Melvin W. (1965) 'Courtly Love: Neurosis as Institution', *The Psychoanalytic Review*, 52:1 (Spring).

Benton, John F. (1961) 'The Court of Champagne as a Literary Center', *Speculum*, XXXVI:4 (October).

Benton, John F. (1968) 'Clio and Venus: An Historical View of Medieval Love', in F. X. Newman (ed.), *The Meaning of Courtly Love* (Albany, N.Y.: State University of New York Press).

Bersani, Leo (1965) *Marcel Proust. The Fictions of Life and Art*. (New York: Oxford University Press).

Bloch, Marc (1940) *La Société féodale*, vol. II: *Les Classes et le gouvernement des hommes* (Paris: Albin Michel).

Blumstein, Andrée Kahn (1977) *Misogyny and Idealization in the Courtly Romance* (Bonn: Bouvier Verlag Herbert Grundmann).

d'Arcy, Martin C. (1945) *The Mind and Heart of Love. Lion and Unicorn: A Study in Eros and Agape* (London: Faber & Faber).

Denomy, Alexander J. (1947) *The Heresy of Courtly Love* (Gloucester, Mass.: Peter Smith).

Donaldson, E. Talbot (1970) *Speaking of Chaucer* (New York: Norton).

Dronke, Peter (1976) 'André le Chapelain: Traité de l'amour courtois', *Medium Aevum*, KLV:3.

Eagleton, Terry (1976) *Criticism and Ideology* (London: New Left Books).

Howard, Donald R., (1966) *The Three Temptations: Medieval Man in Search of the World* (Princeton, N.J.: Princeton University Press).

Huizinga, J. (1924) *The Waning of the Middle Ages* (Harmondsworth: Penguin Books, rpt. 1965).

Jameson, Fredric (1977) 'Imaginary and Symbolic in Lacan: Marxism, Psychoanalytic Criticism, and the Problem of the Subject', *Yale French Studies*, 55/56, 338–95.

Jameson, Fredric (1981) *The Political Unconscious: Narrative as a*

Socially Symbolic Act (London: Methuen).

Kelly, Henry Ansgar (1975) *Love and Marriage in the Age of Chaucer* (Ithaca, N.Y.: Cornell University Press).

Koenigsberg, Richard A. (1967) 'Culture and Unconscious Fantasy. Observations on Courtly Love', *Psychoanalytic Review*, vol. LIV.

Köhler, Erich (1970) 'Les troubadours et la jalousie', in *Mélanges Jean Frappier* (Geneva: Droz), vol. I, p. 543–59.

Leclercq, Jean (1979) *Monks and Love in Twelfth-Century France* (Oxford: Oxford University Press).

Lewis, C.S. (1936) *The Allegory of Love* (Oxford: Oxford University Press, rpt. 1959).

Macherey, Pierre (1966) *Pour une théorie de la production littéraire* (Paris: Maspéro). Tr. by Geoffrey Wall as *A Theory of Literary Production* (London: Routledge & Kegan Paul, 1978).

Moller, Herbert (1960) 'The Meaning of Courtly Love', *Journal of American Folklore*, vol. LXXIII.

Paris, Gaston (1883) 'Lancelot du Lac 2: Le conte de la charrette', *Romania*, 12.

Robertson, D. W. (1962) *A Preface to Chaucer* (Princeton, N.J.: Princeton University Press, rpt. 1969).

Robertson, D. W. (1968) 'The Concept of Courtly Love as an Impediment to the Understanding of Medieval Texts', in F. X. Newman (ed.), *The Meaning of Courtly Love* (Albany, N.Y.: State University of New York Press).

Rougemont, Denis de (1939) *L'Amour et l'Occident* (Paris: Gallimard). Tr. as *Love in the Western World* (New York: Harcourt, Brace & Co., 1956).

Shepherd, Michael (1961) 'Morbid Jealousy: Some Clinical and Social Aspects of a Psychiatric Symptom', *Journal of Mental Science*, vol. 107.

3

A Very Material Mysticism: The Medieval Mysticism of Margery Kempe

Sarah Beckwith

'To the precise degree that the absolute is made to approximate to the finite, the finite is absolutized.'

(Adorno, 1979, p. 177)

'As negative to the man, woman becomes a total object of fantasy (or an object of total fantasy), elevated into the place of the Other and made to stand for its truth. Since the place of the Other is also the place of God, this is the ultimate form of mystification.'

(Rose, 1982, p. 50)

One of the crucial areas opened up by recent developments of critical theory has been the feminist analysis of the imaging, construction and articulation of sexual difference. Frequently this has taken the form of how women are articulated as 'feminine' and what positions are available for them to adopt in a patriarchal society which constitutes woman as 'Other'.[1]

One of the first extant written records in England by a woman must therefore merit analysis, and it is interesting that the *Book of Margery Kempe* (1438), which has been dubbed the first autobiography in England, one which is therefore jointly concerned with the construction of femininity and subjectivity, should also have been produced within the context of medieval mystical Christianity. For if medieval Christianity was so instrumental in the construction and relegation of woman to the place of 'Other' (a construction seen clearly in the traditional polarisation of Eve and Mary as impure flesh and pure soul), it was also the endeavour of the mystical aspect of Christianity to articulate the 'Otherness' of God himself. Female mysticism in the late Middle Ages, which has recently been described by one feminist theorist as the 'only place in Western history where woman speaks and acts in such a public way' (Irigaray, 1974, p. 238) is therefore an area in which the intermingling of God, the 'Other' and woman is complexly overdetermined. Female mysticism is doubly colonised as a focus for the projection of Otherness because both God and woman are seen as the place of a mystified and unrepresentable (but nevertheless constantly represented) otherness.

It is the simultaneous exclusion and construction of the other which is instrumental in the construction of any dominant value system. 'No group ever sets up as the One without at once setting up the Other over against itself,' (de Beauvoir, 1972, p. 17). De Beauvoir's formulation in the *Second Sex* has been redefined by more recent feminist theorists who see women as the otherness which permits the establishment of the norm of a specifically masculine unity. For Luce Irigaray, in her *Speculum de l'autre femme*, the mirroring function of the woman which allows man to reflect and be reflected in his own image operates through the very means by which his subjectivity is structured, linguistically and socially, at the level of the production of meaning itself. Such a process can be seen at work in the medieval ideology of courtly love in which the feudal aristocracy construct woman as the other (the static, voiceless lady of *fin amor*), creating her as the demarcator of their own boundaries and so establishing a confirming and legitimising definition of themselves and their own power.[2]

But if the construction of the masculine as such depends on the repression of the feminine and its relegation to the role of other, the feminine is, for that very reason according to some recent feminist theory, the potential source of subversion, for she is also in the position to return, to dislocate the very unity which posits her as other, to disrupt, disperse and displace the masculine parameters which establish law and reason. She is thus both the support of the dominant value-system (as Mary, perhaps) and the rot in the very foundations of that system (Eve): 'a marginality internal to the system, integrated in it, indispensable' (Feral, 1978, p. 10).

The phenomenon of female mysticism was widespread in the

late Middle Ages. From the thirteenth to the fifteenth centuries it was women who were more likely to be mystics than men, and it was women who encouraged and propagated the most distinctive aspects of late medieval piety—devotion to the human Christ as lover, husband and infant, devotion to the Eucharist in a form of piety which insists on the physical as a legitimate means of access to the spiritual. 'For the first time in Christian history we can document that a particular kind of religious experience is more common among women than men' (Bynum, 1982, p. 172).

One of the aims of this essay is to explore Irigaray's notion of female mysticism ('the only place in Western history where woman speaks and acts in such a public way') as a model feminine discourse, a place in which patriarchy can be mined from within. Clearly such a claim is important, for the Lacanian symbolic order which recent feminist theory both employs and attempts to discard,

> is in reality the patriarchal sexual and social order of modern class society structured around the transcendental signifier of the phallus, dominated by the Law which the Father embodies. There is no way then in which a feminist or pro-feminist may uncritically celebrate the symbolic order at the expense of the imaginary. (Eagleton, 1983, pp. 187–8)[3]

Thus the question posed by the league between God, Christ and woman in female mysticism is one which has been crucial in the debates surrounding French feminist theory—the question as to whether female mysticism is a possible space for the disruption of the patriarchal order, or whether, on the contrary, it exists to act out rigorously its most sexist fantasies, to reinforce the relegation of 'woman' to a transcendent, mystified and mystificatory sphere where female masochism is spectacularly redeployed in the pose of crucifixion/crucifiction.

The *Book of Margery Kempe* is an apt focus for analysis, for Margery is an isolated English example of a widespread continental phenomenon with which she had important connections—connections which were clearly important to legitimise her own form of piety before a disbelieving male clergy. And moreover, whereas most contemporaneous women's writings take the form of revelations (the validity and possibility of women's writing depended on their ability to prove that they were the special witnesses of God's grace), Margery's book is a devotional work which does not exclude the material context of its piety. The book (unusually) contains an account of its own difficult genesis and Margery's difficulties in persuading her male scribe to take down her revelations: 'for þer was so mech obloquie & slawndyr þat þer wold few men beleue þis creatur' (Meech and Allen, 1940, p. 6), testifies to the dangers and difficulties of female authorship at a time when the Church was anxious to control an increasingly literate laity, and where women in particular were the object of a vernacular devotional literature which attempted both to channel, construct and contain feminine spirituality. Indeed one of Margery's commentators has written that the *Book of Margery Kempe* bears, 'besides the marks of a woman's dilemma, the stamp of clerical analysis and controversy. It is a deeply polemical work in a way in which her literary models were not' (Goodman, 1978, p. 349). Margery was a religious woman who refused the space traditionally allotted to religious women—the sanctuary (or imprisonment) provided by the anchoress's cell or the nunnery.[4] Her lack of circumspection, her insistence on living in the world, enables the social dimension which makes her mysticism distinctive. And it is this social dimension, something insisted upon in her life and apparent in her book, which facilitates an account of the material context of mysticism, an examination of the uses to which it is put in relations of power. Such an examination must precede any assessment of the precarious balance between subversion and subservience in the mystical text.

The first part of this paper 'The Discourse of Mysticism: Medieval and Modern' uses the critical reception of the *Book of Margery Kempe* to isolate and analyse the ideology at stake in the representation of mysticism and in particular the problems that consideration of women's mysticism reveal. The second section, 'Mystical Reflections' looks at the mystical philosophy behind Margery's Franciscan mysticism and provides a context for the third section, a fuller re-reading of the *Book of Margery Kempe* which redefines the interests of the book for feminist analysis.

The Discourse of Mysticism: Medieval and Modern

Although this stress on the determination of literary production is a necessary part of any thorough-going Marxist criticism, the historical and material determinations which as it were flow into the literary through the diverse and changing structures which condition the modes of its consumption are of no less importance. (Bennett, 1982, p. 225)

The 'social dimension' apparent in Margery's book has produced a series of critical responses which help reveal important ideological features in the representation of mysticism. When the Butler-Bowden manuscript was discovered in 1934, the initial and dominant critical response was a discussion as to the genuineness or otherwise of Margery's mysticism. Father Thurston, in his series of articles in the Catholic periodicals *The Month* and *The Tablet*, objects, for example, to the preoccupation with self evidenced in her competitiveness in spiritual affairs, quoting Margery's boastfulness about a certain Eucharistic vision which was granted to her but not St Birgitta. He objects to the theatricality of her 'exaltée piety, her disruption of town worship, her morbidity, her boisterousness and lack of decorum, and the publicity of her life: 'If she had really been an ancress, living secluded in her cell, these peculiarities would not have mattered. But she insisted on going everywhere following as she thought the special call of God' (Thurston, 1936, p. 570). It is a response shockingly similar to that of the 'eld monk' in Margery's book: 'I wold þow wer closyd in an hous of ston þat þer schuld no man speke wyth þe' (Meech and Allen, 1940, p. 27). To Thurston, then, Margery's personality, her theatricality, her excess, her sheer loudness, disqualify her as a medium of God's voice. Her book nominally written for the glorification of God ('þis lytyl tretys schal tretyn sumdeel in parcel of his wonderful werkys') is more concerned with the glorification of Margery. And she remains incapable of abasing herself sufficiently for the glory of her maker to shine through. Margery is simply too intransigently present (one reason why her book has been dubbed the 'first autobiography' in England).[5]

Behind such judgements as Thurston's rests a notion of absence, negativity, apophasis, as the only means of access to God. Commentary on mysticism makes the distinction between positive and negative mysticism. Positive mysticism uses imagery and analogy to approximate and approach God, seeing the Incarnation as the type and legitimation of such symbolising, the means through which God descends, and reciprocally the means of mystical ascent to God. This kind of mysticism, most closely associated with St

Bernard and St Francis, was the most popular and the dominant form of late medieval piety. Negative mysticism transmitted to the Middle Ages via the work of the pseudo-Dionysus abjures all symbol which it sees as necessarily inadequate; God's divinity being without limit, he cannot be finitely enclosed within any analogy or symbol, but only by the mystics' *kenosis* or self-emptying, a coming to a cloud of unknowing where no human image will obscure God's divinity. Generally in the representation of mysticism, it is the negative, mystical way that is the model for mysticism, privileged as the superior mystical mode. Clarissa Atkinson, in her book on Margery Kempe, *Margery Kempe, Mystic and Pilgrim* (1983), has suggested that the preference for Dionysian over the affective piety has led to value-judgements which inevitably affect assessment of Margery's mysticism. She cites Dom Knowles, who provides an historical overview of these mystical traditions in *The Religious Orders in England*:

> This stream [of pure spirituality] continued to flow till the reign of Henry VIII but there is some evidence that from the beginning of the fifteenth century onwards it was contaminated by another current, that of a more emotional and idiosyncratic devotion manifesting itself in visions, revelations and unusual behaviour deriving partly from the influence of some of the woman saints of the fourteenth century, woman such as Angelo of Foligno, Dorothea of Prussia and Bridget of Sweden. The most familiar example of this type in England is Margery Kempe. (Atkinson, 1983, pp. 222–3)[6]

The 'contamination' of positive mysticism is one that is generally associated with women, as it is in this quotation:

> the austere mystical theology of antiquity with its negative way on the one hand and its platonism on the other did not lend itself to the feminine temperament which is by nature so much more attracted to the sensible and the personal. (Graef, 1959, p. 242)

The way negative mysticism approaches its objects, and the transformations and tensions it discovers in confronting and recognising the impossibility of its own mystical project, constitute an enormous area which I have no room to deal with in the short space of this paper. The point here is that in the *representation* of mysticism the polarisation of negative and positive mysticism and their accompanying sexual polarisation is a mystification. Negative mysticism, by insisting on the unrepresentability of the Other (God) refuses the return to the social sphere. Indeed, this is the source of its transcendence: a God outside time and language and history is inviolable to change, the perfect legitimation of the system of which He is the transcendental centre and support. Positive mysticism has the potential to embarrass that claim to unrepresentability and reveal the extraordinarily heavy ideological investment in the immateriality, the unrepresentability of God in his function as the Other. Of course, the claims of the mystical project, on an excess beyond the confines of the social and symbolic order, the possibilities it embodies for those dissatisfied with that social order (mysticism then as an 'expression of real distress and the protest against real distress' experienced in society), are vital to those for whom the social order remains so patently inadequate. Indeed, for some modern critics it is the very numinousness and immediacy of the mystical experience that guarantees mysticism as a 'dissident ideology', 'site of the revolutionary possibilities of the Christian religion' (Ozment, 1973, p. 1). And for many influential late nineteenth- and early twentieth-century pioneering theorists of mysticism, it was precisely the loss of confidence in institutionalised religion which led to this view of mysticism as a spiritual experience unsullied by the confinements and compromises of its sanctioned and official incarnation (Gimello, 1983, p. 86). Medieval mystics often presented a source of intense anxiety to the Church which regarded itself as the 'keeper of the Word', an anxiety intensified in a period of increasing lay literacy, where mysticism was a vital form of religious distress and dissent. But often mystics and the mystical experience could just as readily be used as a 'bulwark against heresy'. Fulk of Toulouse's interest in communities of religious women had precisely these aims in mind.[7]

To posit mysticism then as a natural source of resistance to orthodoxy is dangerously a-historical, both because the function of mysticism varies with the social and historical conditions in which it is produced and reproduced and because, over and above this, the very quality of mysticism which can empower its by-passing of official structure, its immediacy, its numinousness, its ineffability —in other words, a conception of it in terms of a direct or supra-linguistic encounter of God with the disembodied human soul— removes both God and the human soul from history. Mysticism has been taken at its Word and the dominant assumption about the discourse of mysticism seems to be imbued with the transcendental trajectory that was mysticism's goal. In the words of one anthologizer of mysticism, this view sees it as a 'perennial philosophy', a 'break through the world of time and history into one of eternity and timelessness' (Happold, 1979, p. 18)

It is in the work of the French feminist theorist, Luce Irigaray, that the most powerful and attractive claims have been made for mysticism, here linked with femininity as a natural source of dissent and a place in which the social and symbolic order is dissolved. According to Irigaray, the feminine is repressed in patriarchal discourse, posited as man's other, the mirror-image that presents to man his own reflection. Incapable of subjectivity herself, she is the static, motionless and emotionless figure whose movement might potentially disrupt the system of patriarchal discourse, reflection and self-reflection. Irigaray argues that mysticism, where the self and subjectivity are dissolved, is particularly attractive to women whom patriarchy places as, in any case, 'outside representation'. And yet it is this very (mystificatory) association which again places 'woman' beyond the pale. For as Toril Moi has argued in a discussion which links Irigaray's notion of mysticism to an accusation of her essentialism: 'is she not caught up in a logic which requires her to produce an image of woman which is exactly the same as the specular constructions of femininity in patriarchal logic?' (Moi, 1985). In a brief but suggestive comment, Moi points out that the frequent use of mirror-imagery in mystical writings represents the re-entry of specularisation into the mystical project. It is via an analysis of mirror-imagery in the works of Margery's contempories and its place in mystical theology that mysticism can be seen as the site of a complex play and interchange of roles, and that far from being the site of a dissolution of subjectivity, it is the place where a new subjectivity is evolved, through the contradictions, rather than the transcendental evasions, of the social and symbolic order.

Mystical Reflections

'We now see by means of a mirror in an enigma; but then face to face.' (St. Paul, I Corinthians 13.12)

The mirror-image was a crucial one in medieval theological writings. Its enormous suggestive power comes partly as a result of the ambivalences it was able to represent within a Platonic philosophical framework which viewed the whole created world itself as a reflection, a shadow of an ideal form. Christian Platonism (combined most influentially in the works of St Augustine) viewed the world as a reflection of God's glory. Thus, as a comment in the entry on the mirror-image in the *Dictionnaire de Spiritualité* indicates, the image represented exemplarity, and existed by virtue of its relation to an origin —God. 'Tout archetype s'exprime par une image dont il est l'origine et qui est son terme. L'image represente ce dont elle procède.' (*Dictionnaire de Spiritualité*, 7.2, p. 1428). But St Paul's words in Corinthians, which echo and re-echo in medieval theological writings, uses the mirror-image to insist both on likeness to and distance from this origin. His use of the image describes and accounts for the necessity of mediation and the possibility of a partial representation of God accommodated to human capacity, yet at the same time laments the very partiality of that mediation in the lack of (and therefore desire for) the heavenly harmony of face-to-face communion. The mirror-image represents and embodies the 'manifestation of the transcendent in the immanent' (*Dictionnaire de Spirltualité*, 10.2, p. 1295). It is because of this manifestation, because of the notion of resemblance between creator and created, that analogy, represented in the mirror-image, can enact the possibility of ascent to and communion with God. The mirror-image is for this reason frequently linked with the notion of the ladder:

> When we wish to ascend we naturally use a ladder, we who are men and are unable to fly. Then let us use a ladder, the similitude of visible things, so that the things we cannot see by direct vision we may come to be able to see from this watchtower and as though in a mirror. (Goldin, 1967, p. 8)[8]

The mirror-image, then, stresses both identity and difference and it is this tension in the ladder of analogy which provides the necessity for and the means of ascent. But it is the human soul itself which must become aware of its resemblance to its maker, must make its mirror mind clear and polished, transparent and receptive to allow and participate in resemblance to its divine origin. The human soul and mind can therefore only come to know itself truly as an image of its maker, and it is this important notion which links the growth of self-consciousness to the knowledge of God. In the words of St Bernard:

> Thus the knowledge of thyself will be a step to the knowledge of God: He will become visible in His Image, which is renewed in thee; whilst thou, beholding with confidence as in a glass the glory of the Lord art changed into the same image from glory, to glory, even as by the Spirit of the Lord. (Eales, 1895, p. 237)

It is both the resemblance and dissemblance of the soul to God that allows the 'self-knowledge' to come into existence.

A similar dialectic of alienation and identification is formulated in the psychoanalytic theories of Jacques Lacan. His notion of the 'mirror stage' is crucial to his account of the birth of subjectivity. According to Lacan, a child undergoes a 'mirror phase' of development between the ages of six to eighteen months in which it comes to see its body, which is still uncoordinated and fragmented, as whole in the mirror-image of itself. The child, who is in reality hopelessly uncoordinated (Lacan's 'hommelette'), and who does not experience his or her body as a defined and discrete entity misrecognises itself as complete, whole and discrete by an identification with its counterpart in the mirror. But this identification is itself dependent on the discovery of difference, of a lack which creates the desire for unity with the image. If the mirror stage participates in the imaginary—Lacan's formulation for the type of apprehension in which factors such as resemblance and identification play a decisive role—it also participates in the symbolic because the process of identification of the self reveals the extent to which the self is not whole or complete but always like an other, radically decentred. Lacan sees the mirror phase as both an identifiable stage in infant development but also one which serves as a metaphor for the way the child identifies with its mother's body and the bodies of other children. It is a stage which is never finally surpassed but forms 'the matrix and first outline of what is to become the ego' (Laplanche and Pontalis, 1973, p. 251).

The mirror phase has been described as the 'vision of harmony by a being in discord' (Wilden, 1981, p. 174). This description simultaneously describes the relation of the mystical subject to her mirror. And the description reveals the similarity of Lacan's terms of reference with the use to which the mirror-image is put in medieval mystical theology. For in medieval mystical theology the soul is both alienated from its maker and yet fantasises its own wholeness by misrecognition of itself with and in its maker.

Lacan's theory of the mirror stage provides the possibility of identifying in the use of the same imagery in medieval theological writings, a series of identifications and resemblances where the ego is constructed not dissolved. Such structures of identification are crucial to mysticism and reveal the extent to which there can be no simple divorce of mysticism from its theologisation, nor from the system of social relationships and identifications which mediate it.

If the Pauline use of the mirror-image deployed in medieval theology indicates the function of the mirror to accomodate God to human capacity and to point out the necessity for mediation in a post-lapsarian world, it is Christ, who, specifically, ideally and flamboyantly comes to fill this role in late medieval mystical writings. God in his Incarnation as Christ has condescended to become human; like the mirror, he unites his 'material nature to a spiritual reality' (Goldin, 1967, p. 8), so that he can function as the means of ascent and communion with God. It is Christ who represents the problematic relationship between spirit and matter, finite and infinite in medieval Christianity. His Incarnation functions like a mirror to accommodate God to human understanding. The book, the *Myrrour of the Blessyd Lyf of Christ* indicates the extent to which Christ's Incarnation, Passion and Resurrection are described for the 'edificacioun of hem the ben of symple understandynge':

> to the whiche soules as Seint Bernard saith contemplacioun of the manhede of God is mor lyking more spedeful and more siker than hige contemplacioun of the godhede. And therefore to hem is principally to be sette in minde the ymage of Cristes incarnacioun passion and resurrection ... so that a symple soul that kan not thenke bot bodies or bodily thinges maye have somewhat according to his affecioun wherewith he may fede and stirre his devocioun. (Powell, 1908, p. 9)

This book, the *Meditationes Vitae Christi*, was an enormously popular Franciscan text, translated into Middle English by Nicholas Love in 1410 in a translation authorised by Thomas

Arundel, Archbishop of Canterbury. The book had an important part to play in the privatisation of devotion in a pedagogic initiative which attempted to limit that space even in its creation. It was part of an attempt by the Church to feed an increasingly literate lay audience who were looking to heretical sources to provide them with reading material in the vernacular. The reader is expected to play the role of spectator at Christ's Passion and he or she is carefully stage-managed in this relationship ('but now be ware ... now with inward compassion behold ... go forth with him') to identify with Christ with the ostensible purpose of realising the extent of Christ's love in his act of redemption.

It is here again that the relationship of the mystic to Christ in this book can be seen to be structured like a re-enaction of the mirror stage. The closed dialectic of spectatorship and identification is repeated in this image of the reader both observing and identifying with Christ in his passion, mis-recognising him or herself. Elizabeth Salter has emphasised the extent to which Love's work constitutes an attempt to counteract Lollard heresies and to co-opt and contain the faithful. Thus the mystical subject is called upon to misrecognise herself as whole in this dyadic relationship with Christ so as to quell the discord of heresy. The ideological function of such a misrecognition is also apparent in the way in which the humanity of Christ is often stressed to counteract prevailing continental heresies where the heretic could all too easily forget his or her creatureliness to assume identity with God. Emphasis on the abasement of Christ's flesh, on his humiliation in the Passion, indeed the very willingness of his subjection, was a useful counter to such tendencies.

The analogy of the mirror stage to the relationship of the mystic to Christ may help to reveal this ideological function—a potentially fluxive relationship is re-presented as a dyadic one of one-to-one imagery identification which encloses and contains a potential otherness in the image of the same. This identification, mimesis, resemblance, never achieves the identity with its creator which is its goal; and it is this gap, this permanent alienation, which perpetuates the mystical desire as it explores the profundity of its own lack of and distance from its creator. However, the relationship of the mystic to Christ cannot be simply typified by a process of one-to-one identification.

The fact of God's Incarnation allows him to be represented in a series of social and familial roles which extend the repertoire and flexibility of the mystical relation to Christ. Much of the pedagogic devotional literature of the late Middle Ages is concerned with the sanctifying and absolutising of social roles, a function that is clearly seen in its deployment of what may be termed the Holy Family Romance. The absolute is domesticated. In particular the female mystic is encouraged to see herself as mother to the infant Jesus, as his wife and sometimes his daughter in ways which clearly solidify her in these social roles. (The most startling example of this domestication of piety is found in the Prussian saint, Dorothea of Montau, who kindly offers her own skin as a suitable nappy for the infant Jesus.) The literature appears to be both a response to the potentially subversive nature of female desire and a way of domesticating and internalising it. Women form a new audience for this kind of literature. Richard Rolle wrote his *English Psalter* and his tracts, *Ego Dormio*, *The Commandment* and the *Form of Living* for nuns or recluses. Richard Misyn translated Rolle's *Incendium Amoris* for a recluse; the first part of Hilton's *Scale of Perfection* was written for a nun. *The Chastising of God's Children*, *Remedies against Temptation* and the *Myrour Of the Blessyd Lyf* all have female audiences in mind.[9] In addition, though much of this literature was translated for nuns or recluses, there is a growing pedagogic preoccupation with those who wished to lead a contemplative life while also remaining in the world. Analysis of wills reveals the extent to which many of these books were found in private houses and were therefore reaching a lay readership. Indeed, such a text as the *Abbey of the Holy Ghost* is 'founded in a place that is clepud conscience' (Blake, 1972, p. 88). Much of this literature was written for the creation and monitoring of that very conscience.

What such texts appear to do is to find an outlet for dissatisfaction but then recuperate that very dissatisfaction by redirecting it towards objects that finally support the social order. Thus Christ functions as a central image of one-to-one imaginary identification but is also used as a figure in a social drama, a way of absolutising and eternalising social norms, in particular deploying the Holy Family to underpin, sanctify and interiorise the emergent bourgeois family space, which itself is both a symptom of and a factor in the changing familial relationships that accompany a nascent mercantile capitalist economy.

The existence of this body of literature is a salutary reminder of the extent to which mystical relationships with God are not immune to relations of power and that far from being direct and unmediated, dissolving subjectivity in an escape out of the social and symbolic order, they only take place through the social relationships that mediate them.

Irigaray's contention that female mysticism celebrates women's specific access to the Imaginary, that subject–object positions dissolve in an undifferentiated mystical *jouissance*, can be seen to have problems when the specific context of late medieval female mysticism is examined. Indeed, it is the image of extreme objectification that remains from this literature as its dominant motif, the extreme objectification that constitutes the spectacle of Christ and the female mimesis of his passion.

Where the lives of Margery's contemporaries and models are available, it is plain that male hagiographers emphasise tableaux which most spectacularly depict the female saint in the pose of suffering, and that without these crucial representations of pain, her visions would be accorded no credibility. Raymond of Capua's account of the life of St Catherine of Siena privileges detailed accounts of Catherine's modes of self-mortification over descriptions of her interventions in the public affairs of ecclesiastical policy. It is clear that women's access to the visionary, far from deriving from their place outside representation, in patriarchy derives instead from the very specific representative function given to them in medieval culture, the specific representation of themselves as associated with the debased matter of the flesh, which they see valorised and redeemed in Christ's torture on the cross, a redemption through physicality.

In *The Second Sex*, Simone de Beauvoir has some interesting comments to make on the particular affinity women found with the crucifixion image:

> In the humiliation of God, she sees the dethronement of man, inert, passive, covered with wounds, the crucified is the reverse image of the white, bloodstained martyr exposed to wild beasts, to daggers, to males, with whom the girl has so often identified herself; she is overwhelmed to see that man, man-God has assumed her role. She it is who is hanging on the tree, promised the splendour of the resurrection. (de Beauvoir, 1976, p. 686)

De Beauvoir sees the identification of the devotional woman with Christ as based on a common identity as excessively vulnerable, passive, victimised. As suggested before I think we can add to this analysis the idea that it is also Christ's physicality, and the Passion as redemption through the carnal that attracted devotional woman, so closely identified with the world, the flesh and the devil.

But mystical women's special attraction to Christ can also be seen to derive from his position in the psychic structure of the Passion story. For in his Passion, Christ is acted upon rather than acting, and his body becomes the site onto which desire is projected. Like woman (as constructed by patriarchal discourse) he is the 'gateway to the infinite and the measure [of a man's] finite nature' (Ibid., p. 175). His submission to the Father acts as a public token that God's power is unchallenged and he functions as an exchange object to guarantee and ratify the mutually beneficial hierarchy of God and man. To understand this as a feminisation, we may trace a series of parallels between these structures and the position of women in medieval patriarchal society. Women were traditionally acted upon rather than acting, their bodies were the site onto which desire was projected (as in the vast literature of courtly love). Marriage for medieval women was an exchange from one man to another, from father to husband. Women's bodies in every way functioned as substitute objects to act as a locus for desire and as a guarantee to underwrite complex property deals between families.

Margery's Passion

This identification of mystical women with Christ is not simply embraced by them; it is also required of them. For Margery identification with Christ has a central enabling function. It is only by virtue of this relationship that she is allowed a voice in the first place. Margery's book was written at a time when literacy and learning was still dominated by a male clergy explicitly trying to maintain this privilege against lay encroachment. To be a lay woman compounded the threat. John Gerson writes:

The female sex is forbidden on apostolic authority to teach in public, that is either by word of mouth or writing. . . . All women's teaching is to be held suspect unless it has been examined diligently and much more fully than men's. The reason is clear, common law—and not any kind of common law—but that which comes from on high forbids them. And why? Because they are easily seduced and determined seducers, and because it is not proved that they are witnesses to divine grace. (quoted in Colledge and Walsh, 1978, p. 151)

Women could not speak as themselves, but only as visionaries (the instruments or medium of God's voice), and even then only with great difficulty, for they always had to convince the male ecclesiastical authorities of the validity of their special relationship to God. One of the guarantees of this special relationship was their own self-abnegation; a demonstration of self-hatred could save the authorities some work. Margery's frequent arrests as a Lollard, her quarrels with the ecclesiastical authorities, derive in part from the problematic nature of self-abnegation. For she refused confinement in an anchoress's cell, yet insisted simultaneously on her claim to a holy reputation. It is her identificatory relationship with the Passion of Christ which is both a demonstration of her self-abnegation and by a typically Christian inversion, a laying claim to a different kind of power.

Margery's book is a dense source of responses to the Passion. For this very reason it is particularly useful in offering a grammar of available female responses to the Passion, from a lay woman who has continued to worship in the world, and so it enables us to examine the potential function of the Passion in a late fourteenth-century woman's life—a potential that can only by realised by choice which involves certain tensions and sacrifices.

Margery identifies with Christ to such an extent in her book, that she claims that he claims that her voice is his: 'þei þat worship þe þei worship me; þei þat deespysenen me, & I schal chastysen hem þerfor. I am in þe and þow in me. And þei þat heryn þe þei heryn þe voys of God' (p. 23). It is an identification bought with a share of his sufferings which engenders a reciprocal caring: 'þu hast so gret compassyon of my flesche I must nede have compassyon of þy flesch' (p. 183). But Margery's sufferings are not simply an accident of her life, a side-effect of her mode of worshipping—they are a constantly sought source of identification with Christ:

Hyr þowt sche wold a be slayn for Goddys lofe, but dred for þe poynt
of deth, & þefore sche ymagynd hyr-self þe most soft deth, as hyr
þowt, for dred of inpaycens, þat was to bounden hyr hed & hyr fet to a
to a stokke & hyr hed to be smet of wyth a scharp ex for Goddys lofe.
(p. 30)

She compels herself to imagine pain to comprehend and share his
Passion. The moment where this identification is most acute is
during Margery's pilgrimage to Jerusalem, where she is taken by
the friars whose task it was to guide the pilgrims to the holy
places, to Mount Calvary, the site of Christ's crucifixion:

> þan þe frerys lyftyd up a cros & led þe pylgrimys a-bowte fro place to
> an-oþer wher owyr Lord had sufferyd hys... passyons ... & þe forseyd
> creatur wept and sobbyd so plentyvowsly as þow sche had seyn owyr
> Lord wyth hir bodily ey sufferyng hys passyon at þat tyme. (p. 68)

As Margery walks the Stations of the Cross, her identification with
Christ becomes a mimesis:

> whan thorw dispensaycon of þe hy mercy of owyr Souereyn Savyowr
> Crist Ihesu it was grawntyd þis creatur to beholdyn so verily hys
> precyows tendyr body, alto-rent & torn wyth scorgys, mor ful of
> wowndys þan euyr was duffehows of holys, hangyng up-on þe cros
> wyth þe corown of thorn up-on hys heuyd, hys blysful handys, hys
> tendyr fete nayled to þe hard tre, þe reuerys of blood flowying owt
> plentevowsly of every membre, þe gresly & grevows wownde in hys
> precyows syde schedynge owt blood & water for hir lofe & hyr
> saluacyon, þan sche fel down & cryed wyth lowde voys, wondyrfully
> turnyng & wrestyng hyr body on every syde, spredyng hir armes
> a-brode as gyf sche xulde a deyd, & not cowde kepyn hir fro crying,—&
> þese bodily mevyngys for þe fyer of lofe þat brent so feruently in hir
> sowle wyth pur pyte & compassyon. (p. 70)

It is here that Margery first begins her tears through which she
visibly participates in the Passion. Margery's identification with
Christ is most explicit in this literal imitation of the Passion as she
stretches out her own arms in the shape of the Cross. And it is an
identification that is highly dramatic, functioning to claim a status
for her as a participant in the drama of the Passion. The first mode
of identification subjectifies Christ's experience. But it is also the
starting-point for a number of developments of her relationship
with Christ which introduce an objectification of Christ (as object

of desire) and so necessarily enter the complexities of social relationships through which any subject–object relationship must be mediated. For inextricably bound up with the initial display of cries is Margery's 'gostly labowr', her conception of spiritual childbirth. After her description of her journey through the Stations of the Cross, and before the climactic description of Christ's torn and bleeding body, Margery specifies that it is here, at Calvary, that her tears begin, and describes the pattern of their development.

And þerfore, whan sche knew þat sche xulde cryen, sche kept it in as long as sche mygth & dede al þat sche cowde to withstond it er ellys to put it a-wey til sche wex as blo as any leed, & euyr it xuld laborwryn in hir minde mor & mor in-to þe tyme þat it broke owte & what þe body myth ne lengar enduryn þe gostly labowr but was ouyrcome wyth be unspekabyl lofe þat wrowt so fervently in þe sowle, þan fel sche down & cryde wondyr lowde & þe mor þat sche wolde labowryn to kepe it in er to put it a-wey, mech þe mor xulde sche cryen & þe mor lowder. (p. 69)

Thus at Calvary, with the onset of her cries, Margery both identifies with Christ and simultaneously gives birth to him. What supports the view of the 'gostly labowr' as a simultaneous identification and parturition is its location in the process of the shifting of the cries from identification to a response to young male children. The sight of a male baby in its mother's arms is enough to trigger off Margery's identification with the Passion, and here she is clearly identifying as a mother to Christ. In Chapter 35, where she discusses her preference for the manhood of God over his Godhood on being asked by the Father to marry his Godhood, she says:

Sche was so meche affectyd to þe manhode of Criste þat whan sche sey women in Rome beryn children in her armys, gyf sche myth wetyn þat þei wer ony men children, sche schuld þan cryin, roryn, & wepyn as þei sche had seyn Crist in hys childhode. And yf sche myth an had hyr wille, oftyn-tymed sche wolde a takyn e childeryn owt of e moderys armys & a kyssed hem in stede of Criste. (p. 86)

She continues:

And gyf sche sey a semly man, sche had gret peyn to lokyn on hym les than sche myth a seyn hym þat was boþe man & god. And erfore sche cryed many tyme & oftyn whan sche met a semly man & wept ful sor in þe manhod of Crist as sche went in þe stretys at Rome.

Here she is clearly identifying herself as a lover of Christ with Christ's attractiveness imaged in attractive men she happens to pass in the streets around her. For once Christ is an object of love for Margery, she is forced into the position of defining the type of loved being that Christ is (son, father, lover, husband, mother), and so her own identity must shift according to the social relationship that love constitutes (i.e. as a mother to the Christ child, as daughter to God the Father, a lover or wife to Christ). The interchangeability of her roles is developed extensively throughout the book. In Chapter 14, Christ makes explicit reference to the permutations of his relationship with her:

> Þerfore I preue þat þow art a dowtyr to me & a moder also, syster, a wyfe and a spowse, wytnessyng þe gospel wher owr Lord seyth to hys dysyples, 'He þat doth þe wyl of my Fadyr in Heuvyn he is bothyn modyr, broþyr & syster to me.' Whan thow stodyst to plese me, þan art þu a very dowtyr; whan þu wepyst & mornyst for my peyn & for my passyon þan art þu a very modyr to me to have compassyon of hyr child; whan thow wepyst for oþer mennys synnes and for adversytes, þan art þow a very syster; and, whan thow sorwyst for þow art so long fro þe blysse of Heuyn, þan art þu a very spowse & a wyfe, for it longyth to þe wyfe to be wyth hir husband & no very joy to han tyl sche come to hys presens. (p. 31)

Christ develops his marital relationship with Margery when he says in Chapter 36:

> And gyf I wer in erde as bodily as I was er I deyd on þe cros, I schuld not ben a-schamyd of þe as oþer men ben, for I schuld take þe be þe hand amongs þe peple & make þe gret cher þat þei schuldyn wel knowyn þat I lovyd þe ryth wel. For it is conuenant þe wyfe to be homly wyth þe husband. Be he neuyr so gret a lorde & sche so powr a woman whan he weddyth hir, yet þei must ly togedir in joy & pes.... Þerfore most I nedys be homly wyth þe and lyn in þi bed wyth þe. Dowtyr, thow desyryst gretly to se me, & þu mayst boldly, whan þu art in þi bed, take me to þe as for þy weddyd husband, as þy derworthy derlying, and as for þy swete sone, for I wyl be louyd as a sone schuld be louyd wyth þe modyr & wil þat þu loue me, dowtyr, as a good [wife]

owyth to loue hyr husbond. & perfore þu mayst boldly take me in þe armys of þi sowle & kyssen my mowth, myn hed & my fete as swetly as þow wilt. (p. 90)

The multiplication of the role of the love object—Christ as lover, son, husband, father—undoes the social codification of desire by its incestuous simultaneity. 'She is no longer capable of separating the sensual from the spiritual,' says Wolfgang Riehle disapprovingly (Riehle, 1981, p. 11).

In a particularly startling mingling of the spiritual and the sensual, she hallucinates what most of her critics have preferred not to see, let alone comment on—'prestys membres'—the genitals of the priestly caste:

> And as sche beforn had many gloryows visyonys & hy contemplacyon in þe manhod of owr Lord, in owr Lady, & in many oþer holy seyntys, ryth euyn so had sche now horybyl syghtys & abhominabyl, for anythyng þat sche cowde do, of beheldyng of mennys membres & swech oþer abhominacyons. Sche sey as hir thowt veryly dyuers men of religyon, prestys, & many þer bothyn hethyn & Cristen comyn be-for hir syght, schewyng her bar membres un-to hir. & þerwyth þe Deuyl bad hir in hir mende chesyn whom sche wolde han fyrst of hem alle and sche must be comown to hem alle .... þes horribyl syghtys & cursyd mendys were delectabyl to hir ageyn hir wyl. (p. 145)

Incapable of repression, the sexuality of the priestly caste returns to plague her in the form of her desire and her fear. One would like to take her hallucination as a symptom of her subversion; just as she insists on the sexuality of God in the rest of the book, upsetting the specious claim of his transcendent impassivity, so here she might be seen as lifting the veil, the priestly skirts that hide the Phallus which reproduces priestly law as God. She shows it to be merely a penis, or in her own words an 'abhominabyal membre'.

But Margery's hallucination is more the sign of her shame than her subversion. It is sent as a punishment, a period of chastisement, because of her difficulties in accepting God's damnation of sinners, all who do not obey his law. It is a sign, less of her transgression, than the unconscious effects of subjection to that very law. Coming from the devil not God, it is juxtaposed with her 'gloryows visyonys' from God, Our Lady and the saints, only to be discarded, appearing in the form it does *because* of the necessity for its sublimation. By returning to and insisting on grating domestic hierarchies against the transcendent, Margery Kempe's positive mysticism embarrasses the myth of God's neutral transcendence. And her embarrassing foregrounding of the insistently physical emphasises the contradictions rather than the miraculous resolution of flesh and spirit in the Passion.

By approximating herself to Christ, misrecognising herself in him, by living a life which is itself a mimesis and remembrance of the Passion, the female mystic may gain access to the Word, or to those more human expedients, words. It is a strategy that never attempts, that is unable to attempt, to break the mould of its subjection. Indeed it cannot, for it is the very equation of victimisation, passivity, subjection with femininity, that allows the Christian inversion its paradoxical triumph. But like a serf becoming king, it is a deposition, a usurpation that changes the terms but never the structure; and so the nature of the change must remain severely limited. Indeed, it may be argued that by underpinning that subjection with a heavenly guarantor, that very subjection is validated and perpetuated on earth, if it is not in the heaven deferred to in these writings.

A feminist analysis of medieval women's mysticism must seek to explain the historical attraction of neo-Franciscanism for women. In doing so it must move beyond the sanctification of the marginal to an interrogation of the structures of power, the boundaries and definitions that enforce marginality onto women.

Notes

1. This term is notoriously vague because of the extended use to which it is put across a diverging range of theoretical discourse, from de Beauvoir's existentialist categorisation to Lacan's psychoanalytic reformulation. The term has been redeployed by French feminist theorists such as Cixous and Irigaray, who use a version of Derrida to deconstruct the sexual hierarchies they see in all binary oppositions. This sense (the one I use here) carries the meaning of the Other as a fantasy, because there is no stable site of meaning over against which a stable identity can differentiate itself. (See second epigraph.)
2. See Toril Moi (Chapter 2, this volume) for a feminist examination of Capellanus's *The Art of Courtly Love*, which demonstrates how this

process of differentiation and construction operates at the level of class as well as gender. There is also a fascinating account of the relationship between the Wife of Bath's Prologue and Tale, read as a redeployment of courtly love from an ideology concerned with the cultural construction of a masculine warrior identity to an ideology concerned with the construction of a new, interiorised, privatised and specifically feminine mode of fantasy and wish-fulfilment, in an unpublished paper by Louise Fradenburg, 'The Wife of Bath's Passing Fancy'. For an account of the mirror analogy in courtly love literature, see Goldin (1967).

3. Lacan's (in)famous divisions are the Imaginary and the Symbolic. The Imaginary is used to designate a pre-linguistic stage (which is not necessarily restricted to any particular chronological moment but intersects with the Symbolic) where the child exists in a state of one-to-one identification with its mother or objects around it, where it cannot think separation but where there is a fluid confusion of its own identity and the people and things around it. With the Oedipus stage the child enters the Symbolic order through the intervention of a third term which by breaking the closed circuit of imaginary identification, subjects the child to language and social imperatives. It is through this process that the unconscious also comes into being. According to Lacan any attempt to live outside the symbolic will render us psychotic. One of the key debates surrounding Lacan's terminology is of course the extent to which it functions as description or prescription.

4. The anchoress's cell was a space attached to a church or monastery in which a woman would be enclosed, after a ceremony in which she would be symbolically buried (to die to the world) and married to Christ, as a way of dedicating her life to contemplation and worship. The anchoress's cell provides an interesting spatial symbolism for the liminal position of women mystics in medieval society, both structurally supporting the church in their position under the eaves and a potential pocket of subsidence. Margery was particularly unpopular with Thomas Netter, the Carmelite Provincial who supported individual holy women on the condition that they were both silent and enclosed. See Allen and Meech, notes to 168/5 and 170/7.

5. Of course, the decentring and destruction of ego that is crucial to the anti-humanist project of establishing a mystical subjectivity make this ascription highly problematic.

6. It is clear from this quotation from Knowles that the exclusion of women saints of positive piety is instrumental in the very construction of a 'pure spirituality'. The one is excluded so that the other can come into being. But it is also clear that even in the very

attempt at this shutting off, this closing down, the forbidden body returns in the latent image of mysticism as a body open to contamination.
7. See Brenda Bolton (1978).
8. The quotation is from Richard of St Victor's *De Trinitate* (V.VI).
9. *Ego Dormio, The Commandment* and the *Form of Living* are available in Allen (1931). For Misyn's translation of Rolle's *Incendium Amoris*, see Harvey (1896). For an edition of the *Scale of Perfection*, see Kuriyagawa (1967). For the *Chastising* see Bazire and Colledge (1957). For the *Myrour*, see Powell (1908).

References

Adorno, Theodor and Horkheimer, Max (1944) *Dialectic of Enlightenment*. (London: New Left Books, rpt. 1979).

Allen, Hope Emily (ed.) (1931) *English Writings of Richard Rolle Hermit of Hompole* (Oxford: Clarendon Press).

Allen, Hope Emily and Meech, Sanford (eds) (1940) *The Book of Margery Kempe* (Oxford: Oxford University Press).

Atkinson, Clarissa (1983) *Mystic and Pilgrim: The Book and the World of Margery Kempe* (Ithaca N.Y.: Cornell University Press).

Bazire, Joyce and Colledge, Edmund (eds) (1957) *The Chastising of God's Children and the Treatise of Perfection of the Sons of God* (Oxford: Blackwell).

de Beauvoir, Simone (1949) *The Second Sex* (Harmondsworth: Penguin Books, rpt. 1976).

Bennett, Tony (1982) 'Text and History' in Peter Widdowson (ed.), *Rereading English* (London: Methuen).

Blake, Norman F. (ed.) (1972) *Middle English Religious Prose* (London: Edward Arnold).

Bolton, Brenda (1978) 'Vitae Matrum': a further aspect of the *Frauenfrage*', in Derek Baker (ed), *Medieval Women* (Oxford: Blackwell).

Bynum, Caroline Walker (1982) *Jesus as Mother: Studies in the Spirituality of the High Middle Ages* (Berkeley: University of California Press).

Colledge, E. and Chadwick N. (1968) 'Remedies against Temptations. *The Third English Version* of William Fulk' (Rome: Edizione di toria e Letteratura).

Colledge, Edmund and Walsh, James (eds) (1978) *A Book of Showings to the Anchoress Julian of Norwich*, 2 Parts (Toronto: Pontificial Institute of Medieval Studies).

Dictionnaire de Spiritualité (1937-79), ed. Marcel Villier *et al.* (Paris:

Gabriel Beauchesne).

Eales, S. J.(tr. and ed.) (1895) *Cantica Canticorum: Eighty Six Sermons by St Bernard of Clairvaux* (London: Elliot Stock).

Feral, Josette (1978) 'Antigone or the Irony of the Tribe', *Diacritics*, 8.

Gimello, Robert M. (1983) 'Mysticism in its Contexts', in Steven T. Katz (ed.), *Mysticism and Religious Traditions* (Oxford: Oxford University Press).

Goldin, Fredric (1967) *The Mirror of Narcissus in the Courtly Love Lyric* (Ithaca, N.Y.: Cornell University Press).

Goodman, Antony (1978) 'The Piety of John Brunham's Daughter of Lynn', in Derek Baker (ed.) *Medieval Women* (Oxford: Blackwell).

Graef, Hilda (1959) *The Light and the Rainbow* (London: Longmans).

Happold, F. C. (1963) *Mysticism: A Study and an Anthology* (Harmondsworth: Penguin Books, rpt. 1979).

Harvey, R. (ed.) (1896) *The Fire of Love and the Mending of Life*, tr. Richard Misyn 1434-5 (Oxford: Oxford University Press).

Irigaray, Luce (1974) *Speculum de l'autre femme* (Paris: Minuit).

Kuriyagawa, F. (ed.) (1967) *Walter Hilton's Eight Chapters on Perfection* (Tokyo: Keio Institute of Cultural and Linguistic Studies).

Laplanche, J. and Pontalis, J. B. (1973) *The Language of Psychoanalysis* (New York: Norton).

Mitchell, Juliet and Rose, Jaqueline (eds) (1982) *Feminine Sexuality: Jacques Lacan and the Ecole Freudienne* (London: Macmillan).

Moi, Toril (1985) *Sexual/Textual Politics* (London: Methuen).

Ozment, Stephen (1973) *Mysticism and Dissent* (New Haven: Yale University Press).

Powell, Laurence (1908) *Myrour of the Blessyd Lyf of Christ* (Oxford: Clarendon Press).

Riehle, W. (1981) *The Middle English Mystics* (London: Routledge & Kegan Paul).

Thurston, Father (1936) 'Review of *The Book of Margery Kempe*', *The Tablet*.

Wilden, Antony (1981) *Speech and Language in Psychoanalysis*. (Baltimore: Johns Hopkins University Press).

4

Reflections on the 'Allegory of the Theologians', Ideology and *Piers Plowman*

David Aers

In the 1960s a sometimes obsessive fascination with the 'allegory of the theologians' (clerical allegory developed in Biblical exegesis) became a prominent feature in studies of medieval literature. This is especially true of those emanating from the United States. It was maintained that the methods of allegorical exegesis practised by theologians and homilists were the key which unlocked the real meaning of all writing from St Augustine to the Reformation, a meaning which remained totally unproblematic and unchanged across these 1100 years of European history. In the words of the movement's leaders: 'all of serious poetry written by Christian authors, even that usually called "secular", is always allegorical when the message of charity or some corollary of it is not evident on the surface' (Robertson and Huppé, 1951, p. 16). This allegory allegedly became 'a habit of mind' and produced, as in the work of medievalists attempting to imitate its methods, 'a kind of continuous present' in which 'temporal sequences acquired something of the nature of an illusion' (Robertson, 1962, pp. 335, 301). Using the apparatus of clerical allegory, Robertson and his followers extracted an unchanging and conveniently simple set of ideas from an extraordinary wide range of texts produced in very different circumstances and contexts. One of the most pleasant ironies in this North American enterprise is that it propagated its monumental disregard for medieval history in all its dimensions— social, economic, ecclesiastical, political, philosophical even theological—under the banner of 'historical criticism' (Robertson, 1951).

Derek Pearsall, (Chapter 7, this volume) discusses some of the major unspoken assumptions in this academic movement, and his observations point towards the kind of analysis it needs. Like any other movement, this seemingly bizarre but influential episode in the history of criticism needs to be located within the social and ideological contexts which fostered it, permeated it, received it, and to whose horizons its practitioners seem to have been quite blind. It would be useful to have a study of the kind Chris Baldick recently made of the social mission of English criticism from Arnold to Leavis, exploring the movement's genesis, its particular kind of moralising, its politics, its class affiliations, its relations to its culture's McCarthyism, Puritan heritage, imperialism and the Cold War (Lentricchia, 1980; Baldick, 1983; Eagleton, 1983). This, however, is not such a study; suffice it here, in conjunction with Derek Pearsall's comments, to mark the radically anti-historical and idealist nature of the school of criticism most devoted to medieval allegory. Perhaps its most powerful long-term influence has been not in its allegorising methods, but in this anti-historical account of a homogeneous age of faith combined with its idealist approach to medieval cultural production—but here it merges with dominant tendencies in Anglo-American criticism, as does poststructuralism or deconstruction, which has shown some interest in allegory (de Man, 1969). The claim here seems to be that allegory affirms the arbitrariness of the sign, so constituting a more adequate discourse than romantic symbolism which, so the argument goes, cultivated a metaphysics of presence. But if this movement ever attracts medievalists, it will not encourage a more serious interest in the relationships between allegorical modes and historical practices. For the version of poststructuralism increasingly fashionable in the USA seems most impressed by Derrida's now famous statement that there is nothing outside the text (1976, p. 158). In this way American poststructuralism merges comfortably enough with now traditional New Critical formalism and its dissolution of the social and historical dimensions of literature, a dissolution accompanied by a refusal to reflect on the social and ideological dimensions of critical practice (Said, 1972; Lentricchia, 1980 and 1984; Ryan, 1982; Eagleton, 1983; Waller, 1983). The openly anti-historical nature of American poststructuralism should make its impact on medieval studies minimal, but its fashionable and easy application to any text (always an advantage in universities demanding that academics pile up publication on publication) together with its political conservatism, will attract some following among medievalists.

Be that as it may, my own starting-point is suggested by some lines in Chaucer's Summoner's Tale:

> I have to day been at youre chirche at messe,
> And seyd a sermon after my symple wit,
> Nat al after the text of hooly writ;
> For it is hard to yow, as I suppose,
> And therfore wol I teche yow al the glose.
> Glosynge is a glorious thyng, certeyn,
> For lettre sleeth, so as we clerkes seyn.
> There have I taught hem to be charitable,
> And spende hir good ther it is reasonable;
>
> (11. 1788–96)

This essay is a meditation on these lines. Obviously enough, it has no pretensions to comprehensiveness, whether in its observations on the allegory of the theologians or poetic uses of these modes. Medieval allegory was extraordinarily diverse, in mode and function. Here I address important aspects of clerical allegory which have been rather ignored, and invite others to pursue the issues raised with a specificity and detail beyond this essay's limited scope. Of course I am *glosynge* Chaucer's lines—'Glosynge is a glorious thyng, certeyn, … so as we clerkes seyn'. How else do 'we clerkes', whether of the Right or the Left, gain our daily bread and wine? But I hope the *glosynge* I offer may encourage a more reflexive approach to the social dimensions of *glosynge*—in the past, present, and in the interaction between past and present.

Chaucer's lines, given to a friar, represent that major clerical practice which so fascinated Robertson and his followers—Biblical exegesis, an activity with allegory at its core. The phrase used here to justify *glosynge* is 'the letter kills'. This phrase comes from Paul's Second Epistle to the Corinthians (Chapter 3) which had long since been wrenched from its context and twisted into a slogan legitimising the allegorical practices of medieval exegetes and their followers. The slogan equated allegory approved by institutionally accredited clerics with the saving, divine Spirit. Simultaneously, it aligned exclusive concentration on the literal meanings of Biblical narratives (at the expense of clerical *glosynge*) with the letter which kills, with the damned Jews who refused to allegorise their sacred Scriptures in accord with Christian dogmatics (de Lubac, 1959–63; Smalley, 1964). A popular fourteenth-century dictionary quoted by Robertson illustrates the commonplace clerical view:

> just as honey is contained in the honeycomb and is clarified and pressed forth, in the same way the letter contains an inner sense which is to be taken forth and held by right understanding reached through appropriate exposition. For this is the letter that kills, the old letter, since he who follows it according to its external appearance is killed by infidelity and made ancient in vices. The spirit, or the spiritual sense, is to be sought, but the literal, indeed, is to be wholly cast aside. (Robertson, 1962, pp. 302-3)

This is the nexus Chaucer alludes to. It is one where the issue of allegory is set within a context where the power of the clerical corporation in determining 'appropriate exposition' is fundamental. Allegory is inextricably bound up with the *power* of a particular social institution. It is not surprising that resistance to allegory is seen as 'infidelity', for 'infidelity', like heresy, was defined as obstinate opposition to the authority of the institution, the Catholic Church and its officials. As Bernard Gui, a fourteenth-century inquisitor, argued: 'one is presumed to be a heretic from the fact of striving to defend error.' And how is error to be determined? Bernard Gui has no doubts: by 'loyal, learned sons of the Church'. The circularity here is to be enforced by a coercive and very material apparatus: the person suspected of dissidence 'may be constrained in various ways: limited in food, held in prison, or chained; or he may even be put to the question [i.e. tortured]' (Wakefield and Evans, 1969, pp. 377, 411, 437). Our understanding of the modes and function of clerical allegory should at least attend to the social and institutional context in which it was generated. It becomes quite understandable that the early Protestant Tyndale should attack the traditional use of Paul's comments on the letter and the spirit, denying that the theologians' allegories were a sense of the Scripture (Greenblatt, 1980, pp. 100-5).

Chaucer's lines insert the practice of spiritual *glosynge* in this institutional context, *one* of the contexts in which we ourselves should always see it. The clerical exegete comments 'I have to day been at youre chirche at messe,/And seyd a sermon...'. It is here, in church, from the authoritative heights of the pulpit that he casts aside the literal sense, selecting the 'spiritual' gloss in approved fashion—'For lettre sleeth, so as we clerkes seyn.' Characteristically, Chaucer shows us how this religious practice has material foundations and consequences which affect the form and content of Christian teaching. He observes that the version of charity taught from the clerical pulpit, with its exegetical apparatus, serves the material interests of the clerical allegorists and the institution which employs them: 'There [in church] have I taught hem [lay people] to be charitable,/And spende hir good ther it is reasonable.' This matrix is also explored in the Pardoner's Prologue and Tale where the preacher relates:

> Of avarice and of swich cursednesse
> Is al my prechyng, for to make hem free
> To yeven hir pens, and namely unto me.
>
> (11. 400-2)

The poet was always intrigued by the way seemingly 'impersonal' discourses of the highest authority relate to specific interests of identifiable social groups, one of whose key strategies is to appropriate for themselves claims to a lofty impersonality and universality. Langland too, like others, had comments on this clerical activity, claiming that friars:

> Glosed þe gospel as hem good liked;
> For coveitise of copes construwed it as þei wolde
> (*Piers Plowman*, B. pr. 58–61)

Not, of course, that the poet himself was hostile to the allegorical grid through which the orthodox were taught to read (Aers, 1975; Goldsmith, 1981).

The allegory of the theologians was a literary form well-shaped to impose orthodox ideology, both to acknowledge and control the diverse potentials of the eclectic writings gathered together and sacralised as the Bible. It was a practice designed both to stimulate and contain imaginative activity within the ideological framework constructed by the Catholic Church, a very material corporation whose 'literal' foundations, according to contemporary critics such as the Lollards and Langland, needed more than allegory to 'spiritualise' them (Aers, 1980, Chs. 2, 3). From this perspective clerical allegory sought to stifle (or at least appropriate) the potential of literature to break through the horizons of the manipulated and ideologically controlled daily world, that potential to 'evoke the words, the images, the music of another reality, of another order repelled by the existing one and yet alive in memory and anticipation, alive in what happens to men and women, and in their rebellion against it' (Marcuse, 1972, pp. 92–3). Such potential the clerics' allegory sought to control.

For those unfamiliar with the standard practices of clerical allegory, examples abound in easily accessible secondary literature (Robertson and Huppé, 1951; de Lubac, 1959–63; Robertson, 1962; Smith, 1966). I have neither the space nor wish to go over ground I have myself ploughed before (Aers, 1975, esp. Chs 1, 2), but I shall include some illustration of clerical allegory when discussing *Piers Plowman*, and it may be worth offering a brief example now in relation to the Song of Songs, or Song of Solomon. That text celebrates a sexual relationship with uninhibited pleasure. But in orthodox Catholic teaching on marriage, *sexual* love and pleasure were condemned even within marriage, and the too ardent lover of his or her own spouse judged as an adulterer. This line is perfectly explicit in Chaucer's Parson's Tale and the tradition is fully described in J. T. Noonan's (1966) major study; there too he amply shows the 'failure to incorporate love into the purposes of marital intercourse' (pp. 256–7). Nicolaus of Ausimo was hardly eccentric when he asserted that there could only be no sin in marital sex if there were no enjoyment of pleasure in it ('hoc est in executione ipsius actus nulla voluptatis delectatione teneatur'; Tentler, 1977, p. 181). Chaucer's Parson would have agreed, claiming that if a married couple 'assemble oonly for amorous love' then they commit 'deedly synne' (940). So clerical allegory had much work to do on the Song of Songs. The carnal and very literal love in the text was read as an allegorical narrative of the spiritual union between Christ and the Catholic Church, Christ and the Virgin, or Christ and the saved Christian soul. The text's celebration of sexual desire was sublimated, and allegorical imagery made a vehicle for ideologically correct statements. For example, when the woman says, 'my beloved put his hand through my opening and my bowels were moved at his touch', clerical allegory sought to make the reader set aside the letter which kills and draw out an approved 'spiritual' sense: the image really meant that the spiritual bride (Church, Virgin, soul) opened the door of the heart to Christ or divine illumination

(Kelly, 1975, p. 311). Or when the male celebrates the body of the woman he loves:

> How beautiful art thou, my love, how beautiful art thou! Thy eyes are doves' eyes, besides what is hid within. Thy hair is as flocks of goats which come up from mount Galaad.
> Thy teeth as flocks of sheep, that are shorn, which come up from the washing, all with twins: and there is none barren among them. (4.1-2)

St Augustine focuses on the letter, the woman's teeth, and initiates us into the spirit, reached through allegory: this discloses that the image relates to the saints of the official Catholic Church who cut men off from their un-Catholic errors, softening their hard hearts (by biting and chewing), and then swallowing them into the body of the orthodox Church (*On Christian Doctrine*, II. 6, 7). In this way clerical allegory sought to impose an ecclesiastically approved grid, to control the interaction between the readers' imagination and the text's diverse potentials. The implications of this enterprise are, quite obviously, political in the broadest sense (one which includes sexual politics, an aspect not broached in the present sketch).

Piers Plowman involves an extraordinary array of medieval literary forms, including a wide range of allegorical modes (Bloomfield, 1961, Ch. 1; Aers, 1975). It is also an unusual medieval religious poem in being genuinely exploratory, one committed to engaging with contemporary social, theological and philosophical problems (Coleman, 1981). Time and again conventional formulations drawn from various traditions of orthodox thought are asserted; but instead of being left as assertions whose meaning is written all over their faces, they are immersed in searching, questioning processes which make them thoroughly *problematic*. Their apparent familiarity, even solidity, is undermined, sometimes in fiercely contested scholastic arguments, sometimes through dramatic figurations of forces and practices in the poet's culture which expose the received pieties as incantations with no significant purchase on the contemporary existence which preoccupies Langland. Fragmentation, ruptures and shifts in poetic modes are central to the meaning of this genuinely dialogic poem, in its own moment and as we re-read it, now. The comments I shall offer on Langland's relationship to clerical allegory can only deal with one aspect of this relationship, albeit one both important and in need of attention. The exemplification of the argument will be compressed and inevitably schematic, but this, I hope, need not be taken as a pitiful relapse into one-dimensional reductionism of Langland's symbolic modes.

In Passus VI (I use Kane and Donaldson's (1975) edition of the B text), Langland introduces Piers, the ploughman. This pious layman sets about organising essential social production, trying to keep it within the bounds of the customary tripartite ideology cherished by the poet. Elsewhere I have analysed the breakdown of the ploughman's enterprise and the multiplicity of subversive meanings this has for Langland's ideology, drawing especial attention to the powerlessness of the knight (Aers, 1980, pp. 12–20). The episode is also replete with theological issues, handled most cogently by Janet Coleman (1981, Chs. 2–3). Here, however, I wish to engage with the issue of allegory through what Langland chose to present as the problem of 'wasters'. His writing in this *Passus* is specifically and densely social, overtly political in its orientation towards contemporary social struggles. It constantly *resists* assimilation to the modes of clerical allegory, modes which would have allowed the poet and his readers to 'solve' the problems by imposing the orthodox ideological grid onto the anarchic field. Such a solution, as Langland knew, unlike some of his modern admirers, would be vapid, a merely solipsistic retreat.

The major agents of the breakdown of the order supported by the traditional ideology Langland favours are people he brands as 'wasters'. The poem explicitly represents this social group as wage-labourers, not as traditional peasants working on family holdings and concerned with accumulation of holdings, forms of tenancy or feudal services. They are dissociated from any fixed, stable community, and they experience labour merely as a commodity to be exchanged for immediate enjoyment of material comforts in the pub. So they reject the employers' work ethic, however it may be supported by clerical ideologues, parliamentary statute and the king. Langland's political judgement against these dissenting labourers is unequivocal, but he never dissolves them into the easily manipulated counters of an allegorical narrative designed to impose his own ideological scheme. They tell Piers to 'go pissen with his plow3' and the poet represents them getting round the knight, ploughman and the repressive post-plague labour legislation just as the gentry in Parliament were currently complaining:

> And þo nolde Wastour werche, but wandered aboute,
> ...
> Laborers þat have no land to lyve on but hire handes
> Deyneþ noȝt to dyne a day nyȝt olde wortes.
> May no peny ale hem paie, ne no pece of becoun,
> But if it be fressh flessh ouþer fissh yfryed,
> And þat *chaud* and *plus chaud* for chillynge of hir mawe.
> But he be heiȝliche hyred ellis wole he chide;
> That he was werkman wroȝt warie þe tyme.
> He greueþ hym ageyn god and grucche þ ageyn Reson,
> And þanne corseþ þe kyng and al þe counseil after
> Swiche lawes to loke laborers to chaste. (VI. 312–18)

The allusions here are to quite specific and deeply problematic social and ideological conflicts in Langland's England, an essential dimension of the poem's explorations. Had the poet deployed the available clerical allegorical apparatus here it would have stifled such explorations, and instead of *Piers Plowman* we would have something like Book I of Gower's *Vox Clamantis*.

Here it seems worthwhile giving two brief examples of clerical allegory around agricultural activity. Jacques de Vitry, delivering a sermon to husbandmen, vine-dressers and other workers, exhorts them to pay their tithes to the Church. This is a literal enough statement to literal workers from a literal and materially interested cleric. The very need to exhort workers to pay tithes reflected a continual conflict between agricultural workers and expropriating Church (e.g. Hilton, 1973, pp. 227–8; Ladurie, 1978, pp. 20–2). But these burning social, political and religious issues are swiftly assimilated in the cleric's allegory. The labour is turned into sowing 'spiritual seed', cultivating 'the land of the church' (nicely unproblematic!) and producing fruit (that is, the word of God) from the field, (that is, man's heart) (Welter, 1927, pp. 457–8). The social and existential world of lay people is dissolved in an allegorical mode which absorbs all it touches into an unquestionable and unquestioning ideological grid. The allegory is truly imperialistic, a medium which denies dialogue in the service of clerical monologue (cf. Bakhtin, 1982).

Another example of the mode: Stephen Langton commenting

on the Book of Ruth comes to the passage where the alien, impoverished and bereaved Ruth goes into the field of Boaz to glean corn after the reapers (Ch. 2). The text is an evocative one, whose potential is certainly polysemous, in semantic and emotional terms. But the clerical allegory presents Ruth as the student disciple; gleaning the ears of corn as extracting the correct message from the Bible; the reapers as the doctors of theology, the clerical élite, from whom the master, Boaz (that is, Christ) asks for a report on the student (*Glosa in Ruth*, pp. 100–1). The allegory works to impose and naturalise a clerical vision of the world, colonising text and, so its practitioners hoped, readers or listeners. And it is the grid through which Robertsonians tried to contain the encounters of contemporary readers with medieval writing, including *Piers Plowman* (for their *glosynge* of the episode I have been discussing, see Robertson and Huppé, 1951, pp. 79–91). Langland's refusal of standard clerical allegory at this point of his poem was essential if he were to engage with problems and conflicts confronting human beings in their daily living. He had to set aside a mode which too readily occluded the material basis of society together with the material foundations of the exegetes' own practices. Unlike many of his academic admirers, Langland confronted the fact that 'man is naturally a social and political animal, destined more than all other animals to live in community', that 'there must be some principle of government within society', but that this was a deeply contested area in his culture (Aquinas, *On princely government*, I.1). All human spirituality, *Piers Plowman* acknowledges, is that of beings whose existence is thoroughly embodied, inescapably social and immersed in a world of political conflicts which permeate arguments about the interpretation or translation of texts (as the Lollards found out) as much as arrangements over the production and distribution of the society's resources.

Nevertheless, there is little doubt that Langland dearly wished Church and society could be reformed to fit the simple terms of traditional tripartite social ideology. Throughout the poem he makes attempts to resolve the massive dislocations his own text represents, often through ideological schemes which would permit a closure to the conflicts and disruptive practices he found so disturbing. It is no coincidence that clerical allegory in its most simple and stable form has a role to play here. (I am not, of course, making the quite untenable claim that Langland was unable to use components of clerical allegory in a more fluid and open way. See, for example, his allegorical writing around the tree of charity, discussed in detail in Aers, 1975, pp.79–109.)

An example of how simple clerical allegory works comes in Passus XIX, the final agricultural scene in the poem, one designed to supersede and spiritualise the earlier anarchic episode already discussed. From Passus XVI Langland's 'visionary forms dramatic' evolve around the Incarnation, the loving acts of Christ and the Holy Spirit, and, characteristically, their efficacy in transforming human lives in the present. The poet returns to the field from which the Church has either been conspicuously absent (Passus VI) or, more frequently, very visible and fully incorporated in the secular fabric of what is presented as a dynamic market society. Once again, Langland tries to organise the intractable reality his poem has so wonderfully mediated. Flowing from the acts of Christ, the primitive Church, inspired by the Holy Spirit, is constructed in the field we now know so well: ('þat hous vnitee, holy chirche', XIX. 328). This seems an appropriate and fulfilling completion on earth to the glorious and kind liberation of imprisoned people from the prison of Lucifer and his 'Dukes' (XVIII. 307–423).

However, it turns out that, for Langland, this ideal activity is inseparable from a reassertion of traditional tripartite social ideology. Yet such reassertion entails a magical dissolution of all the antagonistic practices and aggressive individualism so brilliantly realised throughout the poem. It is just here, in trying to impose the traditionally dominant ideological grid, that Langland deploys the clerical allegory he so conspicuously refused in the earlier Passus. Allegory now transforms the dense agrarian scene of Passus VI, one replete with contradiction and conflict, energy and even tenderness (for the last quality, VI. 199–231). Now the ploughman has oxen which are glossed as the four Gospels; his four bullocks are read as Augustine, Ambrose, Gregory and Jerome; the harrow they pull is the clerical harrow of Biblical exegesis which 'harewede in an handwhile al holy Scripture'. The ploughman sows seeds which are allegorised as 'Cardynales vertues'; while the field is allegorised as 'mannes soule'. The barn for the ripe crop is allegorised in the kind of detail extremely familiar to readers of standard medieval didactic writing, stuffed full of allegorical edifices. For example, the 'morter' of the building here is Christ's 'baptisme and blood'; the roof is 'al holy writ'. The cart in which the crop is transported to the barn is an allegorical image glossed as 'cristendom' and it is pulled by two 'caples' named 'contricion and confession'. The protecting 'hayward' is 'preesthood', while Piers himself takes up the spiritualised/allegorical plough (XIX. 262–335).

Elizabeth Salter classified this episode as 'diagrammatic allegory', and complained that it 'only barely achieves any sort of dramatic presence in contrast to an earlier ploughing scene':

> Such allegory, in which nothing is left to chance, or to the reader's imagination, must be seen as the verbal equivalent of the elaborately inscribed and glossed art of medieval tract illustrations. In fact, it could be said that in its simple, linear quality it bears the same relationship to fully active and rounded allegory (the Meed episodes ... for instance) as the diagram does to the picture, with its deep perspective and its more complex media of communication. (Salter and Pearsall, 1967, p. 16)

This is a typically sensitive response to the formal qualities of the writing here (cf. Aers, 1975, pp. 129–30!). But the 'contrast' she makes in the formal dimension is bound up with ideological issues. For, as I have argued, such allegorical writing in that culture and its institutions had ideological dimensions which were central to its practice. The absence of 'dramatic' exploration Elizabeth Salter observed is intrinsic to the function of the clerics' allegory. It is a literary mode which encourages us to dissolve the embodied and socal nature of human existence and its spirituality, while imposing a schematic form of clerical ideology and the power it mediated. In this mode there is no place for the dialogic imagination. That is why it must have seemed so attractive at this point. The poem had opened itself, in truly dialogic ways, to different forms of life and to conflicting voices. But in doing so it disclosed how the orthodox social ideology the poet cherished was doomed, was already anachronistic.

Now, at a stroke, with the magisterial *id est* of the clerical allegorists, the painfully intractable reality his poem mediates could be swept aside and the desired ideological grids imposed on the field, its institutions and inhabitants. At a stroke the uncontrollable wage-labourers of Passus VI are transformed into

69

passive counters. From being rebellious, exuberant drinkers and singers in the pub, ones who would only 'holpen ere þe half acre wiþ' "how trolly lolly"', ones who substituted secular ballads for clerical and Latin evensong, ones who resisted the Statute of Labourers and the Church which upheld it, the labourers are turned into allegorical 'sheues'. This makes them totally passive. They can now be pulled along in a clerical cart firmly bound up under clerical control ... for their own good, of course. The allegory I have been discussing is very much part of this clerical vision and functions within its ideological framework. 'Glosynge is a glorious thyng, certeyn,/For lettre sleth, so as we clerkes seyn': and so it could, as in 1381!

Langland had tried to use simple clerical allegory to solve these problems before, *substituting* allegorical food for the community's essential material production which generated a host of ethical, political and theological problems (XIV. 29–68). But he was not satisfied with the easy forms of transcendence achieved by the conventional fusion of clerical allegory and its ideological grid. His form of spirituality was reluctant to evaporate the social and intellectual struggles which the poem handled as intrinsic to its dreamer's fundamental demand: 'tel me þis ilke,/How I may save my soule' (I. 83–4). So in Passus XIV, he turned from a comfortable allegorical solution of the problems of material production and social life to a meditation on the situation of the contemporary poor which is utterly resistant to any allegorical 'spiritualisation':

> Ac beggeris aboute Midsomer bredlees þei soupe,
> And yet is wynter for hem worse, for weetshoed þei gange,
> Afurst soore and afyngered, and foule yrebuked
> And arated of riche men þat ruþe is to here.
>
> . .
>
> Ac poore peple, þi prisoners, lord, in þe put of meschief,
> Conforte þo creatures þat muche care suffren
> Thoruȝ derþe, þoruȝ droghte, alle hir dayes here,
> Wo in wynter tymes for wantyng of cloþes,
> And in somer tyme selde soupen to þe fulle.
>
> (XIV. 160–4, 174–8)

Pretty well all the terms in the passage could be looked up in one of the late medieval scriptural dictionaries and cues for clerical allegory found, but that is the mode the poet rejects here. Similarly, in the final agricultural scene just discussed, Langland explodes the allegorical mode and the ideological grid it carries. The poem makes its habitual movement back to the intractable social world and the institutions of market-oriented, thoroughly embodied people:

> 'Ye? baw!' quod a Brewere, 'I wol noȝt be ruled,
> By Iesu! for al youre Ianglynge, with *Spiritus Iusticie*,
> Ne after Conscience, by crist! while I kan selle
> Boþe dregges and draf and drawe at oon hole
> Thikke ale and þynne ale; þat is my kynde,
> And noȝt hakke after holynesse ...
>
> (XIX. 396–401)

The allegorical mode of the clerics cannot order the dynamic and diversified community or its history. The poetry dramatically evokes just those social and psychological drives that proved so resistant to Langland's conservative ideals. It returns to its characteristically dialogic mode; the brewer, whose very 'kynde' is transformed by his occupation, speaks, and with total conviction. Clerical monologue and its allegorical mode is shattered as Langland responds to the overwhelming social and historical forces his own poem has so heroically and so honestly engaged with. The final Passus again shows how these forces have permeated the Catholic Church itself. The allegorical mode of Passus XIX has to be recognised as, at the very best, only possibly relevant to some long-lost apostolic period (XX. 126–8, 332–3, 363–9). The only recourse now is to abandon the institution which allegedly held the monopoly of the means of grace and salvation, to abandon the allegorical mode of its officials, together with the ideological closure they and the poet longed for, and to set out on a quest for the invisible Piers and the hidden Grace outside the visible Catholic Church.

References

Aers, David (1975) *Piers Plowman and Christian Allegory* (London: Edward Arnold).
Aers, David (1980) *Chaucer, Langland and the Creative Imagination* (London: Routledge & Kegan Paul).

Bakhtin, M. M. (1982) *Dialogic Imagination* (Austin: University of Texas Press).

Baldick, Chris (1983) *The Social Mission of English Criticism* (Oxford: Oxford University Press).

Bloomfield, M. W. (1961) *Piers Plowman as a Fourteenth-Century Apocalypse* (Rutgers).

Chaucer, *The Works of Geoffrey Chaucer*, ed. F. N. Robinson (Oxford: Oxford University Press).

Coleman, Janet (1981) *Piers Plowman and the Moderni* (Rome: Edizioni di storia di litteratura).

De Lubac H. (1959-63) *Exégèse Médiévale*, 4 vols (Paris: Aubier)

De Man, P. 'The Rhetoric of Temporality', in *Interpretation*, ed. C. S. Singleton (Baltimore: Johns Hopkins University Press).

Derrida, J. (1976) *Of Grammatology* (Baltimore: Johns Hopkins University Press).

Eagleton, Terry (1983) *Literary Theory* (Oxford: Blackwell).

Goldsmith, Margaret E. (1981) *The Figure of Piers Plowman* (Brewer).

Greenblatt, Stephen (1980) *Renaissance Self-Fashioning* (Chicago).

Hilton, Rodney (1973) *Bond Men Made Free* (London: Temple Smith).

Kelly, H. A. (1975) *Love and Marriage in the Age of Chaucer* (Ithaca N.Y.: Cornell University Press).

Ladurie, Emmanuel Le Roy (1978) *Montaillou* (London: Scolar Press).

Langland, William, *Piers Plowman, The B. Version*, ed. G. Kane and E. T. Donaldson (Athlone).

Langton, Stephen, *Glosa in Ruth*, ed. B. Smalley, *Archives d'histoire doctrinale et littéraire du Moyen Age*, 5 (1931), 86–126.

Lentricchia, Frank (1980) *After the New Criticism* (Athlone).

Lentricchia, Frank (1984) *Criticism and Social Change* (Chicago).

Marcuse, Herbert (1972) *Counter-Revolution and Revolt* (Allen Lane).

Noonan J. T. (1966) *Contraception. A History of its Treatment by the Catholic Theologians and Canonists* (Cambridge, Mass: Harvard University Press).

Robertson, D. W. (1951) 'Historical Criticism', in *English Institute Essays for 1950* (New York: Columbia University Press).

Robertson, D. W. (1962) *A Preface to Chaucer* (Princeton, N.J.: Princeton University Press).

Robertson, D. W. and Huppé, B. F. (1951) *Piers Plowman and Scriptural Tradition* (Princeton, N.J.: Princeton University Press).

Ryan, Michael (1982) *Marxism and Deconstruction* (Baltimore: Johns Hopkins University Press).

Said, Edward (1972) '*Abcedarium Culturae*: Structuralism, Absence, Writing', in *Modern French Criticism* (University of Chicago Press, 1972).

Salter, Elizabeth and Pearsall, Derek (1967) *Piers Plowman* (London: Edward Arnold).

Smalley, Beryl (1964) *The Study of the Bible in the Middle Ages*, revised edition (Bloomington: Indiana University Press).

Smith, Ben (1966) *Traditional Imagery of Charity in Piers Plowman* (Mouton).

Tentler, T. N. (1977) *Sin and Confession on the Eve of the Reformation* (Princeton, N.J.: Princeton University Press).

Waller, Garry (1983) 'Deconstruction and Renaissance Literature', *Assays*, 2 (1983), 69–93.

Wakefield W. L. and Evans A. P. (ed. and tr.) (1969) *Heresies of the High Middle Ages* (New York: Columbia University Press).

Welter, J.-T. (1927) *L'Exemplum dans la littérature religieuse et didactique au Moyen Age* (Paris/Toulouse, 1927).

5

Carnival against Lent: The Ambivalence of Medieval Drama

Anthony Gash

'Objections, non-sequiturs, cheerful distrust, joyous mockery—all are signs of health. Everything absolute belongs in the realms of pathology.'

(Nietzsche, *Beyond Good and Evil*)

Surveying twenty years of academic thinking about medieval drama in 1972, John R. Elliott felt able to assert that 'medieval drama remained at all times a religious drama and derived its characteristic techniques directly from the forms and purposes of Christian worship' (Elliott, 1972, pp. 157–8). This view, which is still current, may be seen, in part, as a reaction against a once prevalent emphasis on the conjunction of sacred and profane which had led A. P. Rossiter to write of 'the uncombinable antinomies of the medieval mind ... two contradictory schemes of value; one standing for reverence, awe, nobility, pathos, sympathy; the other for mockery, blasphemy, baseness, meanness or spite' (Rossiter, 1950, p. 72). I believe, however, that the time has come to rehabilitate Rossiter's view that the evaluated effect of at least some medieval drama is 'ambivalent', and to redefine it in the light of recent historical research into medieval popular culture and belief.

We need to begin by modifying the view of authorship and reception which is proposed by V. A. Kolve in *The Play Called Corpus Christi* (1966), an impressive work which has set the tone and method of much subsequent research. Kolve argues that the anonymous writers of the *Corpus Christi* plays:

were engaged in translating into drama a story whose shape and meaning had already been definitely formulated by the Doctors of the Church. By judicious use of popular religious commentary and by occasional direct reference to the Fathers, we have access to a body of critical thought that was, in fact, instrumental in the making of this drama. ... The authors of the *Corpus Christi* plays were for the most part clerics, and this body of common doctrine was the subject of their formal education. The audience, mostly lay, mostly illiterate, acquired their knowledge of it at second hand, but in several forms. It was the subject of the sermons they heard, and it exercised upon the visual arts—the stained glass, the altarpieces, the wall painting, exactly the same 'selective' authority. (Kolve, 1966, pp. 57–8)

This method of interpretation assumes a consensus of belief among all members of medieval society, and portrays the dramatic process as a one-way transmission of doctrine from authors to audience via the medium of the actors. In fact, both assumptions need serious qualification. Anyone who is familiar with the dynamics of live performance knows that the relationship between written text and performance is a fluid one. The actors comment by gesture, intonation, and sometimes by verbal improvisation, on the written text, generating unprecedented meanings at each new performance, which are, in turn, affected by signals from the audience—silence, heckling, laughter and applause. The tradition of improvisation, particularly comic improvisation, was firmly established in medieval performance (Axton, 1973, p. 23), and we can even eavesdrop on improvisation being put to seditious ends in a report of a May game performed in Suffolk in 1537 'of a king, how he should rule his realm', where 'one played husbandry and said many things against gentlemen, more than was in the book of the play' (Rossiter, 1950, p. 118). Even in approaching the mystery cycles which were perhaps the most rigorously supervised type of medieval play, it is important to bear in mind that the 'books' are at best incomplete guides to what actually took place in performance. All of the surviving cyclical manuscripts were written down late in the history of the *Corpus Christi* performances. Furthermore, the compilation of the individual guild plays into a centralised 'register' may be regarded as itself an implicit act of censorship by the Church and the civic authorities (Beadle, 1982, p. 12).

Even, however, if the letter of the script was adhered to, it was possible for a clerical script-writer, with unorthodox views, to cultivate an ambiguity of tone within an orthodox framework, while allowing the actors to woo the audience's approval for controversial social comments put into the mouths of comic or 'evil' characters. Such, I believe, was a strategy employed by the Wakefield Master who revised an existing cycle of plays in the late fifteenth century.

In the *Mactatio Abel*, for example, he allows Cayn to articulate the frustrations of a ploughman reluctant to pay tithes because he is working poor land with a limited supply of seed and no help forthcoming from his parish priest or neighbours (e.g. 122–6; 84; 104–5). Of course, it is possible to think that in attributing such sentiments to a murderer, he wants to discredit the withholding of tithes by association (Kolve, 1966, p. 104). But such a reading avoids confronting the ambivalent springs of laughter. Cayn's outrageous response to God's speech 'from above' (that honest tithing is rewarded in heaven and dishonest tithing punished in hell (293–96)) must have provoked laughter, as he cups his hand to his ear and asks,

> Whi, who is that hob over the wall?
> We! who was that that piped so small?
>
> (297–8)

It is the flouting of authority that still both shocks and delights and it has to be understood historically in the context of sermons which threatened excommunication for the withholding of tithes—a practice which was deeply resented. Even an orthodox preacher like Bromyard expressed sympathy for the reluctance of parishioners to pay tithes to worldly priests (Owst, 1966, p. 259) and Chaucer's truly Christian parson not only refuses to 'cursen for his tithes' but redistributes the 'offryng' among his poor parishioners (General Prologue, 486–90).

My sense of the play's ambivalence on this issue is reinforced by the oddity of its shape and idiom as a whole. Where convention required a serious treatment of Cayn's eternal damnation, the Wakefield Play interrupts the sequence of God's curse and Cayn's eternal wandering, by the unexpected return of 'mery lad' (2) of a folk-play type who had established a mood of festive reversal at the start of the play by threatening the audience (6–14), trading blows with his master Cayn (51–2) and laying the horses' fodder 'behynd thare ars' (45). Now he joins Cayn in a hilarious parody of a royal pardon, which Cayn proclaims like a town-crier while the Garcio interjects alternating rhymes about his own hunger (417–39).

The parody allows at least three levels of interpretation. Only the first is confined by orthodoxy: namely the idea that Cayn, being risibly stupid as well as evil, has misinterpreted God's refusal to let him be killed as pardon rather than damnation. On the second level, as with the tithing issue, a form of contemporary authority is ridiculed. As the grandiloquent voice of the king interwines with the earthy rejoinders of his starving subject laughter must have been fuelled by social scepticism. Royal pardons, which every member of the audience would have frequently heard cried through the streets of Wakefield, were a cause of corruption, and hence of resentment. They could overrule court indictments, and, since they were frequently granted through the intercession of important men to the king, they enabled criminals in the pay of magnates to escape punishment while poor men driven to crime would be unable to pay. In the reign of King Henry VI, when the play was probably written, the dispensation of royal pardons was dramatically increased for purely financial reasons, in spite of occasional protests from Parliament (Bellamy, 1973, pp. 189–98; Storey, 1966, pp. 210–16).

The third level on which the parody works might be termed counter-theological. The concentration on material needs and the nonsense style defers the frightening prospect of damnation. This implication becomes especially clear when the parody ends with Cayn decreeing that his servant should take a collection from the audience in the manner of the folk-play *quête*. Garcio steps forward and addresses the audience:

> Now old and young, or that ye weynd,
> The same blissing with outten end,
> All sam then shall ye have,
> That God of heuen my master has giffen.
> (444–7)

This subverts the solemn benediction which often ends a Corpus Christi play by ironically inviting the audience to join the community of the damned. Is it supposed to make the audience shudder for the fate of their immortal souls? I think not, for Garcio is a folk-play antibody in the theological drama, subject to neither Divine nor Satanic jurisdiction. It is appropriate that he should end his performance by compounding a curse and benediction, thus offering a temporary reprieve from Christian eschatology. To understand the tone we need to depart from Kolve's 'common body of doctrine' and look instead at the popular genre of the parodic sermon (Gilman, 1974, pp. 16–30). One of these addresses its audience as 'my leve, cursyd creatures' (my beloved, cursed creatures), and nonsensically parodies a blessing by invoking the help and grace of the grey goose, the gallon pitcher, and of salt sausages, to 'be with hus now at our begynning, and helpe hus in our endyng, and qwyte yow of blys and bothe your een, that never shall have endyng' (Wright and Halliwell, 1841–43, pp.82–3). It exhibits many characteristics of the 'mery lad's' idiom—free association, punning, inversion, feasting imagery and scatological humour. It also provides a fascinating example of a fantastic upside-down world, uncharted by Christian cosmology, being abruptly introduced to counter the threat of hell-fire. After a comic dialogue between St Peter and God as to why Adam ate the apple without peeling it, Peter 'saw the fyr and dred hym, and steppud into a plomtre [plum-tree] that hangud full of redde cherys' from which he sees parrots in the sea, hens and herrings hunting deer, haddock put in the pillory for the wrong roasting of May butter, the fox preaching, and so on. (For visual depictions of the popular upside-down world and its social significance, see Kunzle, 1978.)

It is at the very least necessary to qualify Kolve's picture of clerical playwrights' transmitting Bible stories whose meaning had been 'definitely formulated by the Church' by considering the use that certain of the anomymous playwrights made of Biblically unauthorised figures, and by giving due weight to variations in treatments of the same story in the surviving manuscripts. Take Noah's cantankerous wife. She must have answered some deep social and expressive needs for late medieval communities since her rebellious and anarchic behaviour is unauthorised by the Bible. Nevertheless, for Kolve her primary function remains theological: her rebellion restates the theme of fallen mankind and the culpability of Eve, and is contrasted with Noah's solitary obedience to God which prefigures that of Christ (Kolve, 1966, p. 150). Certainly this framework provides a theological point of departure, but it does not exhaust her dramatic significance in practice. In the Wakefield *Processus Noe Cum Filiis*, Uxor herself contests the official reading when she answers Noah's exasperated accusation that she is Eve ('begynnar of blunder!' (406)) by ingeniously mocking his appeal to Biblical authority in rhyme ('man's wonder!' (408)). She also appeals to wives in the audience to take her side in the exchange of blows and abuse: 'We women may wary of ill husbandys' (208), claiming that she has seen many present who long for widowhood 'for the life that thay leyd' (393). The spirit of the combat—

> What with gam and with gyle
> I shal smyte and smyle ...   (214-15)

seems closer to that of the festive combats between husbands and wives that take place after Easter at Hocktide (Phythian-Adams, 1966, p. 13; Mills, 1983, pp. 130–1), than it does to a sermon on wifely disobedience. Rather than describing Noah's wife as a type of Eve, we might conjecture that one source of her appeal was that by rebelling but not being divinely punished, and by being both independent and a wife (like Chaucer's Wife of Bath), she eludes the polarised roles assigned to women in the Bible and in medieval patriarchy. She thus becomes a 'liminal' or threshold figure of the type that Victor Turner has shown, in his studies of ritual, to play a central role in symbolically restoring unity and joy to hierarchical societies threatened by rivalries and divisions (Turner, 1974, pp. 80–118; 172-4). Liminality—the temporary inversion, elusion or mixing of normal social classifications—is a universal character-istic of ritual symbolism: hence a regenerative, reconciling function is commonly attributed to 'unfeminine' female behaviour in rituals, as it is in pre-Christian comedies like Aristophanes' *Lysistrata*. The liminal and reconciling import of Noah's wife is borne out by her behaviour in the Chester play of *Noyes Fludd* where she mediates between the damned and saved by singing a touching and jovial tavern-song with the doomed wives (225-36). Thus, in the middle of a religious play, fear is vanquished in a purely secular dimension in counterpoint to the eschatological scheme of salvation and damnation. The tone and significance of the Wakefield and Chester plays need to be distinguished from that of the Newcastle Flood play where the official polarity of sinful and obedient behaviour is reimposed by the introduction of a devil who prompts the rebellion. The anonymity of the playwrights should not be allowed to mask the possibility of some measure of creative independence; we need to respect variations in form as constituting differences of meaning.

Turning now more directly to the audiences, Kolve's assertion that the audiences ('mostly illiterate, mostly lay') had acquired a common body of doctrine through church-going is questionable, since, as Keith Thomas puts it, 'medieval religion laid its emphasis upon the regular performance of ritual duties rather than on memorising theological beliefs' (Thomas, 1971, p. 196). In view of new evidence of widespread doctrinal ignorance among the lower classes compiled by Thomas and others, we need to take seriously contemporary complaints that audiences would sometimes pay more attention to spectacle than to doctrine. A skilful re-examination of trial transcripts has also revealed that heretical doctrines in the late Middle Ages, throughout Europe, found fertile ground in beliefs of an unorthodox, pantheist or materialist complexion, preserved by the peasantry (e.g. Dickens, 1959; Thomson, 1965; Thomas, 1971; Le Roy Ladurie, 1978; Ginzburg, 1980). In the course of such research, historians have addressed themselves increasingly to the problems inherent in using written clerical evidence to provide a picture of the beliefs of the illiterate majority. The dramatic critic can contribute to this debate by revaluing the vernacular religious drama as an interface or dialogue between literate and oral culture rather than as an offshoot of the former.

A further body of research and theory which is relevant to any consideration of the social meanings of vernacular medieval plays, which were all performed during public holidays, pertains to popular festivities. Where folklorists and anthropologists used to be interested primarily in the pagan origins of medieval festive practices, more recent historians and anthropologists have considered their social function in promoting communal cohesion in a culture which lacked political channels for the expression of social grievances (Gluckman, 1963, Ch. 5). Particular festivals played an important role in symbolically negotiating conflicts between opposing status groups such as masters and servants (Christmas), aristocracy and artisans (Carnival), townspeople and landowners (May day and Midsummer), husbands and wives (Hock-tide) and rival guilds (Corpus Christi) (Davis, 1975;

Phythian-Adams, 1976; Thomas, 1976; Burke, 1978; Le Roy Ladurie, 1979; James, 1983). The counterpoint of hieratic formality and energetic clowning that pervades medieval drama finds its analogue in the cyclical alternation throughout the year of ceremonies which formalised group relations and idealised social distinctions with ones which symbolically inverted norms.

While English historians such as Phythian-Adams and Keith Thomas believe that the subversive potential of rituals of status-reversal and misrule was generally well controlled, and that their meaning was ultimately conservative, Davis and Le Roy Ladurie have shown for early modern France how such rituals could also provide occasions and imagery for artisan protests and revolts against tyranny and taxation. In fact, these apparently contrasting findings are not incompatible since the need for regular ritual celebrations of corporate unity are testimony to the conflicts of interest which they sought, and sometimes failed, to reconcile.

The theory which has attempted most imaginatively to integrate the theme of popular social and religious scepticism with that of festivity is that of Mikhail Bakhtin. In *Rabelais and His World* (1968; written during the war, and first published 1965), he argues that throughout the Middle Ages 'a second life, a second world' of popular festive culture existed in the crevices of official Christian observance. He designates this culture 'carnival', extending the term beyond its usual application to include the Feast of Fools and the 'Risus paschalis' (Easter laughter) as well as fairground and market-place jargon, oaths, riddles and jokes, and learned parodies, all of which he sees as united by a common logic, 'a continuous shifting from top to bottom, from front to rear' (Bakhtin, 1968, p. 11). What distinguishes the carnival world from the extra-carnival life which it parodies was that it was created and apprehended through laughter, in opposition to the Church which sustained its authority by promoting fear and guilt. Where official doctrine directed attention to the eternal fate of the individual soul, and induced shame about the body and about sex, carnivalesque iconography was governed by 'the grotesque canon of the body', coded in hybrid effigies such as those of pregnant old hags laughing, or hell's mouth as a fertile cornucopia, and in the exaggeration of physical processes, apertures and protuberances symbolising the collective, ancestral body of the people which perpetually renews itself (Bakhtin, 1968, pp. 24–30; 303–87).

Where official ecclesiastical language was 'abstract' and 'monolithic', the carnivalesque idiom was 'materialist' and 'ambivalent'. *Parodia sacra* discovered unconscious ambiguities in sacred texts, and transformed them into 'flesh and matter' through punning references to eating, drinking and defecation; macaronics countered the pretensions of scholastic Latin to universality by celebrating diversity of language and dialect; and market-place oaths and hyperboles relativised status through a continuous process of 'crowning and uncrowning', 'burying and reviving'. Ambivalence, in this context, is free from psychoanalytic connotations: its synonyms are 'Janus-faced' and 'dialectical', the point being that, although the comic folk idiom debased authority and abstraction, it retained its connection with fertility rites where negation is inseparable from renewal. Mock-burial and all its verbal homologies—puns, blasphemies, festive curses—does not anathematise its object in the manner of the Church or of modern satire; rather, it casts the isolated, sterile idea or individual into the fertile lower stratum which unites and renews.

In the remainder of this paper I shall turn to a detailed contextualisation and analysis of the fifteenth-century play *Mankind* (1460–65), because it shows the process of 'carnivalisation' in action. By this I mean that the notion of carnival is present in both the uncontroversial, restricted sense (the play alludes to Shrove Tuesday and Christmas customs) and in the elaborated Bakhtinian sense: it is a Janus-faced play in which a stilted, courtly style (aureation) is explicitly associated with the Church as a temporal authority, and set against an 'underworld' of festive, tavern, comic infernal and excremental language which parodies the 'high' language. Usually treated as a morality play, it is more usefully seen as compounding two genres, one official, the other unofficial, by punning between the morality play structure (the fall, repentance and salvation of mankind) and a festive structure (the battle between the licence of Christmas and the prohibitions of Lent).

Certain deductions about *Mankind*'s provenance can be made from internal evidence. The first is that its authors were sophisticated: they were well-versed in theology and law, as well as having a taste for slang and bawdy jokes. It would be easy to take the play for a university Shrovetide *jeu d'esprit* did it not also seriously reflect the hardships and concerns of poor farmers. It even makes specific allusions to a group of villages just south of Cambridge, another group to the east of Cambridge, and a third in Norfolk, a few miles east of Lynn (505–15). It uses a minimum of props, is adaptable to indoor and outdoor locations, and is designed to be played by the usual size of small commercial touring company—six male actors. It seems likely, therefore, that the play resulted from a professional collaboration of learned Cambridge clerics and professional actors, taking the play on tour to East Anglian villages. It indicates that the small professional touring companies, which proliferated in the late fifteenth century, often wearing the livery of a lord to avoid prosecution for vagrancy but escaping the direct supervision of the Church and city guilds (to which the mystery cycles were subject), were important agents of the cross-fertilisation of clerical and popular culture, and of the subtle subversion of homiletic forms from within.

While O. B. Hardison has valuably developed the analogy between Christian rite and Christian drama in terms of the Lent-Easter sequence (the movement from lament at estrangement from God to joyous celebration of redemption) (Hardison, 1965), there is an equally strong case for examining the impact of the Christmas-Lent sequence on medieval experience and imagination. (The term Christmas was frequently applied to the whole season from Christmas Day to Shrove Tuesday.) Such a consideration moves us inevitably towards a sociological perspective since the annual progression from Winter licence to the prohibitions of 'clean Lent' served as a ritual vehicle for dramatising tensions between Church and laity. It was, for example, common for parish priests on Septuagesima, three Sundays before Lent, or Quadragesima, the first Sunday in Lent, to castigate popular winter celebrations as contrary to Christian values, denouncing them as manifestations of sin which required the atonement of Lenten penance (Owst, 1966, p. 483). The Church, as mother to all Christian people, says one of these sermons, sees that her children are 'sore seke yn the sekeness of sin ... þe wheche sekenesse þay have caghte all þys ʒere before, but namely þes Cristynmasse-dayes þat wern ordeynet in holy chyrche for gret solempnyte' (Mirk, *Festial*, 1905, pp. 62–3). In the list of perversions of Christmas solemnity which follows are gluttony, lechery, plays of vanity and 'iapys making of rybawdy and harlottry, so þat he ys most worthi þat most rybawdy can make and spende'. This stylised Lenten outrage at the Christmas reversal of conventional standards of 'worthiness' allows us to glimpse the unofficial and more ancient conception of the winter festival, which promoted natural fertility by reversing norms and transgressing taboos. The 'playes of vanyte' mentioned would include Christmas mummings, and the 'plough games' which took place on the first Monday after the Twelve Days. The latter probably involved considerable 'rybawdy', led by a Bessy (a man dressed as a woman) and a Fool (who carried a phallic stick and bladder), who probably simulated copulation (see Lindsay, 1979, *Ane Satire of the Thrie Estaitis* (1542)). In response to winter weather and the omnipresent threat of starvation, the folk-plays also invoked a utopian, topsy-turvy world where dead men are resurrected, houses are made of food, and birds and animals run about already cooked begging to be eaten—motifs which appear in an anti-clerical context in the fourteenth-century fantasy poem, *The Land of Cockaygne* (see Tiddy, 1923; Chambers, 1933; Robbins, 1959, p. 121).

Another striking instance of tension between official and unofficial mores during the Christmas period was, of course, the Feast of Fools, which usually took place on the Feast of Circumcision (1 January). At this time the sub-deacons (the lowest rank of the clergy) took charge of the church or cathedral and burlesqued divine office, and then processed through the market-place with the mock-bishop and his entourage performing plays and giving mock-sermons and blessings—often obscene ones—to the crowd (Heers, 1983, pp. 177–89). The feast is only well documented for France, and Kolve has argued that it had 'little importance' in England where its place was taken by the more decorous Feast of the Boy Bishop (Kolve, 1966, p. 136). This is, however, an argument from lack of written evidence, always a dangerous procedure where oral culture is concerned, and it makes too little of the fact that the sub-deacons of Lincoln and Beverley continued to 'impede divine office by their shouting, chattering, tricks and games' until at least the last decade of the fourteenth century (and therefore probably later) in defiance of periodic attempts to suppress the feast, which had begun in Lincoln in 1236, under Bishop Grosseteste. It may have been able to survive in Lincoln precisely because of popular support for it, since one striking aspect of the reversing behaviour there was the swapping of garments between clergy and laity (Chambers, 1903, pp. 321–2;

Owen, 1971, p. 111).

Finally, we have evidence for the symbolic contrast between Christmas and Lent being used for political purposes by discontented artisans in fifteenth-century Norwich. Records differ as to whether the insurrection of 1443 took place on the Conversion of St Paul (28 January) or on Shrove Tuesday, but it is clear that John Gladman, a member of the 'Bachery Guild', dressed as the King of Christmas, and other artisans, also in masquerade, led a revolt of the citizens directed against the Prior of Norwich Cathedral and the neighbouring Abbot of St Benet's at Holm. The immediate cause of the riot was an attempt by the Abbot to close two of the city's mills on the dubious grounds that they were obstructing access to his abbey and flooding his lands. Behind this lay protracted conflicts between wealthy merchants and lesser craftsmen for control of the city's government, and between the city and the priory over jurisdictional boundaries. The Abbot and the Prior had the support of the Duke of Suffolk and of Thomas Weatherby, a wealthy merchant, landowner and ex-mayor of Norwich, who had consistently opposed the democratisation of the city council. The fact that, shortly before the riot, a group of citizens had travelled to King's Lynn and elsewhere in Norfolk to enlist support against the Prior is one of the indications that hostility to the wealthier monastic orders was widespread in the region (Storey, 1966, pp. 217–22).

What matters most from our point of view is that the forms of winter games and pageantry have here become inseparable from popular politics. The winter festivities provided not only an opportunity for sedition, but also a symbolism for protest. While the Crown's indictment insisted that Gladman's display was tantamount to treasonable impersonation since Gladman was dressed as the King and his followers carried bows and arrows and wore crowns on their sleeves 'as if they were yeomen of the crown' (Hudson and Tingey, 1906, I, p. 340); a later account, written in vindication of the citizens, maintains that this was no more than the traditional Shrove Tuesday 'in the last ende of Christemess' 'as hath been accustomed in ony Cite or Burgh thrugh al this realme', which contrasted the King of Christmas and his court, comprising the twelve months of the year, with a figure of Lent who was clad in white and red herring skins and whose horse was trapped with oyster shells. The Shrove Tuesday pageantry, according to the later account, betokened that 'all mirthis that seson xuld ende and therafter follow a holy time' (MS Misc. Rolls 9C).

The felt significance of the masquerade in 1443 must have lain, in fact, somewhere between the prosecution's accusation of treasonable impersonation and the defence's disingenuous appeal to custom. The Norwich Shrove Tuesday procession customarily involved 'disportes and pleyes': it is likely that the activities of the King of Christmas and his followers always wooed and gained the crowd's approval at the expense of his rival Lent. We know from York, for example, that the King and Queen of Yule, riding at the start of the Christmas season, drew vast crowds with their bawdry and social satire (Nelson, 1974, p. 50). We know too that effigies of Lent could provide targets for festive missiles on Shrove Tuesday (Brand, 1849, V.i., p. 101). In 1443, in Norwich, under the pressure of urgently felt injustice, jest turned into earnest, ritual into reality, and the seasonal Shrove Tuesday submission of Christmas to Lent was itself reversed to express a rebellion of the laity against the Church.

Usually, of course, Lent emerged as the ultimate victor of the ritualised seasonal *agon*. Christmas revelling, allowed a brief revival in the games and feasting of Shrove Tuesday in February, was solemnly revoked on Ash Wednesday when the clergy laid ashes on the heads of the congregation, intoning the funereal words, 'Memento homo, quod cinis es, et in cinerem reverteris'. Even at this point, however, we have evidence from Europe of the imposition of ashes being sometimes greeted by shouting, singing, drumming and burlesque processions (Heers, 1983, p. 66). The start of Lent was the main annual occasion on which every parishioner was required to receive the Sacrament of Penance (i.e. to confess his sins and receive absolution from a priest) prior to devoting himself to works of satisfaction in the penitential season—fasting and sexual abstinence, prayer, and almsgiving, thus cleansing his conscience for receiving the 'clene body' of Christ in the Easter sacrament (Coogan, 1947, pp. 22–56). Here too, however, the religious and judicial spheres are not easily separated, since civic aldermen were ordered to punish 'bawdry' during Lent (Phythian-Adams, 1976, p. 118), and Ash Wednesday was one of the main occasions for the performance of public penances and floggings imposed by the Church courts. One use of Ash Wednesday for 'solemn penance' and fasting, undergone in

Norwich before the Bishop, which is profoundly evocative of the larger context of *Mankind*, was as a punishment for rural East Anglian Lollards who had organised communal meat-eating in defiance of Church fast-days (Tanner, 1977, pp. 12, 15–16, 23, 29). In a sense, this complements the King of Christmas incident. In one, the symbolic opposition between Christmas feasting and Lenten fasting encodes a rebellion against the Church's authority, and in the other, a punitive reaffirmation of that authority.

The clearest evidence of *Mankind's* debt to Shrove Tuesday customs comes in a trial scene which is a comic *tour de force*. Myscheff, presiding as judge, reads out a parody of a manor roll:

> Carici tenta generalis
> In a place þer goode ale ys
> Anno regni regitalis
> Edwardi nullateni
> On ʒestern day in Feuerere—þe ʒere passyth fully,
> As Nought hath wrytyn; here ys owr Tulli,
> Anno regni regis nulli!

(687-93)

Not only does this give the February date; it also displays typically 'carnivalesque' features of style. Doggerel and macoronic are used to interlard the official legal format of the court record, and even within the Latin, the device of negation—'Edwardi nullateni' and 'Anno regni regis nulli'—suspends ordinary time and puts the court of misrule beyond all authority. The name of one of the vices, Nought, here acting as clerk to the court, falls into place in this context. He is a relation, as it were, of the comic device of Nemo (No one) in the parodic *Sermo de Nemine* which, by the trick of treating No one as a person, festively licenses everything which the law prohibits and the Scriptures taboo. A 'Nemo' sermon from Cambridge, for example, quotes a text from Apocalypse in such a way as to transform Nemo into a comic adversary of God: 'Deus claudit et nemo aperit, et Deus aperit et nemo claudit' (Owst, 1966, p. 64). We know that mock-trials played a part in Christmas celebrations at the Inns of Court (Chambers, 1903, vol. 1, p. 415) and that the English tradition of the trial of John Barleycorn parallels to some extent the European trial of Carnival (Burke, 1978, p. 122). But this is, to my knowledge, the fullest surviving example of the genre. True to the multivalence of folk humour, as well as parodying a manorial court, it simultaneously parodies a wedding service as Mankind intones 'I will, ser'. During the trial, Mankind is clothed only in undergarments while his long 'syde gown' is taken away from him and gradually cut down to a short 'jakett' in another clowning routine. There is a commonplace allegory here to placate clerical exegetes: they could gloss Mankind's garment as immortality and innocence, despoiled by the devil (e.g. *Glossa Ordinaria*: Migne, 1844–64, vol.114, pp.286–7). But transposed to the context of the satirical court where the thieves have become judges, the spectacle of a half-naked farmer making solemn vows and recantations could have suggested, to the less literate, a further Shrove Tuesday debunking of an oppressive institution which was part of their immediate social experience—public penance when the offender against Church law was paraded to public gaze in vest and hose, or clad in a short shirt or vesture (Blomefield, 1805–10, V.iii., p. 140; Owen, 1971, p. 121; Tanner, 1977, p. 23). The joke would be that instead of recanting his infidelity as was customary, here the penitent is solemnly invited to swear disloyalty to the Church and loyalty to the tavern (710–13). Paula Neuss takes this all to allude to the Last Judgement, commenting that Mankind 'agrees to a whole series of acts, any one of which would serve to damn him' (Neuss, 1973, p. 64). But such a comment misses the logic of festive reversal and the mood of sheer Dionysiac release:

> There arn but sex dedly synnes, lechery ys non,
> As yt may be verefyede be ws brethellys euerychon.
> ꝫe xall goo robbe, stell, and kyll, as fast as ye may gon.
> 'I wyll', sey ꝫe.
>
> (705–9)

The rhythm of the chant suggests solemn plainsong; if it were so performed, the contradiction between form and content is likely to have moved the audience to 'wild laughter'. The scene ends with inarticulate whoops and a call for a football—the perennial Shrove Tuesday pastime.

Other parodies of ecclesiastical practices scattered through the play are all paralleled by recorded instances of feast of fools behaviour in France and England: an obscene pardon,

Yt ys grawntyde of Pope Pokett,
Yf ȝe wyll putt yowr nose in hys wyffs sokett,
ȝe xall haue forty days of pardon
(144–46)

a satirical misapplication of a psalm used in ordination ceremonies (324–5); an attempt to make the priest take off his vestments and join the dance (88); an inverted blessing which is surely comic rather than diabolic in the modern sense: 'I blysse yow wyth my lyfte honde: foull yow befall!' (522). If we add to these a scatological 'Crystemes songe' (332) with the refrain 'holyke' (holy and hole-lick), which all the yeomanry are invited to join with the actors in singing, we can guess that the play draws on the practices of several winter holidays.

The play also shows an intriguing cross-fertilisation of learned and demotic idiom. While much of the word-play, usually involving Latin, is very sophisticated, it is accompanied by oaths of popular provenance, which are in themselves ambivalent curses and blessings, like 'God send yow þe gowte!' (702), hinting at venereal pleasure, and criminal slang like a 'da pacem' for a dagger (grant us thy peace!) (714) or a 'manus tuas qweke' (516), one of the many cant terms for hanging in the play: this one interrupts the traditional prayer of the dying with a death-rattle, and also with grim humour suggests an affinity between the public scaffold and Christ's Cross. 'And when Jesus had cried with a loud voice, he said, Father, into thy hands I commend my spirit' (Luke XXIII, 46). In these examples, as in a term like a 'noli me tangere' (512) applied to a hanging Justice of the Peace obviously notorious with the audience, a method of ironical quotations is at work which simultaneously perverts Christian tags, and turns them against the authorities to brand their behaviour as equally un-Christian.

The mumming or plough-play elements were first pointed out by W. K. Smart, and have received attention since, particularly the trick beheading when Myscheff lops off New Gyse's bruised head and puts it back cured (Smart, 1917, pp.21–5). What I think has not been noticed is that again this is a scene of parody with Myscheff as a sort of amoral pagan Mother Nature figure (Erasmus's Folly and Pope's Dullness are her descendants) who practises magical cures and resurrections, as opposed to Mother Church, ruled by Christ, offering an eternal 'remedy' (the word occurs early in Mercy's sermon) to man's ills. Central to Mercy's Lenten preaching is the image of the head governing the body which allegorises the relationship of Christ to the Church (32–5), and also the need for the soul to subdue the rebellion of the flesh (126) by starving it into obedience (243) if it is to be eternally 'crownyd' (224). It is as a festive literalisation and inversion of this Pauline hierarchy of head and body that we can understand the beheading game, which begins with Myscheff's simpering parody of the voice of Mother Church, inviting her children to Lenten repentance:

> Alac, alac! ven, ven! cum hither wyth sorowe
> Pesse, fayer babys, ȝe xall have a nappyll [apple] tomorow!
>
> (426–7)

and goes on to satirise the punitive, castrating patriarchy which the maternal solicitude of Mercy conceals: 'ȝe pley in nomine patris, choppe!' (440) says Nought, comically arresting the sign of the cross at the point where the hand passes from head to genitals. Mother Church caricatured by Mother Nature (Myscheff) is about to lop off her child's (Nowadays') head, which is held between New Gyse's thighs to assist the operations when New Gyse protests, 'ȝe xall not choppe my jewellys ...' (441). To apply the term 'jewellys', usually used of souls, to testicles constitutes, in Bakhtin's terms, a festive crowning of the body and uncrowning of the soul. In keeping too with Bakhtin's notion that carnivalesque humour both 'buries and revives' the subject of its satire is the fact that the body-denying, death-oriented doctrine of the Church is embodied in the decapitation and the threat of castration but also transformed into a comic ritual of healing with a happy *dénouement*, as the vices celebrate their mother's restoration of their damaged members by dancing to 'a Walsyngham wystyll' (452), in which they try to involve Mercy, thus ridiculing another ecclesiastical 'remedy'—pilgrimages to the shrine at Walsingham.

We are beginning to discover that the festive idiom of reversal and parody is being used both to express and conceal anti-clerical sentiments. Even remarks which look at first like sheer nonsense often contain an anti-clerical barb. For example, the vices pose a flippant question to Mercy, the priest, as if it were a serious theological conundrum:

Also I have a wyf, her name ys Rachell;
Betwyx her and me was a gret batell;
And fayn of yow I wolde here tell
Who was the most master.

(135–8)

We have seen that marital battles were regarded as festive and funny in their own right. Here, fused with the old joke, the mocking show of submission to the priest's 'maistrye' becomes a veiled way of expressing scepticism about the celibate clergy's right to pry into the affairs of the married laity at confession.

The picture of Mercy that emerges from the vices' jokes is a disconcerting one. The source of his authority and his motives, they imply, are more secular than divine: 'ʒe are a stronge cunnynge clerke' (128) accuses New Gyse in one of the starkest phrases in the play; and when Mercy goes to seek his errant son Mankind in order to save his immortal soul, Nowadays interprets his action as that of a landlord seeking a writ of arrest; 'a cape corpus' against a criminal or an absconded serf:

Yf ʒe wyll have Mankynde, how domine, domine, dominus!
ʒe must speke to þe schryve for a cape corpus,
Ellys ʒe must be fayn to return wyth non est inventus.

(779–81)

Notice how key words function as puns between temporal and religious authority: dominus is both *the* lord, Christ, and a lord, a wealthy priest. 'Schryve' means both sherrif and confess.

Further support for Bakhtin's thesis comes when we notice that what looks at first like gratuitous scatological obscenity and is regarded by Neuss as 'the most perverted form ... of idle language' (Neuss, 1973, p. 62) is often linked to a sense of the natural, regenerative symbiosis of the earth, animals and the human body. Where official doctrine regards the body as a 'stynkyng dungehyll' (204), the clowns transform the negative into a positive by suggesting that human manure will make 'goode corn' (372–5).

It is important that this kind of joke shares a logic with others that are in no way obscene. We have already noticed that one of the ways in which the vices' parodies work is by undermining exclusive antitheses proposed by Mercy's preaching. This procedure works at the level of casting: Mercy in sombre clerical garb and Titivillus, the folk-play devil, were probably played by the same actor (Bevington, 1962, p. 87); of gesture: the beheading/castration/resurrection; and of language: puns and macoronics fertilise Latin with 'Billingsgate', while the churchman's univocal high style is condemned as constipated (124–5). Another absolute antithesis in Mercy's first sermon has been that of damned and saved. It is particularly painful to a modern, at least to a non-Calvinist, ear when Mercy calls for repentance so 'þat ȝe may be partycypable of hys retribucyon' (16) where the notions of joyful sharing and eternal torture seem unpleasantly mixed. The threat becomes explicit in the closing words of Mercy's first speech: 'The corn xall be sauyde, þe chaffe xall be brente' (see Matt. III, 12; Luke III, 17). Myscheff enters immediately and produces a sort of nonsense patter in which the binary oppositions in Mercy's speech are replaced by syntactic groups of three:

> For a wynter corn-threscher, ser, I haue hyryde,
> Ande ȝe sayde þe corn xulde be sauyde and þe chaff
>   xulde be feryde,
> And he prouyth nay, as yt schewth be þis werse:
> 'Corn seruit bredibus, chaffe horsibus, straw fyrybusque'.
>   (53–7)

Some critics have seen this sequence as a way of impressing upon the audience by repetition the text which Mercy has quoted. Neuss says that Myscheff has failed to recognise the references to the words of John the Baptist (Neuss, 1973, p. 50). But there is surely every difference between failing to recognise and choosing not to. The tradition of literalising metaphorical or paradoxical language as an expression of scepticism is time–honoured. But Myscheff's joke is a more complex one, for not only is he bringing the other-worldly symbolism down to this world; he is also elevating chaff and straw to the same level as corn, just as the child was elevated to the Bishop's level at the Feast of Innocents, or the ass brought into the church at the Feast of the Ass. We might relate this fooling to the rhetorical genre going back to antiquity which praises things without honour like gout, fleas, ashes or dung (Pease, 1926, pp. 27–42). It implies that in nature everything is consumed (no survival of the soul) but that equally everything is to be enjoyed: 'The chaffe to horse xall be goode provente' (61). Hell-fire is transformed into a merry Christmas bonfire to keep out the winter cold, a joke next taken up by New Gyse: 'The wether ys colde, Gode send ws goode ferys!' (323).

What then of the official or dignified aspect of the play, characterised primarily by Mercy's ceremonious, aureate language, which both at the beginning and end of the play is also used by Mankind? Am I arguing that this is merely the pretext for the fooling? Far from it. Some of the most moving lines in the play are spoken by Mercy when the Lenten motif of fasting is transposed from external prohibitions to 'inwarde afflixcyon' which makes eating impossible (734–41). I have termed Mercy's role 'Lenten' not in order to disparage it, but because, as Sister Phillipa Coogan has shown, the religious parts of the play are in complete harmony with the liturgy for the start of Lent (Coogan, 1947, pp. 10–56). Mankind remembers Mercy's Lenten counselling by writing down and fixing to his ploughman's garb the words 'Memento, homo quod cinis es et in cinerem reverteris' (321), the text spoken by the priest at the ceremony of the distribution of the ashes on Ash Wednesday. The vices respond precisely at this point by making the audience sing the excremental Christmas song in a way which may suggest that the same sort of festive profanation of Ash Wednesday which occurred on the Continent also took place in England.

The play then moves gradually towards complete licence in the mock-trial before Mercy rescues Mankind from despair and restores order in a final sequence which is clearly modelled on the sacrament of penance, and Lenten penance specifically, since the priest asks Mankind to say the 'Miserere' (Psalm 50) (831) which was also used in the introit of the Mass for Ash Wednesday (Coogan, 1947, p. 10).

Without reference to festivity, Neuss has related the play to preaching by claiming that the play's formal strategy is first to implicate the audience in the indolence and loose language of the vices, and then to demonstrate how such behaviour leads inexorably to the very brink of damnation (Neuss, 1973, p. 65). This reading strikes me as being only half true because it explains the play's meaning in terms of its ending, not considering how complexities which arise out of a play can be repressed rather than resolved by its formal conclusion. It is only by referring to the dialectical structure of Christmas against Lent that we can point to the play's ambiguity—an ambiguity which as we have shown was fundamental to festive practices themselves.

From the official point of view, Ash Wednesday contains and explains Shrove Tuesday and other popular festivals which have preceded it: the pagan past has been symbolically buried and man's sinfulness, for which he must account in detail to the priest at Ash Wednesday confession, has been abundantly demonstrated during the holiday period. But from another point of view, from inside the revelling crowd, winter festivity contains Ash Wednesday, an impression greatly enhanced by the recurrence of images of atemporality (collages of the annual liturgy at the Feast of Fools; representations of all the months or seasons on Shrove Tuesday; resurrections in the folk-plays): the freedom, equality and feasting of the Golden Age are resurrected, and penance, damnation and fasting are symbolically vanquished via mock-courts and indulgences and comic transformations of hell. Thus winter holidays became an extraordinary pun or palimpsest—the site of a game of equivocation and interpretation, which as we saw in the Norwich incident, could become extremely serious.

Precisely the same is true of *Mankind*. Its meaning would have varied for each performance according to the degree to which the holiday audience's laughter and heckling approved the vices' *double-entendres*, or to which the actor playing Mercy dared to ridicule his verbosity or suggest his cruelty. The vices' strategy is to open up every form of equivocation which the closed formal discourse of Mercy seeks to seal off. Against the hierarchical dualism inherent in the formal structure of the play with Mercy up above, hell down below and Mankind in between, they alert the audience to a continuous ambivalence at every level, often by exploiting the fissure that can occur when an allegorical mode is translated into dramatic form, so that moral abstractions must be rendered as recognisable social types. Mercy is Christ, the Church and a friar: between the three levels there is ideological identity, but experiential discontinuity. Mankind is not only torn between flesh and spirit as Mercy would have it, but between the claims of doctrine and the claims of nature, comically but pathetically evidenced by nature (or the devil) compelling him to 'releave' himself when he is at prayer (560). Allegorically, he is mankind armed with the spade of good works, but it must have been easy for the rural audience to see him as a poor labourer whose toil does not always seem compatible with church-going. The allegory is under most strain in performance when the peasant enters not only with a spade but with a pen with which he writes down a Latin text on a scroll (321). Myscheff makes the relation between literacy and power comically explicit in the satirical court scene:

> Here ys blottybus in blottis,
> Blottorum blottibus istis.
>
> (680-1)

The clowns, of course, themselves the frivolous champions of double-vision, provide a more gritty problem of evaluation for the audience by being both licensed fools and criminals.

It seems probable that the actors could rely on a vein of anti-clerical feeling to be present in some of their audiences, for which one source of corroboratory evidence is the fifteenth-century prosecution of East Anglian Lollards. The intense spate of persecution under Bishop Alnwick in the second quarter of the century must have silenced rather than extinguished heretical beliefs. In 1457, very close to the probable date of *Mankind*, there were two trials led by Bishop Chedworth of Lincoln, and Bishop Gray of the neighbouring diocese of Ely. One of the victims came from Swaffham, and one from Cambridge, both probably places where *Mankind* was performed. One of them was accused of stating that 'a prayer made in a field or other unconsecrated place is just as efficacious as if it were made in a church', a belief to which Mankind subscribes, as he works in the fields: 'Here is my Kerke I knell on my Kneys' (553). All five men charged were sentenced to public recantation and penance in the market-places of Ely, Cambridge, and in their respective parish churches, where they were also disciplined with a rod (Thomson, 1965, pp. 132–3). So we cannot rule out the possibility of topical allusions.

But the more important point to bear in mind is that, as J.A.F. Thomson has shown, what the Church prosecuted under the name of Lollardy consisted of a variety of doctrinal unorthodoxies and anti-clerical resentments which were probably an abiding facet of peasant and plebeian attitudes. In East Anglia particularly, the level of literacy among alleged Lollards was low. Like the vices in *Mankind*, they doubted the efficacy of the sacraments (including Marriage, Penance and Unction). And one of their ways of expressing their scepticism about the Church's costly recipes for salvation was by punning (Walsingham became Falsingham, Wool-

pit Foulpit, and Canterbury Cankerbury) (Thomson, 1965, p. 126).
You did not have to distrust the sacraments, however, to share the
view of Margery Baxter, prosecuted for breaking fast-days in Lent,
who told the court that it was better to eat left over meat than go to
market and run into debt through buying fish (Ibid., p. 128). If the
actors of *Mankind* could rely on the presence of similar attitudes in
their audience, they also had to cater for more orthodox opinions.
These differences of perspective may have had a class basis, since
Mercy's opening sermon makes a point of distinguishing between
'ʒe souerens þat sitt and ʒe brothern þat stonde ryght wppe' (29),
while the vices subsequently challenge this hierarchical division by
making the whole audience sing together. The play does not
declare its allegiance but it exploits divisions within the audience
to intensify the serio-comic game. What is diabolic 'perversion'
from one point of view (192, 296) is festive reversal from another
(119, 323).

Note

My sense of the dramatic potential of *Mankind* owes much to a
performance at the University of East Anglia 1980 by drama
students under the direction of Professor Nicholas Brooke.

Major Primary Texts

'Processus Noe cum Filiis', 'Mactatio Abel', (1958) in A. C. Cawley (ed.),
    The Wakefield Pageants of the Towneley Cycle (Manchester:
    Manchester University Press).
'The Thirde Pageant of Noyes Fludd' (1969) in R. M. Lumiansky and D.
    Mills (eds), *The Chester Mystery Cycle* (EETS).
Mankind (1969) in M. Eccles, *The Macro Plays* (EETS).
All other citations of texts, historical sources, scholarship and criticism
    are listed below under author or editor.

Axton, Richard (1973) 'Popular Modes in the Earliest Plays' in N. Denny
    (ed.), *Medieval Drama* (London: Edward Arnold), pp. 1–39.
Bakhtin, M. (1968) *Rabelais and His World*, trans. H. Isowolsky
    (Cambridge, Mass.: MIT Press).
Beadle, Richard (ed.) (1982) *The York Plays* (London: Edward Arnold).

Bellamy, John (1973) *Crime and Public Order in the Late Middle Ages* (London: Routledge & Kegan Paul).

Bevington, David (1962) *From Mankind to Marlowe* (Cambridge, Mass.: Harvard University Press).

Blomefield, Francis *An Essay Towards a Topographical History of the County of Norfolk*, 11 vols (London: Miller).

Brand, John (1984) *Observations on Popular Antiquities*, 3 vols (London: Bohn).

Burke, Peter (1978) *Popular Culture in Early Modern Europe* (London: Temple Smith).

Chambers, E. K. (1903) *The Medieval Stage*, 2 vols (Oxford).

Chambers, E. K. (1933) *The English Folk Play* (Oxford).

Coogan, M. P. (1947) *An Interpretation of the Moral Play, Mankind* (Washington).

Davis, Natalie Zemon (1975) *Society and Culture in Early Modern France* (London: Temple Smith).

Dickens, A. G. (1959) *Lollards and Protestants in the Diocese of York, 1509–1559* (London: Oxford University Press, 1959).

Elliott, John R. Jr (1972) 'The Sacrifice of Isaac as Comedy and Tragedy', in J. Taylor and A. H. Nelson (eds) *Medieval English Drama* (Chicago: University of Chicago Press), pp. 157–76.

Gilman, Sander L. (1974) *The Parodic Sermon in European Perspective* (Wiesbaden: Franz Steiner Verlag GMBH).

Ginzburg, Carlo (1980) *The Cheese and the Worms* (Baltimore: Johns Hopkins University Press).

Gluckman, Max (1963) *Custom and Conflict in Africa* (Oxford: Blackwell).

Hardison, O. B. (1965) *Christian Rite and Christian Drama* (Baltimore: Johns Hopkins University Press).

Heers, Jacques (1983) *Fêtes des Fous et Carnivals* (Paris: Fayard).

Hudson, W. and Tingey J. C. (eds) (1906) *The Records of the City of Norwich* (Norwich and London).

James, Mervyn (1983) 'Ritual, Drama and Social Body in the Late Medieval English Town', *Past and Present*, 98, pp. 3–29.

Kolve, V. A. (1966) *The Play Called Corpus Christi* (London: Edward Arnold).

Kunzle, David (1978) 'World Upside Down', in B.A. Babcock, (ed.) *The Reversible World* (Ithaca, N.Y.: Cornell University Press), pp. 39–94.

Ladurie, Emmanuel Le Roy (1979) *Carnival in Romans*, transl. Mary Feeney (N.Y.: Braziller).

Ladurie, Emmanuel Le Roy (1978) *Montaillou*, transl. Barbara Bray (London: Scolar Press).

Lindsay, Sir David (1979) *Ane Satire of the Thrie Estaitis* in Peter Happe *Four Morality Plays* (Harmondsworth: Penguin Books).

Migne, J.P., *Patrologiae Cursus Completus*, 221 vols. (Paris).

Mills, David (1983) (1844–64) 'Drama and Folk-Ritual', in A. C. Cawley, M. Jones, P. F. McDonald and D. Mills, *The Revels History of Drama. vol. 1: Medieval Drama* (London: Methuen).

Mirk, John (1905) *Festial*, ed. Theodor Erbe (EETS e.s. 96).

MS Misc. Rolls 9C (Norfolk Record Office: Norwich Corporation Manuscripts).

Nelson, Alan H. (1974) *The Medieval English Stage* (Chicago and London: University of Chicago Press).

Neuss, Paula (1973) 'Active and Idle Language: Dramatic Images in *Mankind*', in Neville Denny, (ed.) *Medieval Drama* (London: Edward Arnold), pp. 41–67.

Owen, Dorothy M. (1971) *Church and Society in Medieval Lincolnshire* (Lincoln: History of Lincolnshire Committee, Lincolnshire Local History Society).

Owst, G. R. (1961) *Literature and the Pulpit in Medieval England* (Oxford: 2nd edn).

Pease, A. S. (1926) 'Things Without Honour', *Classical Philology* XXI, pp. 27–42.

Phythian-Adams, Charles (1976) 'Ceremony and the Citizen: The Communal Year at Coventry 1450–1550', in Peter Clark, (ed.) *The Early Modern Town* (London: Longman) pp. 106–28.

Robbins, R. H. (ed.) (1959) *Historical Poems of the XIVth and XVth Centuries* (New York: Columbia University Press).

Rossiter, A. P. (1950) *English Drama from Early Times to the Elizabethans* (London: Hutchinson).

Smart, W. K. (1917) 'Mankind and the Mumming Plays', MLN XXII, pp. 21–5.

Storey, R. L. (1966) *The End of the House of Lancaster* (London: Barrie and Rockcliff).

Tanner, N. P. (ed.) (1977) *Heresy Trials in the Diocese of Norwich, 1428–31* (London: Royal Historical Society).

Thomas, Keith (1973) *Religion and the Decline of Magic* (Harmondsworth: Penguin Books).

Thomas, Keith (1976) 'Rule and Misrule in the Schools of Early Modern England', The Stenton Lectures, 9 (Reading: University of Reading).

Thomson, J. A. F. (1965) *The Later Lollards 1414–1520* (Oxford).

Tiddy, Reginald (1923) *The Mummer's Play* (Oxford).

Turner, Victor (1974) *The Ritual Process* (Harmondsworth: Pelican).

Wright, Thomas and Halliwell, James (1941-43) *Reliquiae Antiquae* (London: William Pickering).

6

The Social Function of the Middle English Romances

Stephen Knight

I

The romances are the ugly ducklings of medieval English studies.
With rare exceptions, they offer no niceties of style for the New
Critic, no depth of reference for the exegete. They fall between the
elaborate courtesy of their French ancestors and the blunt simplicity
of their junior siblings, the British ballads. Both extremes have
found many to applaud and examine them as models of life and
thought, but the romances as a whole are rarely studied and less
often read.

Yet the romances are there, and there in surprisingly large
numbers for medieval texts that are in English and relatively
unsophisticated—so basically ill-qualified for literary recording. At
least 100 of them have survived (the count varies, depending on
how many quasi-hagiographies and near-novels are admitted), and
while many of the early and shorter romances survive in single
copies, some achieve double figures in manuscripts and early prints,
outperforming many of the poems of Gower, Chaucer and Lydgate.

The romances show variety in form, source and topic, but they
share the figure of the knight and the ethic of chivalry: all
definitions of the genre, however hesitant, recognise that point of
convergence. Since the figure and the ethic belong to a particular
social and economic formation, that of feudalism, an invitation
emerges to investigate the social function of the romance genre.
This approach has been noted by some of the more thoughtful
critics, though hardly pursued very far. Auerbach discerned chivalric

self-projection in the classic French romance and also the contradiction inherent in the birth of the chivalric ideal at the time and place of mercantile take-off (1957, pp. 131, 133, 138). Both of the recent historians of romance considered the possibility of a socio-historical approach. Mehl felt some 'data' might emerge from a geographic and social study (1968, p. 35); Pearsall recognised the approach more fully, but his essentially literary stance made him sceptical of its value (1977, p. 126). Gibbs' introduction to his edition acknowledges Auerbach's initiative but goes only a little further along that line (1966). A more complex study has a more sophisticated vision of the romances in context; Wittig sees them as based on an essentially social myth (1978, p. 183) rather than the much favoured individualist view, offered intrinsically by Stevens (1973) and overtly by Hanning (1977). Finlayson's essay in definition rejects any relation with social reality (1980, p. 54), while Barrow's *The Medieval Society Romances* (1924) is based on naive reflection theory, assuming that feudal society was intensely courteous and employed the romances as handbooks to fine manners.

A different initiative is taken in the undeveloped but refreshingly political comment made by Kettle when positioning himself for his *Introduction to the British Novel* (1951, vol. 1, p. 29):

> Romance was the non-realistic aristocratic literature of feudalism. It was non-realistic in the sense that its underlying purpose was not to help people cope in a positive way with the business of living but to transport them to a world different, idealised, nicer than their own. It was aristocratic because the attitudes it expressed and recommended were precisely the attitudes the ruling class wished (no doubt usually unconsciously) to encourage in order that their privileged position might be perpetuated.

Kettle goes no further, though his colleague in early English Marxism, A. L. Morton, argued out in some detail the basis for the summary given by Kettle (1960). Neither would appeal greatly to modern theoretical Marxism, of course, because of their view that there is an unproblematic 'Real', with which culture should confront people. But the sharply political sense of the role of culture in class conflict should survive from Kettle's pronouncement and should underlie any understanding of the full social role of romance, however much elaboration and modification might be needed.

Two central elements in the recent analysis of culture and its social role need to be incorporated, though Auerbach goes close to subsuming them in his socio-historical asides. The principle of hegemony, stemming from Gramsci's work (Adamson, 1980), has established that culture is not a 'superstructural' or relatively insignificant part of political process, but is a most important pressure helping to create consent to the dominance structured throughout a particular society and reproduced in its cultural forms. This is of special importance in the medieval context, where the appropriation of surplus from producers, in the form of feudal rent, was not brought about by an economic mechanism as in the capitalist appropriation of surplus value, but was primarily made possible by a set of coercions of a political, cultural and religious character (Hindess and Hirst, 1975, pp. 222–3).

Secondly (as part of that hegemony), there is the valuable Althusserian concept of cultures as an 'imaginary' in which people produce for themselves an ideological relationship with actual events and forces (1971). In spite of criticism (Coward and Ellis, 1977, pp. 74–5; Eagleton, 1983, pp. 171–3), the imaginary remains a valuable account of how people make use of and are controlled by a dominant ideology. The corpus of romance evidently filled the role of an imaginary for a complex audience which can be reconstructed to some degree. The use of the English language would exclude from the audience at most the upper aristocracy and royal family, and those not after the mid-fourteenth century. A major role in the audience must have been played by those who actually controlled the economic and social relations of the feudal mode of production, landlords and their families. For them the romances detail a whole range of threats to their tenure of power, and also resolve those threats by employing the values that seem from their viewpoint the most credible—partly the euphemised values of chivalry and partly the realistic values of cavalry.

But the majority of the audience would have been people who were not in positions of power but accepted the values of those who were—that acceptance depended upon cultural persuasions as well as more tangible coercions, as is normal in such situations. The broader audience (to whom the feudal threats and values were both an ideological imaginary and a structure of false consciousness) would include many who have been wrongly thought outside the world of feudal social and cultural relations. Marx showed that pre-capitalist formations such as primitive manufacturing (weaving for instance), local circulation of goods for cash (carrying trade) and urban artisanship (guild and journeyman crafts) do not in any way breach the economic and social bases of the feudal mode of production (*Grundrisse*, 1973, p. 512; *Capital*, I, 1975, p. 510). The fact that mercantile values are seen as a threat in many of the romances only points to the dialectic and historically developing nature of the feudal mode of production; similar strains are to be found within the culture of the capitalist mode of production.

It should be said at this stage that the term 'feudal' has a distinct value, in spite of problems raised by some historians. The concept functions valuably as the description of a specific economic and social structure, perceived in medieval Western Europe as dominant both in its time and by historians since then (Mukherjee, 1985). The texts to be discussed here will be considered in terms of their relationship with feudality, not in terms of their chronological historicity, genre or literary form, though those features can help to reveal the parts played by various romances in feudal hegemony— central to it, peripheral to it or, in some cases, critical of it.

II

This paper will give first a brief general account of the inherent and centrally ideological structure of the romances, followed by a more detailed account of the realisation of that pattern through three major romance types. The first is that in which a lonely hero wins honour, wife and property; the second is that in which a whole family is disrupted and through difficulties re-establishes itself in honour and power; the third type contains romances which in both theme and form interrogate and cast doubt upon the ideological pattern of most romances. While some from the first two types do contain aspects of social critique, there is a distinct third category of critical romances; they have been traditionally regarded as having special 'literary critical' value. It will be argued here that such 'quality' is actually a function of their socially critical role.

First, a general summary of romance ideology. The romances confront problems seen from the viewpoint of a landowning, armed class, and resolve those problems with values felt to be potent and admissible. Threats and values are coded to produce a self-concept for the powerful and to present an acceptable image of power to those without it. But the coding and generalising into a cultural form of political dominance does not sever it from a traceable historicity. In the classic romance, the knight establishes his authority over property and creates a family; he excludes enemies and challengers from his land just as the texts exclude from their purview the productive classes; he is his own lord, honoured by the king, but not in any way ruled by him. Those three familiar features act out dynamically what Hindess and Hirst find to be the three crucial and particular features of the Feudal Mode of Production (1975, pp. 235–7). Title and exclusion form the dual mechanisms by which the lord appropriates surplus; the absence of centralised state power is the overarching political factor that typifies the world of feudal relations. Those basic patterns of urgent and structural value in medieval secular society are ideologically central in English romance, and so is the consistent representation of a basic contradiction of feudalism, the public and honorific concept of a knightly class in dialectic with the actual one-to-one relations of lord and liege (Ullman, 1966). The result is a pattern of 'competitive assertiveness' (James, 1978, p. 1)—feudal knights reacting in that basic way towards others who are either of their class or aspire to their position. That structure underlies romance and is its central dominant ideological feature, validating the practices of the feudally powerful, and persuading the non-powerful of the authenticity of the whole imaginary. A classical example of a hegemonic culture.

A paper like this one might well examine individual romances in terms of title, exclusion, devolution of power, as the structure within which competitive assertiveness was the personalised response. That would compile an historical and political analysis of the genre, and be of some interest. However, there is another area of operation, and so of analysis, in an ideological imaginary. The detailed and manifold ways in which the central pattern is realised in varying human instances, these construct the system through which a total imaginary is produced in human subjects, the creation of what Jameson has thoughtfully described as the 'political unconscious' (1981). This paper will take as established the inner ideological core that has just been described and will move towards an understanding of the detailed realisation of the romance imaginary.

III

The best-known pattern of romance deals with an unmarried hero who wins his way to a wealthy wife and so establishes both a family and his own honour: this will be called the knight-alone structure. The threats realised are multiple—at first, isolation, poverty, lack of honour, physical opposition. It is also usual, later in the story, to derive some form of threat, or at least embarrassment, from the need to have female company in order to be both honoured and wealthy.

The values that stand against these problems are those of courage and martial skill (prowess is the quasi-technical term) and endurance and fidelity to duties or goals (loyalty, or 'leute'). Sometimes chivalrous behaviour towards men is a value, and often the texts prize feelings of love towards the propertied women, but both aspects of courtesy exist in awkward tension with the need to be a ferocious warrior and the negative aspects of the woman's power. However, in the English romances courtesy and love are very rarely instrumental; they are at best masking values. Christianity, however, is sometimes presented as a force which does bring results, through prayer or Christian deeds. In fact, Mehl (1968, Ch. 5) identifies a category of 'homiletic' romances, but while these do at times approach validation of the Church as an institution rather than the feudal class, as in the 'hagiographic' versions of *Amis and Amiloun*, his instances are mostly feudal romances which incorporate Christian values.

The hero-alone pattern is familiar from a famous and very early romance, Chrétien de Troyes' *Le Chevalier au Lion* (also known as *Yvain*). The pattern of a hero's progress towards honour and wife is standard in culture from epic to folk tale, but it has been argued that the particular isolation of the hero in this type of romance takes its force from circumstances in France in the early Middle Ages, partly from changes in inheritance laws which left younger sons of the knightly caste quite without financial support (Duby, 1977) and also from social conflict within an expanded aristocracy (Köhler, 1974; Knight, 1983, Ch. 3).

The 'fair unknown' story is a major hero-alone structure which reveals the complexity of romance ideology: it both expresses and euphemises the theme of social *arrivisme*. It was the basis of Chrétien's late twelfth-century *Le Chevalier au Lion*, and was still powerful in Malory's late fifteenth-century 'Tale of Sir Gareth'. The vitality of the pattern suggests it realises important forces: Mills provides a good survey of its main versions in his edition of *Libeaus Desconus* (1969, pp. 42–64).

The 'fair unknown' is at first and in French a threatening figure, uncouth but strong and determined; he learns to be courteous as well as powerful, wins a lady, property and honour (not always in that order, as will be discussed below). Somewhere along the way he becomes known, and it is revealed that he is not the incursionary thug that his presentation has implied, but in fact a member of the aristocracy. A crucial point is that the later this revelation comes, and the more abuse and anxiety aroused by the figure on the way, the stronger is the realisation of social advancement through martial force. Through the 'fair unknown' there rises to consciousness the reality of social *arrivisme* in its threatening reality; but the threat is also culturally resolved. A similar use of an imaginary at work is found in the 'lost heir' stories which in the nineteenth century both faced and dissolved the fear of inexplicable (and so disturbing) sudden wealth and power: it is the fable which Dickens offers and then withdraws in the searching and socially critical, rather than simply ideological, structure of *Great Expectations*.

Libeaus Desconus, the English romance which owes its name to the 'fair unknown' structure, is a good example of the knight-alone romance, with telling socio-historical relations. Popular in England (six manuscripts survive against only one of the earlier French version), this seems a suitable choice for a moderately detailed analysis. The purpose is to show just how much ideological material is suspended in these narratives, how passages and motifs fill out in specific detail the basic structure of the imaginary. The earlier French concern with *arrivisme* is much reduced in *Libeaus Desconus*; the threat of the 'fair unknown' himself is much less in English. The hero is immediately named as Gyngelayne, Gawain's illegitimate son, and the 'damsel maledisaunte' becomes friendly and admiring after his very first victory. Like other English 'fair unknown' patterns, *Sir Percival, Sir Degare* and (in variant form) *Ywain and Gawain*, the story develops a series of problems associated with a knight's rise to power and maintenance of that position, exploring the fourteenth-century specifics of title, exclusion, devolution and competitive assertiveness.

Gyngelayne moves swiftly through the battles that establish him (Benson called this a 'proving' pattern, 1976, pp. 99–101). A malicious knight is disposed of, and his vengeful relatives follow suit. They all submit to the hero and take themselves to court as tokens of his power and honour—a neat model of the weak central authority in feudalism. Then Gyngelayne deals abruptly with two giants who are oppressing a young woman.

None of this action has presented major problems for the hero or demanded emphatic treatment in the text. But from here on the episodes grow in length and impact as they explore more thoroughly and anxiously the threats and values of the feudal imaginary. The hero now defeats the knight of the falcon, who insists his lady is more beautiful than all others. This sort of sequence is common in romance and is treated by most commentators as nothing more than escapist material. In fact, it has an important effect in ideologically sealing the hero's attainment of high status. He no longer brawls with giants or knightly thugs; this is graceful and courteous fighting, and in service of a lady's honour. The whole network of chivalry and courtesy provides a euphemistic cover for the brutal practices of feudal cavalry, and this type of episode enacts that function within their imaginary. Morton (1960) offers some analysis along these lines, and I have done so elsewhere (1983, Chs 3, 4): the masking effect itself still operates in conventional and idealistic treatments of chivalry, recently exemplified in Keen's work (1984).

There follows a movement towards real problems. Arthur hears of Gyngelayne's honour and sends him the huge sum of a 100 pounds. With it the hero establishes a feast in Cardiff while Arthur rules in Carlisle. The life-style that brought together show, honour and so the authority of title and local rule had to depend on extra income; here the need for cash surplus is realised, but its origin is alleged to derive through honour alone and from a willing royal acceptance of devolved authority, not from the actual feudal appropriation of surplus in cash form. The sequence elegantly condenses real patterns and their euphemisations.

But the text is not always as blandly and confidently ideological as that. The actual source of luxury-producing surplus is indicated in the following passage. In a firmly emphasised sequence of action, Gyngelayne takes a fancy to a dog that crosses his path , and seizes it. Its owner and his men pursue dog and catcher, but they are all defeated. As a result the hero wins not only a dog but

> Tresure, land and rente
> Castell, hall and boure.
>
> (1272–3)

This startling episode cuts through the cultural coding of tournaments and royal presents as the source of feudal authority. Feudality was based on violence and self-interest, and all the romances at some stage recognise this disturbing reality, in order to make valid their cultural concealment of it.

Libeaus Desconus is now well-established; he is no longer the property-less knight needing for his success to win a lady—the early French emphasis on culture. It was an historical possibility as well, and continued to be so—Edward III's sons tended to marry very rich women. But his romance, like most of the English 'hero-alone' stories, exhibits a sturdily self-reliant patriarchy in social ascent. Yet that does not exclude from the text the embarrassment caused by women and love in the earlier pattern. Rather it is dealt with more confidently and starkly than before—and more briefly than in the French version.

In the next sequence the hero meets a woman named nothing less the La Dame Amoure. She entraps him through specifically-named powers of sorcery and makes him forget his knightly quest: this topic was treated with more subtlety and more anxiety in the cases of Yvain and Erec. Time after time in romances that have so often been accepted by conservative critics as idealistic and courteous it appears that love-service of women actually functions either as a specific rationale for gaining their property or as part of a more general sophistication, part of the chivalry that concealed the brutal reality of cavalry.

Gyngelayne is reminded of his knightly and non-amatory duty by his faithful and distinctly asexual (so non-embarrassing) guide. He next encounters a new enemy whom he fights but who then becomes his helper. This is the steward of Synadoun, the city of the woman he has come to rescue. Stewards themselves as court officials, masters of a knight's material needs, are often treated with hostility in romance—Sir Kay is the archetype. This one, though, means more than the usual figure, for he is named Sir Lombard. If Lombards were known at all in the period, it was for banking, not their ancient military history; this figure is a potent condensation of the court official and a man who controls cash, two figures the feudally powerful had many reasons to regard with caution, and needed to neutralise or, preferably, make into allies. The story continues to range through the intimate enemies of the knightly class as Gyngelayne makes his promised rescue. The woman is held not by the usual villain knight—they have long been disposed of, before the story moved to a more searching level of threat and resolution. Two 'clerks' have her under control in a 'paleys queynte of gynne' (1763). The hero's final act is to release the lady from the cunning power of a learned and non-military class. This seems to encode feudal anxiety about on one hand the Church and its legalistic threat to property, and on the other the increasing dependence of the landed classes on trained lawyers—a fact glancingly referred to in the description of the Manciple in Chaucer's 'General Prologue' (576–83); I have argued elsewhere that the same problem underlies 'The Franklin's Tale' (Knight, 1980).

The resolution of this threat to feudalism is, as so often in romance, condensed with escape from a patriarchal fear. Released by the hero's courage, the lady turns from an enchanted serpent into a submissive wife. From a sexually hideous and threatening Lamia she becomes the ideal and property-bearing wife. She is final testimony to the historical relevance and imaginative vigour of the motifs and structures found throughout the Middle English romances and typified by *Libeaus Desconus*.

Another interesting case is the story of *Sir Amadace*, an unjustly ignored romance. He owes money because of his rash generosity— a feudal fortunate flaw. He goes into exile with his remaining 40 pounds, and encounters the corpse of a merchant who failed because he was not mean-minded enough. His creditor, a successful merchant, refuses his body burial because his debt is outstanding, so Amadace pays the 30 pounds owing and, with his last 10 pounds, arranges a funeral. Then he organises a huge feast, at the expense of the merchant who lives by meanly mercantile values. Finally, Amadace retires, ruined, into the forest.

So much seems a neat and firm response to mercantilism from a feudal viewpoint. But the story, like *Libeaus Desconus*, grows more searching as it continues. A White Knight appears, supports Amadace spiritually and financially, and says they must share everything. Through his knightly efforts (a proving pattern again)

Amadace wins a wife and will inherit a kingdom after her father dies (a rare and rather credible feature). When the White Knight reappears he rejects all shared goods except half the wife and child, and he means a literal half of their bodies. The wife urges Amadace to dismember her to keep his oath. As he is about to do so, the White Knight calls it all off and a happy, though hardly unstrained, ending follows.

After the easy victories over the bourgeoisie, this Abraham-Isaac motif appears to outline the difficulty of living in a collective fraternal system, as feudality is alleged to be, and emphasises the danger of ever having to rely on anyone else's help. Knighthood is shown in crisis because of the clash of private acquisition and public duties, mediated through the ever-present oath—and the poem seems to have the power to interrogate, by its imagination and emphasis, its own ideological positioning. This self-criticism is a feature of the most powerful and long-lasting of the romances, a version of 'critical realism' as Lukács called it (1972), the power of the historically aware imagination to present an essentially radical critique from an essentially conservative position.

Some aspects of this process appear in other hero-alone romances which are usually dismissed as no more than 'conventional'. In *Sir Degrevant* the hero's initial nadir is caused by an unusually realistic oppressive neighbour; *The Squire of Low Degree* is exiled because of a jealous royal steward; *Sir Launfal* suffers from the Queen's hostile power and then from mercantile fickleness; *Sir Gowther* is at first a terrible model of unrestrained knightly savagery. In all of these cases, however, the penetratingly real threat is resolved in a fully ideological way. *Sir Degrevant* comes to love the neighbouring villian's daughter; *The Squire of Low Degree* has a stong-minded princess for a lover and she waits seven years for his return; *Sir Launfal* relies on that folk-tale fantasy, a fairy mistress who prohibits any revelation of her existence (so indicating her status as private compensation); Sir Gowther's violence is neutralised from the beginning by making him the child of a diabolic incubus, and yet he is able to reform his ways into a remarkable piety.

If those romances explore problems inherent to the feudal world, others seem to be at best peripheral to that social context. *Havelock* shows 'lower-class' features in its village games and physical work, royal myth in its hero and his revelation, urban connections as an origin legend for Grimsby. This text is much broader than the specifically knightly and feudal world, being both older than and marginal to the main romance pattern. A similar example of uneven development is *Gamelyn*. About a dispossessed younger son, it does not activate the values of chivalry or even cavalry in his quest for title. He becomes leader of an outlaw band and they help him establish some very unknightly rough justice. The problem of title seems to have transposed itself to the world of the Robin Hood ballads, which have recently been identified as native to neither the peasantry nor the gentry, but texts in which urban craftsmen constructed a new imaginary to handle their new and troublesome socio-economic status (Tardif, 1983).

IV

Though the hero-alone story has been seen as 'the basic paradigm of the romance' (Finlayson, 1980, pp. 55), the family-based pattern is both very common and ideologically rich. In this structure, at the beginning, the knight already has a family and a disruptive force separates its members. They must struggle through many trials to enjoy reunion; the knight's own role is often important, but never total, and may indeed be marginal; wife or son can be the main agents of re-establishment. The family structure is likely to be the underlying pattern in romance, as it is dominant in ballad and folk-tale; apparently the special circumstances of late twelfth-century France brought forward the hero-alone pattern but other contexts saw the re-emergence of the family-based form.

When Wittig saw the basic romance pattern as 'Separation and Reunion' she made the family structure primary (1978, p. 179), but it might be better, and consistent with her view of romance as an essentially social myth, to recognise the two major types in such a structural summary. If her two categories were represented as 'social dysfunction' and 'social function', then in the first segment the hero-alone story offers 'Lack' and the family-based pattern reveals 'Crime'. This is to borrow terms for the initiating narrative function from Propp (1968); his analysis is of considerable value in romance study, as is suggested by Bordman's intriguing motif index of romances (1963).

Significant differences between the knight-alone and the family-based patterns are located in their threat and resolution structures. Threats to the family may be in part the same as those of the knight-alone type—exile, isolation, shame. But many of the family-based romances involve threats to more than a single hero. The wife often plays a major role, she may be 'calumniated' as the folklorists call it—exiled, threatened with various oppressions. The child or children may also be of an age to suffer consciously; if very young, they may be abandoned, stolen by animals, or put in the care of merchants or infidels.

The values which rescue the feudal family from these terrible fates are also wider than in the knight-alone romances. True, fighting does often play a major part, but it may be conducted by a son as well as (or instead of) a father, so embracing the reproduction of title and authority as well as their re-imposition. The wife's virtues are often substantial and instrumental—endurance, fidelity, courage, shrewdness, but also physical action and intervention. Her overarching virtues of passivity and loyalty to her menfolk locate the stories in a patriarchal context, but some romances, such as *Emaré* or *The King of Tars*, depict women in something approaching historical terms; that is, they operate with genuine power and impact, provided that the limits of patriarchy are not breached (Haskell, 1973).

A good example of the family-based romance would be *Sir Eglamour of Artois*, a popular mid-fourteenth-century production with six manuscripts and four early prints surviving. This is basically a 'giant's daughter' story: many folk-tales follow this pattern and so do Celtic stories such as *The Wooing of Emer* and *Culhwch and Olwen*, featuring Cuchulainn and Arthur. *Sir Eglamour of Artois* is not a hero-alone story because he and the giant's daughter have a child before he is sent off on the task-fulfilling quest which always precedes (and, as the giant hopes, might prevent) the marriage. She is exiled with their son; he is stolen by a griffin and is adopted by the King of Israel. These are stereotypical family romance disruptions, a striking mixture of exotic projections and the mundane uncertainties of life in the military caste. Then this story, like so many romances, turns the screw and enacts a starker drama. The son meets his mother unknowingly, woos her and wins her in joust. Only when they are approaching sexual intimacy does a recognition scene occur. In the following action the father, equally unknowing, wins her by defeating his son.

Romance often euphemises conquest through courtesy, but here the calming motif becomes the mechanism of a dark threat inside the family itself. But things grow no worse: recognitions flourish and the family is reunited after its extraordinary strains. The hero-alone romance was quite capable of realising private tensions within its social pattern: the masculine fear of woman is deeply etched in Yvain's imprisonment in Laudine's gatehouse; Erec's visit to the Joie de la Court; Launcelot's trip across the sword bridge; his (and Tristan's) adventures with Guinevere's bedroom window—all these present in condensed form both deflowering and castration. But the family romances realise sexual anxiety and disturbance not in terms of one-off images and incidents, but as a thoroughly structured part of their meaning; the family's dangers do not come all from outside.

Other family-based dramas lay different emphases. *Emaré* makes the woman most important; she has to avoid the incestuous wishes of her father, and go through trials with her child with little help from husband or son—the story pattern found, in distinctly restrained form, in the story of Constance used by both Gower and Chaucer. Women play a large role in other family romances, especially *Lai le Freine, The Erl of Tolous, Le Bone Florence of Rome* and *Sir Triamour*. Although a general deference to the male is evident, the neurotic control of feminine power found in the hero-based structure does not seem to be a feature here.

The long and arresting romance *Octavian* is full enough to involve a mercantile theme. At first the malicious mother-in-law (a recurring figure of familial strain) brands the Queen as adulterous for having twins. She is exiled and they are stolen by an ape and a lioness. The ape-child becomes a butcher, sponsored by a money-lending merchant called Clement le Vileyn; the lioness-child (the nobler beast of the two, of course) goes straight into a slot as an adopted prince. A complex double-plot ensues, involving the butcher as a 'fair unknown' fighting the giant of Montmartre (so rejecting his urban connections) and meeting his family through various chivalric actions. *Octavian* could be seen as combining the family-based and hero-based patterns, which is certainly true, almost programmatically so, of *Sir Degare* and *Sir Beves of Hamtoun*.

Other versions of the family-based romances are origin legends like *Sir Beves of Hamtoun, Guy of Warwick* and, in their European origins, *Partenaye* and *William of Palerne*. A non-familial grouping is the basis of fraternal romances such as the very popular *Amis and Amiloun* (some of its versions become distinctly hagiographical), *The Avowing of Arthur* and, in basis, *King Horn* and *Athelston*. In each of these competitive assertiveness is the inner strain upon the fraternal bond. Some of the group-based romances seem, like a few hero-alone stories, quite outside the feudal world, either before it like *Athelston* or after it like *The Tournament of Tottenham* and the 'King and Subject' romances (sometimes wrongly seen as ballads) where the emergent sense of class is both the social bond and the challenge to the feudal and royal authority: examples are *King Edward and the Shepherd* and *Rauf Coilyear*.

V

There are other romances and types of romance whose functions lie largely outside the central knight-alone and family-based patterns that have been discussed. One particular group of texts seems to privilege learning more than usual: the 'epic romances' (Pearsall, 1965, p. 92) are *Arthour and Merlin, Richard Coeur de Lion* and *Kyng Alisaunder*. Written in the later thirteenth century and perhaps by the same man, they load their narratives with information and moralism, envisaging an audience which values informational and didactic culture more highly than that of the mainstream feudal romances. Mehl sees these texts as early 'novels in verse' (1968, Ch. 7), but some clerical connection appears a likely social setting.

The later fifteenth century offers two different sorts of non-feudal romance. There are the major literary popularisations of chivalric material, either in manuscript like Lovelich's *Holy Grail* and Malory's 'Arthuriad', or in print like Caxton's 'torrent of Burgundian-style chivalric prose romances' (Pearsall, 1976, p. 72) which includes Malory's *Le Morte Darthur*, the first editing of his work. In this 'Indian Summer of English Chivalry' (the title of Ferguson's somewhat general book, 1960), feudally originated texts found an expanding and literate audience in the complex mixture of aristocrats and businessmen (not exclusive categories) who valued the ideology of chivalry most urgently at a time when what reality it had contained, or subsumed, was rapidly disappearing. Lovelich the skinner and Caxton the wool-merchant are typical purveyors of chivalry and romance to a world for which it was an inauthentic but valuable force; just as, in different ways, it had always been.

At the same time the spread of literacy recorded a very different sort of romance, the popular versions that are usually derogated with some metaphor such as 'debased' or some partial evaluation such as 'vulgar'. Several romances exist in a ballad version such as *Hind Horn*, *The Marriage of Gawain* or the *Guy of Warwick* cut-down which enmeshes the noble hero with the Dun Cow of Dunsmore Heath (Crane, 1915, p. 180). It is a matter of some doubt whether all of these do (as is usually assumed) post-date the 'high'—or at least long—romance forms, that is, forms which treat in more focused detail the concerns of the powerful. In *Kempy Kay*, for example, regarded as extremely debased and even an 'unpleasant piece' (Child, 1884, vol. I, Part 2, p. 301), Arthur's peppery Seneschal is presented in something much like his form as a Celtic warlock. The theory that ballad and popular story are 'down-sinking cultural goods' (the phrase sounds less threadbare in its original German) may be consoling to conservative scholars, but has no credibility. The popular forms have their own vitality and function which are separate from the special 'high' forms and so may precede, parallel or follow them with equal ease.

VI

There remains another important type of romance. It is found in the texts which are most often discussed, namely *Sir Gawain and the Green Knight* and Malory's 'Arthuriad'. These 'quality' romances have a subtlety of style and theme which has provided raw material for academic labours, but the texts do not belong to some new 'good' category: they are, in fact, another socially functional variant. They do not simply promulgate an ideology, as do most of the romances, whether naively like *Sir Launfal*, or with some complexity like *Libeaus Desconus*. These literary favourites are critical texts in the sense that they show both an instinctive grasp and a distinct critique of the social structures of feudal England and its cultural projections.

Some other romances come close to doing this. Tragedies like *Sir Tristrem* and the stanzaic *Morte Arthure* have, by virtue of their endings, a serious and sombre tone, but seem to go no further than an austere view of fatefully conflicting loyalties. Some of the happy ending texts are closer to being critical through the complex patterns they suggest: *Sir Amadace's* uncomfortable success and *Octavian's* turbulent path to reunion both leave strain and disturbance in the mind. The classic text of this kind is Chrétien's *Le Chevalier au Lion*; its critical sting is quite absent in the English *Ywain and Gawain*, together with the second half of the action. Some critics have felt that the alliterative *Morte Arthure* treats its imperialist theme in a sceptical way (Matthews, 1960; Finlayson, 1967) but this seems a modern re-reading (Kelly, 1986). *Sir Gawain and the Green Knight* and Malory's 'Arthuriad' go further than any other English romance in treating their world and its values critically; they grasp its inherent socio-cultural structures and also—the aperture for merely literary criticism—they realise that critical position in imaginative and purely formal terms as well as in suggestive thematic statement.

Sir Gawain and the Green Knight is based on a structure familiar in the Arthurian romances, especially in those encyclopedic ones which provide a series of adventures stemming from Arthur's court. Some disruption occurs just as the court is about to feast, to celebrate its honoured unity. A challenger-knight rides in, a woman reports some distant oppression, some strange occurrence indicates disruption of the Arthurian and feudal stasis—on one occasion a rout of hart, hounds, woman and knight; on another, the grail with its varied attendants. The hero of this particular adventure will travel out, resolve the disorder and return to his portion of honour and the renewed Arthurian calm.

The Gawain poet resists the easy consolation of this bland threat-resolution structure. The threat he provides in the Green Knight most formidably and directly questions the heroic values of Arthur's court. Then he is found to have an alternative court, equal or even superior in courtesy to Arthur's world, one marked by vigour and natural activities against which even the Christmas sport of Camelot seems both artificial and immature. An alternative must imply critique, just as Parzival's court of the grail surpasses Arthur's court of earthly chivalry. But it is primarily from Gawain's own viewpoint that the challenge to traditional feudal values is made. They are first of all exposed as vulnerable. When Gawain is told he just cannot be the real and publicly known Gawain, when servitors gather to watch his fabled performance of courtesy, when he is the prisoner of his reputation, in all these instances the external system of honorific value is denaturalised, made to seem a culture-specific and so a set of values capable of being altered. (A similar process occurs, in a more theoretical mode, in *The Book of Fame* (Knight, 1986).) The key critique of the feudal and chivalric values is Gawain's own dissent when the court interprets his journey as a success but he insists it is failure. All wear the green baldric, but one is a nonconformist.

It is only from the position of internalised Christianity that this judgement can be made. Gawain is Mary's knight, but she is on the inside of his shield, she is his guide in personal extremity, not part of any public religious performance. Wyclif's emergent idea of a desocialised religion, between God and believer alone, is an inherent critique of both the public wealth of the Church and the public role of the priest, and such a position makes it possible for dissent to be raised against the feudal matrix of values. That point of contact between religious and social protest was clearly observed in the period, in terms of Lollardy and the Peasants' Revolt (Aston, 1960).

There is a social as well as an historical context for the Gawain poet's critique. Bennett (1979) has located its language and geography as belonging to the upwardly mobile professional soldiers of fourteenth-century Cheshire, hard-handed, self-made barons like Knolles and Calveley. There is *no* North-West Midlands aristocratic court, that product of reflection theory over the decades. Though Bercilak's castle, as an alternative Camelot of hard hunting, true hospitality and clear-eyed, non-traditional assessments, may well enshrine the projected self-consciousness of that new class fraction of *arriviste* soldiers. One very striking thing is the resemblance between the social context and function of this poem and that of Chrétien de Troyes's *Le Chevalier au Lion*: both deal in elaborate and questionable chivalry for an audience whose power and wealth depended on quite unchivalric practices but had need of a new imaginary because of their new position.

The thrust of the poetic form in *Sir Gawain and the Green*

Knight, that artistic power that clearly separates it from the bulk of the romances, is itself convergent with the poem's innovative and proto-humanist critique of traditional ideology. Dynamic physical detail, sharp naturalistic focus, vivid realisation in sound and syntax of a tactile world, this deep-laid sense of tangible form invokes a material and sense-available ontology and epistemology. In *Sir Gawain and the Green Knight*, as in most late medieval art that has been valued in bourgeois society, there is an emergent individualisation in the form. That pattern meshes with the inherent critique of feudal ideology and its cultural projection in romance; it also relates to economic and socio-cultural aspects of the post-feudal world, which are evidently both detected and realised through the imagination of the major artist.

Malory has rarely been considered as acute and perceptive a writer as the Gawain poet, and yet a structural conflict between feudal collectivity and an opposing privacy is much more thoroughly developed in his 'Arthuriad'. By his selection and treatment of episodes from 'The Tale of King Arthur' onwards, he appears to be instinctively aware of the contradiction at the heart of feudal life, that its collective honorifics are both the result and the concealment of the pattern of 'competitive assertiveness'. The impact of the grail story on his work, and perhaps on his imagination, is to oppose a Christian system of internalised values to the external values of honour and shame, previously the only, and rather frail set of sanctions available in his Arthurian world. The pattern closely resembles that of critical evaluation in *Sir Gawain and the Green Knight*.

In Malory's last two tales a complex presentation of the private and public worlds is undertaken, showing that they are not merely opposed, but become dialectically interwoven, as Launcelot, then Arthur, then Gawain (and perhaps even Aggravayne) all act on grounds of honour and seriously exacerbate a matter which was inherently private, and untroublesome while it remained so. The issue, and Malory's consciousness of it, is clear in sequences he expands from his sources such as the argument between Guinevere and Launcelot immediately after his return from the Grail quest; at the end of 'The Knight of the Cart' the matter is presented in an extraordinary dumb show as the lovers are unable to speak when they both wish Meleagaunt dead: their private world is becoming public and so must be constrained.

Like the White Knight in *Sir Amadace*, the contradictions of the feudal structure are eventually appalling. They are also formally realised. Malory juxtaposes Launcelot's Christian final speech with the famous elegy by Ector, and both are high points of complexity and art. Malory realises at the level of form the tensions of his text, as did the Gawain-poet: both speeches bring to a head the two polar styles of the 'Arthuriad'. Launcelot speaks in the thoughtful, hypotactic, analytic style that is normally wielded by Merlin, hermits and, finally, Arthur, by those who can internalise and judge. Ector speaks in a heightened version of the declarative, paratactic style that has so often chronicled battles and knights' instinctive, unreflective feudal responses to feudal threats.

Although the impact of the tragedy and the tone of the last tale are that confusion, sin, private interest on many parts has brought down the public Round Table, the book does not rest with a glum prospect of tragedy as do other English 'Arthuriads'. Malory shows how the system of feudal organisation and public values is itself a major element in its catastrophe, and he amplifies its contradictory destructive mechanisms, as in the crucial scene where Gawain abandons his fraternal loyalty to Launcelot and in the long speech where Launcelot defends himself before his peers in language which is definitely noble but on the question of Guinevere, unavoidably false. The text demonstrates both its ideological adherence to Arthurian and feudal values and at the same time their radical instability; it also transmits through its formal meaning an underlying prediction of value in the individualised sphere. Again like *Sir Gawain and the Green Knight*, the form conveys values that the theme cannot ideologically encompass and inscribes a process of history and social change within the text. In an increasingly novel-like structure, in an increasingly individuated presentation of personality and speech, the 'Arthuriad' finally implies that a personalised ontology and epistemology are not only counter-feudal, but are also positive forces, a proper topic for art. Malory's tendency to move towards the novel has long been evident: that such a pattern arises from his imaginatively critical response to his social world and its forces has not so readily been recognised.

Like its poetic partner as a critical romance, Malory's text has an evident context. Other challengers for the authorship have faded, and the Warwickshire Malory appears to be the man. He was a

Warwick man too, a member of the Kingmaker's powerful and turbulent affinity. As such, this Sir Thomas was part of the violent and acquisitive politics of the period. There are specific ways in which this experience shapes an ideological treatment of the clash between Warwick and Edward IV, as I have argued elsewhere (Knight, 1983, Ch. 4). But there is also a general relation between the text and its social matrix. Malory has the imaginative power to project his experience of an increasingly privatised world into the romance genre, and so to dramatise the inherently personal aspects of the knightly world as well as the historical inadequacy of chivalric and feudal structures to contain that socially destructive force.

Those texts that have been seen as 'the best' by critics who use 'literary' values to protect themselves from society and history are in fact the most historically and socially attuned of all. They bring into full artistic and critical focus the strains and tensions that have been evident at times but quickly resolved or concealed in most of the romances. Taken as a whole, read in their historical position and their social function, the Middle English romances are a wide-ranging and powerful body of cultural production. They are the best testimony to the hopes and fears of the medieval English ruling class, and a part of the cultural pressure on those who permitted them to rule. The romances deserve more attention.

Bibliography

Texts

Mehl gives a full list of romance texts (1968, pp. 287–9), but some of these editions are now not easy to obtain. Several anthologies have recently been published or republished. The largest remains W. H. French and C. B. Hale, *Middle English Metrical Romances* (New York: Prentice-Hall, 1966), and A. V. C. Schmidt and N. Jacobs, *Medieval English Romances* (London: Hodder & Stoughton; 1980). M. Mills' smaller edition, *Six Middle English Romances* (London: Dent, 1973) has a thoughtful introduction and unconventional selection of texts; A. C. Gibbs' *Middle English Romances* (London: Arnold, 1966) also has a worthwhile introduction.

References

Adamson, W. (1980) *Hegemony and Revolution* (Berkeley: University of California Press).

Althusser, L. (1971) 'Ideological State Apparatuses', in *Lenin and Philosophy*, (London: New Left Books).

Aston, M. (1960) 'Lollardy and Sedition, 1381–1431', *Past and Present*, 17, 1–44, reprinted as Chapter 15 of Hilton, R. H. (1976) *Peasants, Knights and Heretics* (Cambridge University Press).

Auerbach, E. (1957) *Mimesis: The Representation of Reality in Western European Literature* (New York: Doubleday).

Barrow, S. F. (1924) *The Medieval Society Romances* (New York: Columbia University Press).

Bennett, M. J. (1979) '*Sir Gawain and the Green Knight* and the Literary Achievement of the North-West Midlands: The historical background', *Journal of Medieval History*, 5, 63–88. Incorporated into Chapter 10 of Bennett, M. J. (1983) *Community, Class and Careerism: Cheshire and Lancashire Society in the Age of Sir Gawain and the Green Knight* (Cambridge University Press).

Benson, L. D. (1976) *Malory's Morte Darthur* (Cambridge, Mass.: Harvard University Press).

Bordman, D. (1963) *A Motif-Index to the English Metrical Verse Romances* (Helsinki: FF Communications).

Buchan, D. (1972) *The Ballad and the Folk* (London: Routledge).

Child, F. J.(ed.) (1882–98) *The English and Scottish Popular Ballads* (Boston: Houghton Mifflin; rpt. New York: Dover, 1965).

Coward, R. and Ellis, J. (1977) *Language and Materialism* (London: Routledge).

Crane, R. S. (1915) 'The Vogue of Guy of Warwick from the Close of the Middle Ages to the Romantic Revival', *Proceedings of the Modern Language Association*, 30 125–94.

Duby, G. (1977) 'Youth in Aristocratic Society', in *The Chivalrous Society* (London: Edward Arnold).

Eagleton, T. (1983) *Literary Theory* (Oxford: Basil Blackwell).

Ferguson, A. B. (1966) *The Indian Summer of English Chivalry* (Durham, North Carolina: Duke University Press).

Finlayson, J. (ed.) (1967) *Morte Arthure* (London: Edward Arnold).

Finlayson, J. (1980) 'Definitions of Middle English Romance', *Chaucer Review*, 44–60, 168–81.

Gibbs, A. C. (ed.) (1966) *Middle English Romances* (London: Edward Arnold).

Hanning, R. W. (1971) *The Individual and Society in Twelfth Century Romance* (New Haven, Conn.: Yale University Press).

Haskell, A. (1973) 'The Paston Women on Marriage in Fifteenth-Century England', *Viator*, 4, 459–71.

Hindess, B. and Hirst, P. (1975) *Pre-Capitalist Modes of Production* (London: Routledge).

James, M. (1979) *English Politics and the Concept of Honour, 1485–1642* (Oxford: Past and Present Monographs).

Jameson, F. (1981) *The Political Unconscious* (London: Longman).

Keen, M. (1984) *Chivalry* (Baltimore: Johns Hopkins University Press).

Kelly, H.A. (1986) 'The Non-Tragedy of Arthur', in *Medieval English Religions and Ethical Literature: Essays in Honour of G. H. Russell*, ed. G.C. Kratzmann and J. Simpson (Cambridge: Brewer).

Kettle, A. (1951) *Introduction to the English Novel* (London: Hutchinson).

Knight, S. (1980) 'Ideology in Franklin's Tale', *Parergon*, 28, 3–35

Knight, S. (1983) *Arthurian Literature and Society* (London: Macmillan).

Knight, S. (1986) *Geoffery Chaucer* (Oxford: Basil Blackwell).

Köhler, E. (1974) *L'Aventure chevaleresque: Idéal et realité dans le roman courtois* (Paris: Gallimard).

Lukács, G. (1972) *Studies in European Realism* (London: Merlin).

Marx, K. (1973) *Grundrisse* (London: Penguin Books).

Marx, K. (1975) *Capital* (London: Lawrence & Wishart).

Matthews, W. (1960) *The Tragedy of Arthur* (Berkeley: University of California Press).

Mehl, D. (1968) *The Middle English Romances of the Thirteenth and Fourteenth Centuries* (London: Routledge).

Mills, M. (ed.) (1969) *Libeaus Desconus* (Oxford: Early English Text Society, No. 261).

Morton, A. L. (1960) 'The Matter of Britain', *Zeischrift für Anglistik und Amerikanistik*, 8, 5–28; reprinted in Morton, A.L. (1966) *The Matter of Britain* (London: Lawrence & Wishart).

Mukherjee, S. N. (1985) 'The Idea of Feudalism from the Philosophes to Karl Marx', in Leach, E., Mukherjee, S. N. and Ward, J. (eds), *Feudalism, Comparative Studies* (Sydney Association for Studies in Society and Culture).

Pearsall, D. A. (1965) 'The Development of Middle English Romance', *Medieval Studies*, 27, 91–116.

Pearsall, D. A. (1976) 'The English Romance in the Fifteenth Century', *Essays and Studies*, 29, 56–83.

Pearsall, D. A. (1977) *Old and Middle English Poetry* (London: Routledge).

Propp, V. (1968) *The Morphology of the Folktale*, 2nd revd edn (Austin: Texas University Press).

Stevens, J. (1973) *Medieval Romance* (London: Hutchinson).

Tardif, R. (1983) 'The "Mistery" of Robin Hood: A New Social Context for the Texts', in Knight S. and Mukherjee, S. N. (eds), *Words and Worlds* (Sydney: Association for Studies in Society and Culture).

Ullmann, W. (1966) *The Individual and Society in the Middle Ages* (Baltimore: Johns Hopkins University Press).

Wittig, S. (1978) *Stylistic and Narrative Structure in the Middle English Romances* (Austin: Texas University Press).

7

Chaucer's Poetry and its Modern Commentators: The Necessity of History

Derek Pearsall

The purpose of this paper is to make some brief remarks about the reflection of contemporary historical actuality in Chaucer's poetry and, more specifically, about the manner in which this reflection has been perceived by his modern commentators through the lens of their own historically conditioned values and attitudes; more briefly, and perhaps in the idiom of the present volume, to look at the ideology of an ideology. It may be thought that the superimposition of a shifting historical perspective upon a finite historical relationship will lead to some blurring of the image of that relationship, but the advantage sought is a greater degree of objectivity, or at least a more self-conscious and shamefaced subjectivity.

The assumption I make that the question of the relationship of history and literature is an important one needs no elaborate defence, I take it. The 'historical approach' is acknowledged by Morton Bloomfield, in his essay 'Contemporary Literary Theory and Chaucer' (1981, p. 23), to have 'a certain priority' (though he does not avail himself of it), and literary commentators of widely different persuasions will agree on the pre-eminence of the historical. So Roy Harvey Pearce (1969) writes, from the point of view of the liberal humanist: 'Literary works have as a necessary condition of their own intrinsic value the fact that they both implicate and are implicated in the conditions of the time and place in which they were created—in their history, that is to say' (p. 48); and Terry Eagleton (1976), with an emphasis on 'major art' directly comparable with Pearce's idea of 'intrinsic value', writes thus as a historical materialist: 'Any art sealed from the significant movements of its epoch, divorced from some sense of the historically central, relegates itself to minor status' (p. 57).

Likewise, the assumption I make that the views of modern literary commentators, on this matter and others, are historically and otherwise conditioned, would meet with widespread support from various quarters. An epistemologist would speak of the impossibility of any but 'theory-impregnated' knowledge (Popper, 1972, p. 72); a phenomenologist of the impossibility of 'presuppositionless' interpretation (Palmer, 1969, pp. 135, 182) a structuralist of the manner in which knowledge and understanding are insensibly structured by the systems of code of which language is one. A more specific, and more specifically historical, account of this conditioning, of 'the determination of consciousness by social reality' (Jameson, 1971, p. 206), is given by Raymond Williams (1977) in his description of 'alignment':

> It is a central proposition of Marxism ... that writing, like other practices, is in an important sense always aligned: that is to say, that it variously expresses, explicitly or implicitly, specifically selected experience from a specific point of view ... Such a recognition is crucial, against the claims to 'objectivity', 'neutrality', 'simple fidelity to the truth', which we must recognise as the ratifying formulas of those who offer their own senses and procedures as universal. (p. 199)

This looks like a Marxist version of the hermeneutic circle, and not too easy to get out of. How Williams gets out of it can be seen in an earlier passage in the same book, where he is describing 'hegemony'. It is, he says, a way of talking about the depth of penetration of ideology; it is

> a saturation of the whole process of living—not only of political and economic activity, nor only of manifest social activity, but of the whole substance of lived identities and relationships, to such a depth that the pressures and limits of what can ultimately be seen as a specific economic, political, and cultural system seem to most of us the pressures and limits of simple experience and common sense .... It thus constitutes a sense of reality for most people in the society, a sense of absolute because experienced reality beyond which it is very difficult for most members of the society to move, in most areas of their lives. (p. 110)

The rather unreflecting shift from 'most of us' to 'most people' is what most of us (or most people) would regard as the unhistorical face of historical materialism. The alternatives, though, to what can be seen as a kind of honest fudging on Williams' part, are difficult: either a notion of the total estrangement of the individual from the roots of his being through the historical forces (expressed through ideology) which shape his perception of all things; or the acceptance of the view that historical materialism is not 'a canon of historical interpretation' (Jameson, 1971, p. 362), but a mode of thought that contains all other modes of thought, one that has the advantage of claiming to contain a 'theory of the genesis, structure and decline of ideologies' (Eagleton, 1976b, p. 16) and not merely to be one. It is, in fact, in this formulation, not even a mode of thought, since if it ever found itself in the position of becoming such a 'mode', with an objective and systematic body of ideas and a recognised and accepted set of mental processes, it would instantly dissolve itself. Marxism is (not 'is in') a kind of permanent mental revolution, potentially false whenever it freezes into a system (Jameson, 1971, p. 326; cf. p. 161). There is something a little disconcerting about the proximity of Jameson here to the deconstructionists, who would similarly aver that 'Critical concepts are ceaselessly transformed or undone by the activity of self-conscious writing' or assert 'the critic's freedom to exploit a style that actively transforms and questions the nature of interpretative thought' (Norris, 1982, pp. 12, 16). Perhaps we can keep our footing, in this heady air, if we go back to one of Jameson's more sober claims for dialectical thought, that it is to think and at the same time to observe our thought-processes, 'to reckon the position of the observer into the experiment itself' (1971, p. 340). This has a solid scientific ring to it, can be reconciled with old-fashioned demands for 'self-awareness' as well as more recent demands for 'self-reflexiveness', and may find a pragmatic echo in Postan's observations (1983, pp. 74–5) that the historian who realises that his interpretations are the product of certain value-based and socially-determined theories is in a better position to understand what he observes than the historian who does not, or who thinks, foolishly, that they are not.

There is another assumption made in the opening sentence of this paper which has so far gone unexamined, and which will have struck any reader at all experienced in the literature of the subject as naïve. This is the assumption that the rendering of historical reality in a literary work can be adequately represented in the image of 'reflection'. The assumption is false, but the image has an interesting history in Marxist literary criticism, where alone it has been subjected to systematic scrutiny, and it is worth examining.

An early chapter in the critique of Formalism written by Medvedev and Bakhtin in 1928 begins with a section entitled, 'The Reflection of the Ideological Environment in the "Content" of the Literary Work'. The authors are working with the familiar model of 'base' (mode of production of material life) and 'superstructure' (the social, political and intellectual process in general) established by Marx, and with the notion of 'ideology' as the mediation of the former through the latter, what Eagleton (1976) briskly describes as 'that complex structure of social perception which ensures that the situation in which one social class has power over the others is either seen by most members of the society as "natural", or not seen at all' (p. 5). Medvedev and Bakhtin understand fully the complexity of the relationship (literature-ideology-history) with which they deal, and, in explaining it, deliberately multiply the optical metaphors so as to disestablish the simplistic mode of operation of the metaphor of reflection:

> The literary structure, like every ideological structure, refracts the generating socioeconomic reality, and does so in its own way. But, at the same time, in its 'content', literature reflects and refracts the reflections and refractions of other ideological spheres (ethics, epistemology, political doctrines, religion, etc.). That is, in its 'content', literature reflects the whole of the ideological horizon of which it is itself a part. (pp. 16–17)

Allowing for what does not come through in translation, one can still see here the strenuous effort to impart some sense of mobility and activity and generative force to all elements in the relationship, and also to identify the literary structure as 'in its own way' special, if not specially privileged.

Despite such efforts, the notion of reflection, or 'reflectionism', as it inevitably came to be called, has not been regarded as a satisfactory image for the relationship of literature, (ideology) and history. Its unsatisfactoriness is perceived to be in the inertness which it imparts both to the reflected image (the literary work, and the mental process of the writer in his work) and to the reality of which it is the reflection (the material process of history); and also in the absence of any indication that the reflecting medium has the power to shape anew what is supposed from the reflection to be reality (broken or distorting mirrors might allow a weary image to maintain a little life, but they lack the vigorous self-repairing power and the ductility of a vigorous ideology); and, finally, in the elimination of the observer. The function of literature in its relation to history, according to the crudest 'reflectionist' model, is to create a special world of representations in which the individual imagination moves untrammelled, intuitively, much as a spectator capsule moves among the simulacra of a Disneyesque exhibition, cries of 'How like life!' fading as soon as uttered.

Raymond Williams, therefore, spends some pages tinkering with and finally dismantling the reflectionist model. There is no inert reality called history, knowable from other sources, which literature can be congratulated on for conforming to, though a concept of history as active process in accordance with the laws of historical materialism would allow art to be 'seen as reflecting not separated objects and superficial events, but the essential forces and movements underlying them' (p. 96). This contrast between (dynamic) realism and (static) naturalism allows some legitimate range of imaginative activity to the individual writer (and accommodates nicely the influential interpretation of Balzac's achievement by Georg Lukács), but is perhaps too close for comfort to the lazy intuitionalism of Arnold Kettle (1972), who, dismissing the idea of 'reflection of reality' (p. 160), claims that great writers are always 'highly critical, in some way or other [not necessarily conscious or explicit] of bourgeois society and its values' (p. 166), and concludes: 'What gives art its value is not the abstract correctness of its message or its conscious ideology but the concrete richness of its expression of life in its full complexity' (p. 174).

Williams understandably goes on to try out some other ideas of 'reflection'. Art can be defined as reflecting the laws of operation of the material social process (a version of the Medvedev–Bakhtin hypothesis); or the relationship may be one of mediation, though this still implies a pre-existent dualism, and encourages 'vulgar Marxists' in that kind of reductive analysis which consists in unmasking in literature the class-based distortions of ideology (p. 98); or the relationship may be one of homology or typification, the reflection of the essential or underlying or general reality of history (p. 101). Happy with none of these, Williams returns, as always, to *language* as the determinant of relationships between literature and history, language not as expressive of or equivalent to reality, nor as an undifferentiated medium through which reality may 'flow', but as 'a socially shared and reciprocal activity, already embedded in active relationships, within which every move is an activation of what is already shared and reciprocal or may become so' (p. 166).

Terry Eagleton is less patient with the reflectionist theory, though he often uses it as an anvil on which to beat out something more durable. He sees as 'vulgar Marxism' the idea that literature reflects ideology (as for instance that *The Waste Land* reflects the exhaustion of bourgeois ideology), but equally so the idea that literature penetrates through the obfuscations of ideology to the essential historical reality (1976, pp. 17–18). Literature gives, to the critical consciousness, access to the history that constitutes ideology, but the text cannot by-pass ideology and connect itself to history; if ever it seems to, and to stand in close natural relation to what it represents, the task of the critic is 'to refuse the spontaneous presence of the work—to deny that "naturalness" in order to make its real determinants appear'.[1] Generally, though, these refusals and denials are made imperative in the text, and Eagleton draws on a number of writers (Trotsky, Althusser, Macherey) for the elaboration of the idea that literature liberates consciousness by deforming history. It creates awareness of ideology by 'making strange' (in the famous phrase of early Formalism) the object of representation; it constitutes 'a deflection, a changing and transformation of reality, in accordance with the peculiar laws of art' (1976, p. 50, quoting Trotsky); it breaks up the familiar apparatus of theatrical representation in the work and theory of Brecht, assuming the task not of 'reflecting' a fixed reality but of demonstrating 'how character and action are historically produced, and so how they could have been and still can be different' (ibid., p. 65). The concluding formulation is carefully phrased: 'Literature is a peculiar mode of linguistic organisation which, by a particular "disturbance" of conventional modes of signification, so foregrounds certain modes of sense-making as to allow us to perceive the ideology in which they inhere' (1976b, p. 185).

Frederic Jameson speaks similarly of the function of literature as the creation of dialectical consciousness through 'an assault on our conventionalized life patterns, a whole battery of shocks administered to our routine vision of things, an implicit critique and restructuration of our habitual consciousness' (1971, p. 374). An image for this activity might be the breaking of the mirrors that our 'routine vision' has grown used to, and it is not surprising that Jameson is scornful of reflectionism. He associates it, in fact, with that most degraded activity called 'the sociological study of literature', in which the relationship of literature to history will be seen as 'a *reflection* or a *symptom*, a characteristic *manifestation* or a simple *by-product*, a *coming to consciousness* or an imaginary or symbolic *resolution*' (p. 5); in which literary history will be sorted out according to the classic periodisation of Marxist literary history (decay of feudalism, emergent capitalism and bourgeois individualism, etc.); in which raids will be mounted into socio-economic history to bring back some isolated detail that will then be set in revealing metaphorical conjuction with some literary fact;[2] in which literary texts will be annexed to some supposedly significant sociological consciousness through the identification of the literary characters as types of class-affiliation (p. 398). Jameson would presumably exclude from his strictures that more innocent activity, also often called the sociology of literature, which has to do with the recovery of facts about the author's life, audience and text, and which may properly be regarded as the foundation of critical consciousness (like learning the author's language), not the mode. Jameson's complaint, familiar enough now, is that what he denigrates as sociology stabilises the observer (the critic, the artist) and the observed (history) as fixed quantities, ignoring the unconscious value-systems that permeate the vision of the former and the conversions worked on the image of the latter by ideology. The work of art certainly reflects something, but that something is not fixed and autonomous, nor is the activity one of mere reflection. Some more active sense of the relationship is needed, and it is essentially one that demands we get closer to the writer and to the reality he 'reflects' (p. 382).

Pierre Macherey (1978), finally, has a good deal to say about mirrors, especially in his essay on Lenin as a critic of Tolstoy. He presents first Lenin's orthodox Marxist view that Tolstoy's relationship to the history of his time was not determined by his individual position but was mediated by a specific ideology: 'Between Tolstoy's work and the historical process which it "reflects" there is the ideology of the peasant' (p. 115). Macherey shows how Lenin arrives at this conclusion through a critique of reflectionism ('Lenin teaches us that it is not so simple to look in the mirror: he has undertaken a rigorous scrutiny of mirrors', p. 134), in which particularly Lenin draws attention to contradictions in Tolstoy: 'On the one hand, the remarkably powerful, forthright, and sincere protest against social falsehood and hypocrisy; on the other, the jaded, hysterical sniveller called the Russian intellectual ... on the one hand, merciless criticism of capitalist exploitation ... on the other, the crackpot preaching of submission ... On the one hand, the most sober realism ...' etc. (p. 300). These contradictions are the fissures in the text through which the ideology may be perceived, or, as Macherey puts it, the contradictions signal the text's silences: 'The mirror is expressive in what it does not reflect as much as in what it does reflect. The absence of certain reflections, expressions—these are the true object of criticism' (p. 128).

There would be more to say, but this summary of what some writers in some of their books have said about reflectionism is not intended to provide a history of the subject nor a methodology for what follows. It will have served its purpose if it ensures that the present writer and his readers never again use the word 'reflection', in this context, unreflectively. In that sense it provides, not a framework for the ensuing discussion, but a foghorn to keep it off some familiar sandbanks. However, there are one or two points, drawn from the history of reflectionism, that I want to emphasise before proceeding. The universal agreement on the mobility and generative force of both literature and history, and the dynamic nature of their relationship, is striking. The determinant in that relationship is ideology, which mediates history fully in terms of its own class-based perceptions, but which shows faults and cracks in certain of its literary manifestations. This may have to do with language, and the (hoped-for) impossibility that any language could ever be an instrument of complete ideological containment; or with the placement of the individual writer at certain key moments of shift in the ideological formation (Eagleton, 1976b, p. 181); or with the power of imagination of the individual writer to penetrate that ideological formation and bear witness to the real moving forces of history. The last two are not at odds:[3] both require a precise attention to the particular form and moment of historical conjuncture, the text, line by line, set with the daily newspaper (or nearest equivalent), day by day.

What is left out of these formulations is the 'historicalness' of literature itself, the historicity of literary forms, literary history. Medvedev and Bakhtin (1928) declare the inadmissibility of studying the literary work 'directly and exclusively as an element of the ideological environment' without understanding 'the place of the work in literature and its direct dependence on literature' (p. 27), though they do not fail to point out that 'the effect of literature on literature is still a sociological effect' (p. 28). Jameson (1971) acknowledges that 'every work of art is perceived against a generic background' (p. 313): no work stands in autonomous relation with its history, any more than with its author.

These observations are of great importance, and they are elaborated by Hans Robert Jauss (1982) in his 'Theory of Genres':

> It is unimaginable that a literary work set itself into an informational vacuum, without indicating a specific situation of understanding. To this extent, every work belongs to a genre—whereby I mean neither more nor less than that for each work a preconstituted horizon of expectations must be ready at hand ... (p. 79)

These genres 'cannot be deduced or defined, but only historically determined, delimited and described' (p. 80). Jauss regards his theory of genres as an answer to the necessary question of relationships between literature and history, and as a superior answer to 'the classical theory of reflection [*Wiederspiegelungstheorie*]'. He observes that Marxism has to accept the importance of genres (as we have seen), and that, from the point of view of the historical materialist, generic stability may be a significant point of strain in moments of historical crisis (p. 91). Jauss would not relish a role as the builder of an annexe to Marxist literary scholarship, but he does not deny compatibility (p. 75).

The interpretation of Chaucer's poetry, to turn now to more specific instances of the relationship of literature and history, was dominated for many centuries by the neo-classical notion that the value and interest of his work was as a representation of general nature. The idea was introduced by Thomas Speght and his associates, in the Chaucer edition of 1598, strengthened there by appeal to the Latin tradition of satire, and sustained chiefly by illustration from the General Prologue. Dryden fixed the critical canon in the Preface to his *Fables* in 1700, much on the strength of Speght's hints. 'Chaucer follow'd Nature everywhere,' he declares, 'but was never so bold to go beyond her':

> We have our Fore-fathers and Great Grand-dames all before us, as they were in Chaucer's Days; their general Characters are still remaining in Mankind ... for Mankind is ever the same, and nothing lost out of Nature, though everything is alter'd. (quoted in Spurgeon, 1925, I. 276, 279)

A string of writers in the eighteenth and nineteenth centuries repeat Dryden's praises. William Blake, for instance, declares that the characters of the General Prologue remain for ever unaltered, being 'the physiognomies and lineaments of universal human life, beyond which Nature never steps' (Spurgeon, II. 43). The essential impulse of recognition is vividly exposed by Hazlitt: 'It would be a curious speculation ... to know what has become of this character of the Sompnoure in the present day; whether or not it has any technical representation in existing professions ...' etc. (Spurgeon, II. 101). Matthew Arnold, though he speaks a more refined idiom, speaks the same language: 'he has gained the power to survey the world from a central, a truly human point of view ... a large, free, sound representation of things ...' (Spurgeon, II. 127). Arnold, like the others, bases most of his remarks on the General Prologue, which always stood at the beginning in editions of Chaucer.

It is not a distortion of the facts or a prejudgement of the matter to see the existence of such a systematic body of interpretation, over so many centuries, as evidence of the hegemony of a certain class of readers. It is an educated class, in which reading is instilled as an expected occupation, and with money enough to buy books; its view of society is a stable and 'natural' hierarchy of relationships; literature will be seen to endorse those socially cohesive categories and declare their permanence through its portrayal of 'general nature'; even those who do not share the benefits of the class will aspire to its views. The denial of history will be acclaimed: the poet transcends the 'merely historical' and communicates with all ages by connecting up with the current of the universal. The extraordinary power of ideology is well demonstrated in the long and vigorous life of this system of interpretations and its determinate fixedness (in contrast to the Protean nature of literature itself). It would be wrong to regard it as mere stereotyped repetition: as a system of interpretation it suited very well, and it remains strong today even though a variety of sciences have demonstrated that its propositions are false.

Meanwhile, it was accepted that Chaucer had a life (though Speght was anxious to ensure that it was a suitable one for a classic English poet), and that that life was part of history. As far as Chaucer's poetry was concerned, however, this was chiefly important as a series of opportunities for dating his works. Chronology once established, a poetic career could be deduced in which Chaucer drew away from artificiality and rhetoric (medieval accidents) and towards nature, from foreign influences towards a natural Englishness. So the neo-classical canon of interpretation could be confirmed, as in J. M. Manly's famous essay (1926) on 'Chaucer and the Rhetoricians'. History more broadly considered was treated as a fixed set of events and relationships to which Chaucer's poetry stood related as copy to original. In the essays by J. Leslie Hotson (e.g. 1924), in which occasions are assigned to certain poems by Chaucer and a topical allegory drawn out, history is treated no differently from a body of scientific knowledge such as astronomy. Historical scholarship in its saner moments assumes that its task is to understand the past, in accordance with T. S. Eliot's dictum, 'If one can really penetrate the life of another age, one is penetrating the life of one's own' (1928, p. 11). This may be so, but the activity of interpenetration has to be demonstrated, if a form of 'historical reductionism' is not to take over:

> If I say that the importance of the *Divine Comedy* lies in the fact that it gives me an understanding of the state of mind of certain classes in a certain epoch, this means that I transform it into a mere historical document ... (Trotsky, cited in Eagleton, 1976b, p. 169)

History, in whatever form, is a minor consideration, however, for Chaucer critics in the pre-modern era. Kittredge (1915), in paying some attention in his discussion of *Troilus* to 'the mediaeval system' of courtly love, suddenly sweeps it aside impatiently in his famous avowal: 'Give me forty-eight hours, and I will translate every mediaeval symptom into modern journalese, and my version shall keep step with the daily records' (p. 124). Elsewhere, looking for the 'knitting-up' of the marriage debate in the Franklin's Tale, Kittredge offers this endorsement of the Franklin's point of view:

> He is no cloistered rhetorician, but a ruddy white-bearded vavasour, a great man in his neighbourhood, fond of the good things of life and famous for his lavish hospitality. He has been sheriff of his county and Member of Parliament, and is perpetual presiding justice at the sessions of the peace. Such a man lies under no suspicion of transcendentalism or vague heroics. When *he* speaks of mutual forbearance and perfect gentle love between husband and wife, we listen with conviction. The thing is possible. The problem need puzzle us no longer. (p. 210)

Even C. S. Lewis, writing one of the important modern works of literary and cultural history (*The Allegory of Love*, 1936), and exercising much pioneering restraint in his interpretation of the social-historical and literary process, finds himself resorting to 'general nature' (or his version of it) in order to explain Pandarus:

> Every one has met the modern equivalent of Pandarus. When you are in the hands of such a man you can travel first-class through the length and breadth of England on a third-class ticket; policemen and gamekeepers will fade away before you, placated yet unbribed; noble first-floor bedrooms will open for you in hotels that have sworn they are absolutely full; and drinks will be forthcoming at hours when the rest of the world goes thirsty. (p. 190)

Lewis speaks mockingly, of course, but the mockery only adds an ironic edge to the impulse of desire to belong to the class of readers who can live, and read, like that.

The collapse of this world of pliable gamekeepers and rooms with a view in the aftermath of the First World War did not have an immediate effect on Chaucer criticism. In fact, it was not until 1957 that Muscatine published *Chaucer and the French Tradition*, and, in announcing this 'exploratory effort toward a modern criticism of Chaucer' with emphasis on the 'complex whole' of form, style and rhetoric (p. 1), brought the New Criticism to the old poet.

The New Criticism, as has often been explained, is essentially a response to the break-up of the old consensus of values concerning the relationship of literature and history. Uncertain of the model of society to which they preferred to relate literature, critics worked to extract literature from politics and history, and to establish the text as a 'verbal icon' in which history was contained and subsumed, and in which the decisions that the events of the day seemed to demand could be avoided. The fences are built high, topped with the broken glass of irony and ambiguity, sufficient to keep out any naive and impudent inquirer after 'relevance'. Within the fence, the game of interpretations can go on, the players having detached themselves, not from history (how could that be?), but from the recognition of the history that permits, organises and gives the rules of their game (there being no irony without a supporting ideology). The game was invented just in time to allow for the large increase in the number of players after the Second World War. For the students who were brought into universities by mass education, who lacked the traditional leisures of an educated background and the patience to tolerate philology, the New Criticism promised a somewhat quicker 'mastery of the cultural goods' (Hartman, 1978, p. 495). A seminar on one of the *Canterbury Tales* which offers the same privilege of interpretation, perception of irony, elucidation of ambiguity and embroidery of paradox to every one of its intelligent members is going to 'go' better than one which requires the demonstration of hard-won linguistic and historical knowledge.

Muscatine himself seems to stand free from some of the criticisms that attach to the New Criticism, as does Donaldson, despite the manner in which the latter's gleeful pursuit of the multiple ironies of the unreliable narrator tends in the end to pull the text in on top of him. Many of their followers, however, have lacked charm and eloquence as well as a sense of the need to relate literature significantly to history. Psychological fantasising has been rife, with literature acting as no more than an arrow shot from nowhere and quivering in the reader's sensibilities. An intelligent critic, eager to assert of Chaucer that 'almost everyone feels or senses an author's unique mind present in and behind his work', can give vent to this extraordinary assault on history:

> Criticism of 'the text itself', especially with older poets, almost always ends appealing to 'the background'. To explicate a text we must dredge up contemporaneous meanings of words, analogous forms or

conventions, iconography, topoi, motifs, ever here and there a real live historical event. This kind of 'objective' criticism leaves one with the impression that 'the background' gets silted into poems by natural erosion, though I doubt any critic believes it. (Howard, 1976, p. 23)

One would have to ask, if the critic does not like his own geomorphological image of the process by which history ('the background') gets into literature, what image would he prefer, since process, indubitably, there is? Further, if we are not to attend to the 'contemporaneous' meanings of words, what meanings should we attend to? Their present-day meanings, or those meanings, uncontemporaneous and maybe even unattested, that we intuitively deduce to inhere in the text *qua* text?

The containment of the New Criticism within the accepted values of the society that sponsors it, whether that sponsorship be construed as the pursuit of advantage or the consignment to harmless activity of potential delinquents, is not infrequently made explicit. The straining, for instance, toward a moral (as distinct from a social or political) relevance for literature is often strong, and is particularly marked in the version of the New Criticism that took hold in England under the influence of F. R. Leavis, and which is represented in books on Chaucer by Speirs, Robinson and Whittock. The last-named emerges from time to time as a full-fledged Christian humanist, a reminder of the tendency of text-confined criticism to push through to universal values, indeed the necessity of its nature that it should do so, given that meaning must be located *somewhere*. Cleanth Brooks, answering rather tartly the charge that formalist critics had made poetry into an *ersatz* religion, expressed himself on the matter with some satisfaction: 'I think it no accident that so many of the formalist critics either hold, or are sympathetic to, an orthodox Christian faith' (1953, p. 135). It should come as less of a surprise, therefore, that Muscatine, who in 1957 (p. 243) drew towards a generally relativistic account of the conventional pieties at the end of the Nun's Priest's Tale, if not towards the mischievous subversiveness of Donaldson, should in 1972 accept the 'inner' meaning of the exhortation as the true one:

> The logic of his ironic structure, pushed toward a consideration of ends, ultimate realities, provided in fact a justification of orthodox faith. Serious irony can be made finally to expose the instability of this

brittle world and by implication to turn our attention to a stable world of faith in God. (p. 113)

One could see this as the critic simply changing his mind: but the inbuilt tendency of the critical system is a factor in the direction of change. A somewhat different response to the crisis of the inter-war years can be seen in European medievalists, closer to the zone of catastrophe (see Stock, 1973). Both Auerbach (1946) and Curtius (1948), conscious that the world was falling about their ears, tried to shore it up intellectually in their different ways by compassing the whole Western literary tradition in a single book. Both dispense with history, or rather recreate it, through hope, from within literature. Auerbach speaks of that 'clearly formulable and recognized community of thought and feeling' which provided a writer, up to the early twentieth century, with 'reliable criteria' by which to organise his representation of reality (p. 486): and of how a new Europe, 'unsure of itself, overflowing with unsettled ideologies and ways of life, and pregnant with disaster', produced writers who dissolved reality 'into multiple and multivalent reflections of consciousness' (p. 487). But he does not despair: the more the emphasis on the significance of the little movements of consciousness that all men have in common, the more the chance of the future unity of mankind. By contrast with this heroic and poignant vision, communicated to Auerbach while writing his book in Istanbul during the war years (1942–45), there is the more austere purpose of Curtius, who published a pamphlet in 1932 attacking the 'barbarization of education and the nationalistic frenzy which were the forerunners of the Nazi regime' (p. vii), and subsequently, with the coming of 'the German catastrophe', settled to the writing of his great work (1933–48). 'It grew,' he says, 'out of a concern for the preservation of Western culture', and a belief that the unity and continuity of that culture derived from medieval Latin tradition: 'In the intellectual chaos of the present, it has become necessary, and happily not impossible, to demonstrate that unity' (p. viii).

An important resemblance, however, between these great European literary historians and the Anglo-American New Critics is the secondary, or in certain cases non-existent, place given to history as the condition of literature. It was into a vacuum that the 'historical criticism' of D. W. Robertson and his followers rushed in the early 1960s. At the beginning of *A Preface to Chaucer* (1962), Robertson quotes David Hume's recommendation of history as the eliciting of 'the constant and universal principles of nature' (p. vii). He rejects this, arguing that human nature changes with changes in human relationships and in society, and that people in the past may have been *essentially* different. The task of the critic is to examine and understand its differentness. We find, when we do this, that 'the medieval world was innocent of our profound concern for tension' (p. 51). It was a world of stable hierarchies:

> We project dynamic polarities on history as class struggles, balances of power, or as conflicts between economic realities and traditional ideals .... But the medieval world with its quiet hierarchies knew nothing of these things. (p. 51)

The limitations of the 'historical criticism', as both history and criticism, have been frequently rehearsed: the collapsing of ten and more centuries of history and historical change into a single monolithic world-view; the insistence on the permeation throughout vernacular literature of this world-view, not as an ideology but as a body of doctrine directly or indirectly (allegorically) expressed through all literature; and the subordination of all forms of interpretative activity to the enforcement of two premises—that nothing means what it says, and that everything means the same thing. Nevertheless, the historical role of such a criticism needs also to be understood, and it can be seen thus: deeply disturbed by certain developments in modern society, particularly those that tended towards moral relativism, the proponents of the historical criticism had no hesitation in setting up their interpretation of the Middle Ages not merely as historically correct, but as a model of a superior society and culture, suitable for the correction of a depraved age. Non-medievalists will often express their surprise that the historical criticism, which seems to them a naive form of homilectics at best, has exerted such a powerful influence in North America (it has had very little influence in England). The explanation must be in some such terms as those outlined above: the seeking of an expression in the Middle Ages of traditional American values of domestic and social hierarchy, prompted by shock at the threat to those values. The vogue amongst modern Catholic apologists for medieval scholastic theology may have had a bizarre tributary effect. The flourishing of the historical criticism was further assisted by the manner in which it offered opportunities for instant scholarship, under academic pressures certainly more severe in North America than in England. Not many things in medieval scholarship are easier than to multiply annotations from the *Patrologia Latina*, and the sanctification offered to every literary interpretation derived therefrom does away with the need, and then the desire, for flexibility and sophistication in a specifically literary response.

In his later scholarship, D. W. Robertson has insisted on the study of fourteenth-century social and agrarian history as the necessary means to a preliminary understanding of Chaucer. There is no question, as he says of 'documentary realism' (or reflectionism) on Chaucer's part (1977, p. 572), only the necessity of understanding the nature of the society he describes and the meanings and connotations of the words he uses. This is altogether admirable, and a shrewd move too, since a number of familiar interpretative positions can be thereby fortified. The Franklin, for instance, is identified by Robertson (1974) as a social upstart, not because this is the necessary conclusion from the available evidence—indeed it is opposed by two extended recent historical studies (Specht, 1981; Coss, 1983)—but because it suits Robertson's interpretation of the Franklin's Tale to see the teller as a *parvenu* who is as flawed morally as he is unstable socially. There is a moment in another essay (1977) when brief allusion is made to the 'povre wydwe' of the Nun's Priest's Tale, who was, we are told, 'a maner deye'. Robertson explains the duties of the *deye* or *daya*, emphasising (though it needs no emphasis, since it was the seasonal occupation of every available farm-hand) her responsibility for winnowing. He comments, with delightful *insouciance*:

> Those who wish to see the widow as a figure for the Church will be happy to know that one of her duties was to separate the chaff, which the Priest tells us to disregard, from the grain. (p. 580)

Since this exegesis of the widow is the keystone of the 'Robertsonian' interpretation of the Tale, it seems to be more than an accident that the supporting evidence has been lit upon so happily.

Finally, there is the essay in which Robertson (1979) attempts to demonstrate that the Wife of Bath was a bondwoman. The historical evidence that he adduces does not deny that she could have been, but the momentum of argument comes from the demonstration of a status for the Wife 'consistent with the iconographic overtones of the Wife's character' (p. 403). In other words, she will be better able to be seen as a spiritual bondwoman (Galatians 4. 22) if she is a real one (p. 415).

Robertson is not the only one to have started trucking in history in order to provide foundations for particular interpretations. If he represents anti-historical medievalism, there is also a more familiar kind of anti-historical modernism, in which history will be ransacked for clues and indications that support an interpretation already, for specifically modern reasons, decided upon. Terry Jones's book on Chaucer's Knight (1980) is an example. It was not to be supposed that modern readers would long continue to stomach the glorification of war and chivalry when modern war had lost its nationalist colouring, and when mercenaries had re-emerged in the 1960s. If Chaucer is to be admired, he must share the political and social view of his modern admirers, and the means by which he can be made to do so, infallibly, is irony. Irony thus becomes a technique of interpretation through which the whole 'meaning' of a text can be refuted, and the structure of the *Canterbury Tales*, with its Donaldsonian multiplicity of unreliable narrators as well as its generally unreliable Chaucerian narrator, seems actually to encourage such practice. The notion of the relationship of literature to history embodied in such practice is, however, naive: it is not far from simple reflectionism, with the image automatically inverted.

In one respect, perhaps, there is more in such studies than mere reflectionism, or at least more than is present in those books which describe the social and historical background of Chaucer's poetry and which have titles alluding to the imagery of reflection, and pictures, for instance, of artefacts mentioned in his poetry. A book such as Jones's, like the essays (e.g. Scattergood, 1981) that have found signs of anti-militarist sentiment in *Melibee* and *Thopas*, has some sense of historical change and of the dynamic relationship of literature to those processes of change. It was Muscatine, particularly in his book on *Poetry and Crisis in the Age of Chaucer* (1972), who made the most influential contribution to the establishment of the now commonplace idea of the late fourteenth century as an age of social, political and spiritual crisis, and of the poetry of the age as implicated in that crisis. Though traditional critics may believe that not everything in the literature of the period has to do with the break-up of feudalism and the emergence of bourgeois capitalistic individualism, and though they may feel that, if all literary works stand necessarily in relation to history, some stand in more significant relation than others (and *Thopas* hardly at all), yet there can be no doubt that the idea of the immersion of literature in a dynamic process of historical change is a source of understanding as well as of excitement. The excitement is certainly there in Janet Coleman's *Writers and Readers 1350–1400* (1981), which presents a broad picture of the shifting tectonic plates of the ideological formation in the late fourteenth century, with much attention to the history of ideas as well as history. The book is one in a series on 'Literature in History' edited by Raymond Williams, and is by a medieval political historian, which is perhaps a comment on the generally unreflective anti-historicism of much traditional scholarship.

There is also much excitement and insight in the book by David Aers on *Chaucer, Langland, and the Creative Imagination* (1980), perhaps the most systematic and selfconscious attempt to bring the perception of a Marxist-influenced historical understanding to medieval English literature. In the face of the traditional distinctions made between Chaucer and Langland in terms of their relationship to the history of their time, and the congratulations generally extended to Chaucer on having avoided mere topicality and gone for universality, Aers recognises that the comparative absence in Chaucer of direct references to the events of his day is not a sign that he is to be detached from history. History goes deeper than that, and Aers has some excellent accounts of the historical deforming power of ideology on the individual consciousness as it is presented by Chaucer through a character like the Wife of Bath. Aers, however, is not quite content with the 'insertion' of the writer at moments of crucial ideological shift, as it is described by Eagleton: 'It is not that a "progressive" ideology thrusts through the constrictions of the hegemonic formation', but that important writers stand at 'a particular dissentient conflictual position within it', where the 'fault-lines' of the formation are thrown into relief (1976, p. 181). Aers adds to this a Lukácsian sense of the power of the idealised poetic imagination to penetrate the outwardness of ideology-seen-as-reality and to discover the dynamic forces of change at work within history. There are problems and vulnerabilities with this approach, not so much with *Piers Plowman*, where it produces important new understanding, as with Chaucer, who often eludes the embrace of the historical critic. At such moments, when the text will not readily yield the meaning appropriate to the activity of the idealised poetic imagination, the demonstration of the inadequacy of 'the narrator' saves the day. So it is with the account of the Franklin's Tale in Aers (1980, p. 168) and there must be some doubt about the validity of an interpretative technique used by different kinds of historical critics, in the same way, to produce diametrically opposed results. It is also not impossible to believe, in relation to this tale, or the Knight's Tale, that a writer may, on reflection, without being the victim of false consciousness, assent to the ideas and beliefs of a ruling class or group, to which he may or may not belong, and may because of that (not nevertheless) produce important poetry.

Sheila Delany (1971, 1974) is another writer who uses the Marxist model of relationship between history and literature, and specifically of 'the social origin and social function of cultural forms' (1974, p. 259), to throw light on the history in Chaucer's poetry. She attempts to explain the absence of allegory in Chaucer by pointing to the appropriateness of allegory, with its systematised analogical relations, to the fixed and permanent social structure of the feudal ruling class, with its similar analogical relations; and by describing further the growth of social disturbance, the lack of certainty, the greater concern with the complex ambivalences of the individual free will, which made allegory inappropriate in the late fourteenth century. The historical brush is a broad one here, and there is much that is only sketchily covered. It seems, in a way, an odd task to set oneself as an historical critic, to explain the *absence* of something. Perhaps these are not so much historical readings of Chaucer's poetry (or absence of poetry), or readings illumined by a knowledge of history (do we know enough in detail about the history of his time to make them?), as excitements injected into his poetry from a reading of history. Delany evidently has little time for allegory ('Allegory simplifies experience by systematizing it', she says, 1971,

p. 50) and suspects that Chaucer, sensible fellow, shared her views. It might be more profitable to think of allegory in a different kind of historical perspective, as a literary form from whose 'surprising otherness' we may learn 'the perception of an inner world which represents everything which for the modern reader is the expression of subjective feeling, as the play and conflict of objective forces' (Jauss, 1978, p. 186).

Of Stephen Knight's essay, 'Chaucer and the Sociology of Literature' (1980), what is to be said? It should be a centrally important document in the present inquiry, and indeed should have made it unnecessary. One gets the impression, though, that when Knight says that 'it is high time Chaucer criticism availed itself of some of the techniques, skills, and insights which these thinkers [i.e. Macherey, Lacan, etc.] have developed' (p. 23), he really means that it is high time other people read them, as he has. There is much intelligence at work, and some valuable comments contributing to the understanding in Chaucer's poetry of the formation of 'subjectivity', of a notion of the individual as a nexus of social conflict (in the Wife of Bath and Criseyde, for instance). But even the well-disposed reader will be put off by the magpie-like nature of Knight's Collection of 'thinkers', and by his intoxication with the jargon of modern literary theory. ('It is,' we are told of the Nun's Priest's Tale, 'so full of reference, wit, and seductive skill that its ultimately naturalizing and disarming stasis predicts the passivist triumphs of bourgeois relativist art', p. 36.) There is no need to deny that specialised language can have its function in temporarily denaturalising the object of discourse and creating attention; complaints about jargon do not always forget this.

There is something worrying here, about the manner in which investigation of the most real and historically-rooted aspects of a literary work (rooted in the writer's history and in the critic's) gets set adrift and becomes another mode of theorising. It is something which Edward Said describes in the Preface to *Literature and Society* (1980): the merry-go-round of academic critical theory, with ideas first formulated in the context of a real history and society being taken up as fashions, orthodoxies 'mindlessly followed by a whole band of academic enthusiasts' (p. ix). It is a subject that needs a new *Voyage to Laputa*: what it gets is the lollipop comforts of David Lodge (*Small World*), scampering about among the undergrowth of critical theory like a puppy among toilet-tissue. Mostly it is the high-powered steel-and-glass academicism of France, Germany and America that keeps the merry-go-round whirling, and throwing power and privilege to those who manage to stay on. The English University, by contrast, with its 'churchy conservatism' (Burrow, 1978, p. 386), presents the appearance of a farmyard, with homely fowl pecking away at odd ears of hermeneutics. The strength of the English tradition, however, is worth stressing, for it is attention to the language of medieval literature, to the minutest detail of synchronic semantics, for instance, and to the architecture of connotation (e.g. Burnley, 1979), that promises best a way through the babble of theorising, and a securely rooted understanding of the manner in which history is embedded in the language of literature

Notes

1. Eagleton (1976b), p. 101. With synchronic functions substituted for diachronic, and 'structural man' detached from his history, there is something similar in Barthes (1972): 'Structural man takes the real, decomposes it, then recomposes it' (p. 215).
2. Jameson (1971), pp. 375–9. This is what Trotsky, as cited by Eagleton (1976b, p. 171), calls 'adjacentism'.
3. Both appear in Medvedev and Bakhtin (1928): 'Literature often anticipates developments in philosophy and ethics (ideologemes), admittedly in an undeveloped, unsupported, intuitive form. Literature is capable of penetrating into the social laboratory where these ideologemes are shaped and formed. The artist has a keen sense for ideological problems in the process of birth and generation' (p. 17).

References

Aers, David (1980) *Chaucer, Langland and the Creative Imagination* (London: Routledge & Kegan Paul).

Auerbach, Erich (1946) *Mimesis: The Representation of Reality in Western Literature*, trans. Willard Trask (Princeton, N.J.: Princeton University Press, 1953; rprt. Doubleday Anchor Books, 1957; originally published in German in Berne).

Barthes, Roland (1972) 'The Structuralist Activity', in *Critical Essays*, trans. Richard Howard (Evanston: Northwestern University Press).

Baxandall, Lee (1972) *Radical Perspectives in the Arts* (Harmondsworth: Penguin Books).

Bloomfield, Morton W. (1981) 'Contemporary Literary Theory and Chaucer', in *New Perspectives in Chaucer Criticism*, ed. Donald M. Rose (Norman: Pilgrim Books), pp. 23–36.

Brooks, Cleanth (1953) 'A Note on the Limits of "History" and the Limits of "Criticism"', *Sewanee Review*, 61, 129–35.

Burnley, J. D. (1979) *Chaucer's Language and the Philosophers' Tradition*, Chaucer Studies II (Cambridge: D. S. Brewer; Totowa, N.J.: Rowman & Littlefield).

Burrow, J. A. (1978–79) 'The Alterity of Medieval Literature', *New Literary History*, 10, 385–90.

Coleman, Janet (1981) *English Literature in History 1350–1400: Medieval Readers and Writers* (London: Hutchinson).

Coss, P. R. (1983) 'Literature and Social Terminology: The Vavasour in England', in *Social Relations and Ideas: Essays in Honour of R. H. Hilton*, ed. T. H. Aston *et al.* (Cambridge: Cambridge University Press).

Curtius, Ernst Robert (1953) *European Literature and the Latin Middle Ages*, trans. Willard R. Trask, Bollingen Series XXXVI (New York: Pantheon Books; originally published in German in Berne, 1948).

Delany, Sheila (1971–72) 'Undoing Substantial Connection: The Late Medieval Attack on Analogical Thought', *Mosaic: A Journal for the Comparative Study of Literature and Ideas*, 5, 31–52.

Delany, Sheila (1974) 'Substructure and Superstructure: The Politics of Allegory in the Fourteenth Century', *Science and Society: An Independent Journal of Marxism*, 38, 257–80.

Eagleton, Terry (1976a) *Marxism and Literary Criticism* (London: Methuen).

Eagleton, Terry (1976b) *Criticism and Ideology: A Study in Marxist Literary Theory* (London: New Left Books).

Eliot, T. S. (ed.) (1928) *Ezra Pound: Selected Poems*, Introduction (London: Faber & Faber; rev. edn, 1948).

Hartman, Geoffrey H. (1978–79) 'A Short History of Practical Criticism', *New Literary History*, 10, 495–509.

Howard, Donald R. (1976) *The Idea of the Canterbury Tales* (Berkeley, Los Angeles and London: University of California Press).

Jameson, Fredric (1971) *Marxism and Form: Twentieth-Century Dialectical Theories of Literature* (Princeton, N.J.: Princeton University Press).

Jauss, Hans Robert (1978–79) 'The Alterity and Modernity of Medieval Literature', *New Literary History*, 10, 181–229.

Jauss, Hans Robert (1982) 'Theory of Genres and Medieval Literature', in his *Toward an Aesthetic of Reception*, trans. Timothy Bahti (Minneapolis: University of Minnesota Press).

Jones, Terry (1980) *Chaucer's Knight: The Portrait of a Medieval Mercenary* (London: Weidenfeld & Nicolson).

Kettle, Arnold (1972) 'The Progressive Tradition in Bourgeois Culture', in Baxandall (1972), pp. 159–74.

Kittredge, George Lyman (1915) *Chaucer and his Poetry* (Cambridge, Mass.: Harvard University Press).

Knight, Stephen (1980) 'Chaucer and the Sociology of Literature', *Studies in the Age of Chaucer*, 2, 15–51.

Lewis, C. S. (1936) *The Allegory of Love: A Study in Medieval Tradition* (Oxford: Oxford University Press).

Macherey, Pierre (1978) *A Theory of Literary Production*, trans. G. Wall (London: Routledge & Kegan Paul).

Manly, John Matthews (1926) 'Chaucer and the Rhetoricians', *Proceedings of the British Academy*, 12, 95–113.

Medvedev, P. N. and Bakhtin, M. M. (1928) *The Formal Method in Literary Scholarship: A Critical Introduction to Sociological Poetics*, trans. Albert J. Wehrle (Baltimore and London: The Johns Hopkins University Press, 1978; originally published in Russian in 1928).

Muscatine, Charles (1957) *Chaucer and the French Tradition: A Study in Style and Meaning* (Berkeley, Los Angeles and London: University of California Press).

Muscatine, Charles (1972) *Poetry and Crisis in the Age of Chaucer* (Notre Dame and London: University of Notre Dame Press).

Norris, Christopher (1982) *Deconstruction: Theory and Practice* (London: Methuen).

Palmer, Richard E. (1969) *Hermeneutics: Interpretation Theory in Schleiermacher, Dilthey, Heidegger, and Gadamer* (Evanston: Northwestern University Press).

Pearce, Roy Harvey (1969) 'Literature, History, and Humanism', an essay originally published in *College English* (1963) and reprinted in the author's *Historicism Once More* (Princeton, N.J.: Princeton University Press).

Popper, Karl (1972) *Objective Knowledge: An Evolutionary Approach* (Oxford: Clarendon Press).

Postan, M. M. (1983) 'Feudalism and its Decline: A Semantic Exercise', in *Social Relations and Ideas: Essays in Honour of R. H. Hilton*, ed. T. H. Aston *et al.* (Cambridge: Cambridge University Press), pp. 73–87.

Robertson, D. W. Jr (1962) *A Preface to Chaucer: Studies in Medieval Perspectives* (Princeton, N.J.: Princeton University Press).

Robertson, D. W. Jr (1974) 'Chaucer's Franklin and his Tale', *Costerus:*

Essays in English and American Language and Literature, new series, vol. 1, ed. James L. West III (Amsterdam: Rodopi), pp. 1–26.

Robertson, D. W. Jr (1977) 'Some Disputed Chaucerian Terminology', *Speculum*, 52, 571–81.

Robertson, D. W. Jr (1979–80) '"And for my land thus hastow mordred me?": Land Tenure, the Cloth Industry, and the Wife of Bath', *Chaucer Review*, 14, 403–20.

Said, G. W. (1980) *Literature and Society: Selected Papers from the English Institute 1978*, new series, no. 3, ed. Edward W. Said (Baltimore and London: The Johns Hopkins University Press).

Scattergood, V. J. (1981) 'Chaucer and the French War: *Sir Thopas* and *Melibee*', in *Court and Poet*, ed. Glyn S. Burgess (Liverpool: Francis Cairns), pp. 287–96.

Specht, Henrik (1981) *Chaucer's Franklin in the Canterbury Tales: The Social and Literary Background of a Chaucerian Character* (Copenhagen: Akademisc Forlag).

Spurgeon, Caroline F. E. (1925) *Five Hundred Years of Chaucer Criticism and Allusion*, 3 vols (Cambridge: Cambridge University Press).

Stock, Brian (1973–74) 'The Middle Ages as Subject and Object: Romantic Attitudes and Academic Medievalism', *New Literary History*, 5, 527–47.

Williams, Raymond (1977) *Marxism and Literature* (Oxford: Oxford University Press).

8

Interpretation and Imitation in Chaucer's Franklin's Tale

Judith Ferster

There has been much interest lately in the use of modern literary theories for interpreting medieval literature (see *Medieval Literature and Contemporary Theory*; and Ridley, 1981). The discussion is a continuation of the older debate between those who try to recover and apply medieval methods of interpretation (such as patristic exegesis) and those who use modern methods of close reading. What is at stake in both controversies is whether modern readers can shed their modernity to view the past as the past viewed itself, or whether, since all interpretation is historical—that is, since interpreters have a particular place in history that shapes their interpretations—we might as well use whatever critical tools the intervening years have managed to invent. In the 1950s and 1960s, Robertson and Jordan argued that the aesthetic of the Middle Ages was so different from ours that to look for literary values that please us (e.g. organic unity, irony, paradox, and other New Critical concepts) is to prevent understanding. It is, in fact, to rewrite the poems as modern poems. With a minimum of theory and a maximum of sensibility, Donaldson in numerous articles (some of which are collected in *Speaking of Chaucer*, 1970) used close textual analysis to support the claim that modern critical tools work, that is, they seem to reveal the 'richness' of the poems. They were not arguing for anarchic anachronism—many of these critics had been philologically trained and intended to discover medieval meaning. They often had a sense of the difficulty of separating reconstruction of the past from appropriation of it for our own purposes. In 1976, Donald R. Howard's description of the

148

relationship between medieval and modern minds presented an undeclared version of the hermeneutical circle (pp. 15–20). The two 'schools' were equally concerned with 'the medieval mind', but their definitions of it and of our access to it differed.

In the latest version of the debate, which takes in (under the rubric of anarchic anachronism) semiotics, deconstruction, and phenomenological hermeneutics, what is at stake is again fidelity to (and therefore definition of) the medieval mind. Cries of 'They didn't think like that in the Middle Ages' are again being heard. And again, there are no living witnesses to come to the aid of either side. Since most of the modern 'methods' have something to do with language, however, the case can be made that 'they' did indeed think like that. The recent interest in linguistically-based modern theory has occurred simultaneously with great interest in the linguistic Middle Ages.[1] This scholarly dialectic is a version of the hermeneutical circle: we impose our modern preoccupations on the Middle Ages, but should not be surprised to find the Middle Ages mirroring us because some of our modern concerns come out of the western tradition's preoccupation with language. We create our own Middle Ages, but not solipsistically, because it has created us.

My particular concern in this essay is the usefulness of modern phenomenological hermeneutics for interpreting medieval literature, especially Chaucer. This intention raises an immediate question because phenomenological hermeneutics explicitly shuns 'method'. Gadamer's title, *Truth and Method* (1975), is notoriously ironic: There is no *method* that will guarantee truth. How, then, can the theory be applied? One way is that of Hans Robert Jauss, who focuses on the relationship between literary works and the tradition from which they spring, and the relationship between literary works and their audiences. Thus, he is interested in genre and the history of reception.

Another way to apply the theory is to find the hermeneutical themes in medieval literature by using the techniques of close reading. This is the method I wish to discuss and, through a reading of Chaucer's Franklin's Tale, to demonstrate here. I argue in this essay that modern hermeneutics is useful in interpreting medieval literature, especially in calling our attention to the explicit medieval interest in interpretation. Modern hermeneutics reminds us that we shall always be modern, never see the medieval period as medieval people saw it. Paradoxically, modern hermeneutics also reminds us that we share with the Middle Ages a concern for the problems of interpretation. In section I, I list some of the tenets of modern hermeneutics and a few pieces of evidence of the medieval interest in these same ideas. In section II, I give a reading of the Franklin's Tale to show how it is, in an important way, *about* interpretation.

I.
Hermeneutical Principles, Modern and Medieval

These are some principles of modern hermeneutics (drawn from Chapter 1 of my *Chaucer on Interpretation*, 1985):

1. All judgement is based on prejudgement—on assumptions, biases and anticipations of what one expects to find. Prejudice comes out of the interpreter's context, the place in which he stands to view the other. His location determines what he will see. All interpretation is thus historical because the interpreter is standing in a specific place in history that cannot be neutralised. This is not a correctible flaw in interpretive practice, but part of the human condition.

2. The source of prejudgement is tradition: Each age, each person, is shaped by what has gone before. But each age selects parts of the past to be shaped by. According to Gadamer, tradition 'is not simply a precondition into which we come, but we produce it ourselves, inasmuch as we understand, participate in the evolution of tradition and hence further determine it ourselves'(1975, p. 261). Thus, understanding is circular. When interpreting a piece of writing from the past, for instance, the interpreter sees it with and through his prejudices, but at the same time those prejudices have been created by the writings of the past, including the very text he is reading. This is true of all interpretation, not just interpretation of the past. The circle is unavoidable and unbreakable.

3. The dream of knowing the other in a way that is free from the influence of the interpreter's own time and place—seeing the past as it really was—is futile. Nevertheless, to recognise the otherness of the other and to *attempt* to interpret the other as if it had its own intention (i.e. to interpret in good faith) is preferable to cynical imposition of one's own will.

4. The circle means that the model of totally separate subject and object is inadequate. Subject and object are separate, but are also part of a dialectic in which they mutually influence each other.
5. The hermeneutical circle, though unavoidable, is none the less not necessarily vicious. We are not trapped for ever in a stalemate, locked away from knowledge of the world. In so far as we attempt to know the world, and in so far as it does not meet out expectations, we learn about it and about ourselves—at the very least, we learn about our prejudices. Encounter with the world brings bias to consciousness. Therefore interpretation is not a sterile imposition of the interpreter's will upon the world, but a cause of discovery and self-discovery for the interpreter. Interpretation thus rebounds upon the interpreter, and leads to awareness of the self and the conditions of interpretation. The discomfort we feel in the confrontation with the other—the hermeneutical equivalent of culture shock—leads to discovery. Hermeneutics, the study of interpretation, follows naturally from the process of interpretation.

Although I formulated these principles in terms borrowed from Gadamer and Ricoeur, they express concerns familiar to the Middle Ages. St Augustine's view of Scriptural interpretation, for instance, reflects both the desire to find the author's intention and the recognition that the author's intention may not be recoverable through the text. Each reader may impose his own meaning on the text. Lest this tendency of the text (to function as a mirror in which each person finds his own truth) should lead to interpretive anarchy, Augustine requires three safeguards. First, each reader of Scripture must try to discover the author's intentions. The fact that readers produce different interpretations is acceptable as long as 'each of us tries as best he can to understand in the Holy Scriptures what the writer meant by them' (12.18). This is good faith interpretation. Second, each person must recognise the partiality of his own view—that it is not complete and that he loves it because it is his own (12.25). Third, the truth that a person finds in a passage of Scripture must be consistent with the truth obtained from other sources—other passages of Scripture and other kinds of revelation. The dependence on other passages of Scripture is a version of the hermeneutical circle: each part is interpreted in the light of the others. The dependence on revelation is a version of the circle of faith and understanding. Revelation can 'correct' partial interpretations, but for revelation, faith is necessary; understanding is sometimes the basis for faith (Augustine's leap of faith is preceded by his years of study). Understanding needs faith; faith needs understanding. These safeguards are analogous to the principles of modern phenomenological hermeneutics. The difference is, of course, that modern hermeneutics admits of no revelation and no institution that can end interpretation by providing an authoritative answer.

Nor is there an authoritative interpretation of non-Scriptural texts. This is perhaps one reason why medieval secular writers were sensitive to the threat of interpretive anarchy. Another is the ability of literature to affect readers' and hearers' behaviour. This is the other side of the dialectic. Not only does the mind of the interpreter influence the meaning of the text, but the text may influence the interpreter. Hugh of St Victor says of Scripture and saints' lives that they teach 'what it delights us to know and behooves us to imitate' (1961, 5.6, p. 127). That texts could inspire imitation fascinated many writers in the Middle Ages, partly because they knew that there is no guarantee that readers will be influenced in the way writers intend to influence them. Two examples will illustrate medieval awareness of the power of stories to inspire imitation: Augustine's story of his conversion in the *Confessions*, and Francesca da Rimini's story of her 'conversion' in Canto 5 of Dante's *Inferno*.

St Augustine's conversion is mediated in several ways by the story of St Antony, who is converted when he hears a portion of the Bible read in church and takes it 'as a counsel addressed to himself' (8.12). Augustine's awareness of St Antony, and of another man who had been converted when he learned about St Antony, leads him to interpret the voice in the garden as a command and to choose a passage of Scripture and apply it to himself. On the basis of the text he chooses, he transforms his life. Thus the conversion is doubly mediated by the imitation of stories: Augustine has the example of Antony, and the example of how to use Antony by imitating him.

The influence of story on Dante's Paolo and Francesca is more dangerous because of the model they select and how they use it. They lose their lives and souls by imitating the adulterous passion of Lancelot and Guinevere. As Francesca says, 'A Galeotto [pander] was the book and he who wrote it' (*Inferno*, 5.137). Whatever the author's intention, Paolo and Francesca short-circuit them by acting before they have read the book's tragic end, which might have warned them of their own danger: 'That day we read in it no farther.' As Susan Noakes (1983) shows, they have made a mistake about how to read and how to use their reading.

Another reason medieval writers may have been attuned to the way in which reading is really rewriting is that they themselves were readers who *literally* rewrote what they read. Since the typical medieval mode of composition was the rewriting of old works, writers themselves demonstrated the reader's power to transform a text.

Furthermore, the conditions of reception in the fourteenth century increased the reader's responsibility for interpretation. As paper became cheaper and literacy spread, ownership of books increased, thus allowing readers access to texts apart from authors' public readings or recitations.[2] Oral performance of texts controls the audience's experience of them more than a written text can, and therefore also controls interpretation to a greater degree. The performer determines the selections, order, pace, tone and accompanying gesture. Of course, his hearers can still miss his meaning or disagree with him, but when they take the book home and read it for themselves, they can do so even more. When the writer is absent, the readers are in charge. Chaucer acknowledges the reader's freedom in a number of places—for instance, his narrator's famous advice to the squeamish to avoid the Miller's Tale: 'Turne over the leef and chese another tale' (I[A], 3177).[3] Here Chaucer shows his awareness that readers can control their experience of his book, shaping the book to suit their own individual needs and wishes. In his Retraction, Chaucer worries that some of the tales 'sownen into synne' (X[I], 1085), but he does not list the ones he suspects. The reader chooses how he will be led astray. The Retraction is Chaucer's attempt to get himself off the hook, by reminding the reader of his own power to use or misuse the text. It is the writer's attempt to control the reader's (and hearer's) uncontrollable power of interpretation by pointing out its existence. This attempt to communicate, like the tales themselves, cannot be guaranteed, but it may be all that a writer can do.

II.
The Franklin's Tale

The Franklin's Tale is an examination of the interpretation of stories and the imitation that stories often inspire. Imitation is the link between stories and the lives of their readers and hearers. People adopt the story as a model for their own behaviour. But the link is not necessarily direct; it passes through interpretation and is affected by the interpreters' prejudices. Paolo and Francesca's fatal prejudices are their susceptibility to passion and their willingness to imitate the book before they reach its cautionary conclusion. In the Franklin's Tale, one of Dorigen's prejudices is her ignorance of magic and deception. She accepts Aurelius's contention that she must fulfil her promise (to 'love hym best of any man') because 'She nevere erst hadde herd speke of apparence' (1602). The Franklin has a prejudice against 'apparence': he shows his distrust of fiction when he intrudes on the narrative to say that 'swich folye' as magic

> ... in oure dayes is nat worth a flye,—
> For hooly chirches feith in our bileve
> Ne suffreth noon illusioun us to greve.
> (V[F], 1132–4)

This rejection of illusion fits nicely with the Franklin's rejection of rhetoric in his prologue (716–28): both passages choose the real over fantasy and adornment. The Franklin seems to be trying to protect his audience from the dangers of Dorigen's prejudice by inoculating them with his own. He demonstrates the ill-effects of her ignorance. He is warning them of the dangers of his own medium: stories are illusion, and can have unpredictable and unsafe results.[4] His intrusion calls attention to the artificiality of the medium of story-telling.

What is surprising about Dorigen's problem of 'trouthe' is that it comes from her perfect understanding with Aurelius in the garden. Aurelius speaks, she shows that she understands, she answers, and he shows that he understands. She is a good reader, correctly interpreting his 'Have mercy, sweete' (978):

> 'Is this youre wyl,' quod she, 'and sey ye thus?

Nevere erst,' quod she, 'ne wiste I what ye mente.
But now, Aurelie, I knowe youre entente ...'
(980–2)

She mentions two parts of communication—a speaker's will and
the audience's understanding of it. She then tries to communicate
her intent by giving her 'fynal' refusal. Even her playful promise to
love him if he removes the rocks is expressed in terms of clearing
the sea-lanes for ships (she wants to make her husband's return
easier; 994). She says she has asked this because 'it shal never
bityde' (1001), and Aurelius shows that he understands her
intention by declaring sorrowfully that 'this were an inpossible'
(1009). The only other example of such clear understanding in the
Franklin's Tale is the magician's understanding of why Aurelius
and his brother have sought him out (1176–8), and that feat of
insight is supernatural. We must pay attention to how Dorigen
and Aurelius manage to turn their carefully achieved clarity into
melodrama.

Some of the difficulty comes from Dorigen's second refusal,
made 'in pley' (989). Pitying Aurelius's pain at her refusal, she sets
him the seemingly impossible task of removing the rocks from the
coast, as if to comfort him. Examination of the tale's other uses of
the word 'pley' will help us see why play is so troublesome. When
Dorigen and her friends

> ... hadde maad hir ordinaunce
> Of vitaille and of oother purveiaunce,
> They goon and *pley* hem al the longe day.
> (903–5; emphasis mine)

As Harry Berger notes, the balance between 'purveiaunce' and
'pley' is the balance between necessity and amusement, practicality
and ornament, Fact and Rhetoric (pp. 137–40). The garden,
'peynted' by May and 'Arrayed' by the 'craft of mannes hand,' full
of 'beautee with pleasaunce', fit for after-dinner dancing and
singing, comes down on the side of play. Although based squarely
on adequate provisions, it offers respite from black rocks. The
friends who try to comfort Dorigen for the absence of her husband
choose the garden as an escape from the sea, a place 'to pleyen
somwher elles' (897). But not only is play entertainment, it is also
imitation: the garden has no equal 'But if it were the verray

paradys' (912). If the garden is not the true paradise, it is an imitation paradise. The passage that leads up to (912) delicately establishes the dichotomy:

> And craft of mannes hand so curiously
> Arrayed hadde this gardyn, trewely,
> That nevere was ther gardyn of swich prys,
> But if it were the verray paradys.
>
> (909–12)

The sentence pauses momentarily at 'trewely', briefly suggesting that the garden was arrayed curiously but truly. However, 'trewely' is also the Franklin's assertion of sincerity, and the sentence then moves on to the true paradise, in comparison to which the crafty, painted garden is implicitly 'untrue'. Dorigen cannot be seduced by Aurelius, but she is apparently seduced by the garden, where she lets 'hir sorwe slyde' (924). She makes her untrue promise in an untrue paradise.

Another reference to play is in Aurelius's brother's plan to find a magician to help Aurelius: he will resort to 'tregetoures pleye', which can 'maken diverse apparences' (1141, 1140). This usage does nothing to detract from the bad reputation that play is accumulating in this tale.

Comparison of the Franklin's Tale with Boccaccio's *Filocolo*, which many have taken to be Chaucer's source,[5] highlights an illusion the Franklin could have avoided. In Boccaccio, the magician does actually produce what the lady requests: a summer garden in winter. The wonder of the garden is that it *is* true and we know it is true because we follow Tebano as he gathers materials on his travels to Spain, Greece, Africa and India in his dragon-drawn chariot and as he plants the garden and makes it grow with his rituals and custom-mixed potions. We see the garden bloom. Even the dragons are rejuvenated by his magic, and the lady and her friends walk in the garden and taste its fruit. Boccaccio's real garden is in contrast with the *Franklin's Tale* with its untrue paradise and the untrue disappearance of its rocks. The subject of the illusion that makes rocks disappear is the occasion for the Franklin's intrusive judgement of magic, which I have already quoted. Comparison of Boccaccio's real garden and the Franklin's unreal garden and the unreal disappearance of the rocks emphasises how the troubles in the tale come out of play and illusion.

Another cause of the difficulty is interpretation. When Aurelius comes to Dorigen to announce the disappearance of the rocks, he interprets her. In the garden, he read her playful promise for what it was—an impossibility trope—and responded with appropriate despair. Now he paints a picture of her that he hopes she will take as a mirror; he treats her as though she were a woman who had made a promise:

> For madame, *wel ye woot what ye han hight*—
> Nat that I chalange any thyng of right
> Of yow, my sovereyn lady, but youre grace—
> But in a gardyn yond, at swich a place,
> *Ye woot right wel what ye bihighten me*;
> And in myn hand *youre trouthe plighten ye*
> To love me best—God woot, *ye seyde so*,
> Al be that I unworthy am thereto.
> Madame, I speke it for the honour of yow
> Moore than to save myn hertes lyf right now,—
> I have do so as ye comanded me;
> And if ye vouche sauf, ye may go see.
> Dooth as yow list; have youre *biheste* in mynde ...
>   (1323–35; emphasis mine)

Aurelius describes his concern for her honour (1331), calls her action in the garden a 'biheeste' (1335), and tells her that *she* knows she has promised and that *God* knows she has promised. Dorigen accepts Aurelius's interpretation of her and internalises it. She accepts as a mirror what is really a caricature. When she repeats the story to Arveragus, she again imitates it, as does Arveragus when he accepts it as true. Interpretation and imitation lead Dorigen into her dilemma.[6]

The Franklin may be motivated to protect his audience from the kind of muddle generated by illusion and interpretation because he, too, is a story-teller. Stories can endanger audiences in just the way that the story of Lancelot and Guinevere endangered Dante's Paolo and Francesca. It is precisely the turning of 'trouthe' (promise) into 'trouthe' (reality) that worries the Franklin.

The Franklin's rejection of illusion and his emphasis on the priority of the audience are related because his own art is a kind of

157

illusion-making. He is like his character, the magician, in his ability to conjure up illusion out of books. And (as Kee says, 1975, pp. 6–7) despite his claim of ignorance about the 'termes of astrologye' (1266), he demonstrates his knowledge by his detailed description of the magician's calculations (1273–97). He shares more of the magician's art than he is prepared to admit. The tale insists on the similarity between the Franklin and the character he values least.[7] Boccaccio's magician is not a student: he has a book but never refers to it. When doing his work, he abandons all equipment, including his clothes, to pray to the night, the stars, the moon, Hecate, Ceres, breezes, other elements of nature, and countless gods. There is no text. In contrast, the Franklin's magician is a student whose hallmark is his book. Aurelius's brother, in fact, remembers the book before he remembers its owner:

> He hym remembred that, upon a day,
> At Orliens in a studie a book he say
> Of magyk natureel ...
> And whan this book was in his remembraunce,
> Anon for joye his herte gan to daunce ...
> (1124–6, 1135–6)

The Franklin and the magician both mention the book by describing the magician's study as the place where the book is (1207, 1214). Unlike Tebano's garden, the magician's illusion of the rocks' disappearance is based on texts: the Toledan Tables (1273) and three other kinds of compiled computations. This is no wild, naked invoker of animistic spirits, but an astronomer, a mathematician, a calculator, a master of the astrolabe.

The magician's use of books makes him very like both of his authors: Chaucer was a writer of a treatise on the astrolabe which was to have included 'diverse tables' (80; the introduction predicts them, but they do not actually appear) like those the magician uses. And Chaucer also had a book out of which he conjured up the Franklin's Tale, though he does not name it. The Franklin freely refers to *his* book: the lai he claims as his source is written (713–14), and he mentions it several times. (Schofield (1901), Hume (1972) and Yoder (1977) discuss the problem of whether Chaucer actually knew and used Breton lais.) Compare Boccaccio's narrator, who remembers his story as an event that happened in his home

town (Miller, 1977, p. 122), not as a story in a book. The Franklin
is, in contrast, a reader. For instance, just after Aurelius concludes
his bargain with the bookish magician, the Franklin intrudes on
the narrative:

> And this was, *as thise bookes me remember,*
> The colde frosty seson of Decembre.
>
> (1244–5; emphasis mine)

In the *Filocolo*, Menadon remembers what happened; the
Franklin remembers his book (see also (813)).

There follows a highly rhetorical, ten-line description of
December, which is unnecessary to the plot and contrary to the
Franklin's rejection of rhetoric in the Prologue. His intrusion of
December reminds us of Boccaccio. In the *Filocolo*, winter matters.
I have already mentioned that the garden is a miracle because it
produces May fruits and flowers in the dead of winter. The
Franklin notes carefully that winter 'Destroyed hath the grene in
every yerd' (1251). This rhetorical interruption also displays the
Franklin's information about astrology (1246–8). Thus, if the
Filocolo is indeed Chaucer's source, the levels of narration collapse
into each other as the Franklin's Breton book reminds him of
Chaucer's Italian story, and the Franklin reveals his interest in
both the disowned rhetoric and the disowned astrology. This
convergence reinforces the connection between the three
magicians who conjure illusion from books, language and the stars.

The relationship among the characters in the tale and the
relationships between the Franklin and his source and Chaucer
and *his* source are figured in the nymph Echo, when Aurelius
claims as an analogue when he cannot confess his love to Dorigen:

> ... dye he moste, he seyde, as dide Ekko
> For Narcisus, that dorste nat telle hir wo.
>
> (952–3)

When Aurelius likens himself to Echo, he is not like her at all. She
does speak her love and her woe. She is nothing if not a speaker—
in fact, she becomes nothing and is still a speaker. When she pines
away, what is left is her voice, and she will answer anyone who
speaks to her. It is true that she can only repeat Narcissus's words
back to him, but in Ovid's version of the story, she manages to

make herself quite clear. She works on the principle of selection and the words she repeats carry not only Narcissus's message but her own. For instance, when Narcissus cries, 'I would die before I would have you touch me,' she answers, 'I would have you touch me' (*Metamorphoses*, 3.390–2; Innes trans., 1983, p. 91). What seems to be mere repetition is really the creation of new meaning. Aurelius is quite unlike her when he claims to be like her, but he is very like her in the later confrontation when, in essence, he is repeating Dorigen's words back to her, but with the new meaning he gives them. His interpretation of them changes them from 'pley' into a promise. Aurelius is a sly Echo, interpreting his 'source' while imitating it. So is the Franklin, and so is Chaucer.

Thus the problems that Dorigen, Arveragus and Aurelius find themselves in are inherent in the medium of story-telling. The Franklin tries to mitigate these problems in several ways. He presents more neutral or even positive images of fiction. For instance, he includes examples of stories that do not lead anywhere. Dorigen is also a reader and a story-teller. Her long suicide speech is an attempt to use stories to kill herself (1342–456): in imitation of the honourable ladies, she will die rather than dishonour her marriage. However, she *really* uses the stories to keep herself occupied until Arveragus returns, scraping the bottom of the barrel for very dubious examples of wronged virtuous women. Since imitation is a matter of choice, she can choose not to imitate. Her stories do not mediate action; they defend against it.

The ending of the tale is a partial defence of stories. At least if fiction causes the problem in the first place, it also manages to solve it. The plot turns on a chain of imitation as each man takes the story of another's generosity and decides it can apply to himself. Aurelius lets Dorigen go because he appropriates the story of Arveragus's generosity and chooses to imitate it. The clerk hears the story of Arveragus's and Aurelius's generosity and chooses to imitate them both.

If illusion is a problem, one way to defend against it is to undercut it. The Franklin does this by treating his characters rather cavalierly. His references to the amount of time Aurelius suffers as a lover and Dorigen suffers in her dilemma are so vague that he cannot care much for their suffering. Aurelius pines silently for Dorigen 'In langour and in torment furyus/Two yeer and moore ...' (1101–2). Anyone who had any sympathy with 'torment furyus' would be more precise, but the Franklin has already said,

> Lete I this woful creature lye;
> Chese he, for me, wheither he wol lyve or dye.
>
> (1085–6)

Dorigen considers suicide 'a day or tweye' (1457). The Franklin's refusal to project himself into her suffering is a way of undercutting our sense of her reality. A day more or less of her suffering somehow does not matter much. The Franklin also leaves room for the reader to question her dedication to suffering. Since Arveragus comes home on the third night, we might wonder what she was doing on the third day.

The most important method of protecting the audience against fiction is to emphasise the *context* of the fiction itself. The Franklin does this by referring to his source (Bloomfield, 1982, p. 195) and directly addressing his audience (Kee, 1975, p. 3; Magnus, 1983). He also emphasises his (and his audience's) distance from the tale when he makes transitions between the different parts of the tale. He uses most of these occasions to turn attention away from his characters and toward himself. He spotlights his own activity as narrator and our experience as audience at the expense of his characters. For instance, when he turns his attention from Arveragus's quest for honour in England back to Dorigen, alone in Brittany, he announces,

> Now wol I stynten of this Arveragus,
> And speken I wole of Dorigen his wyf ...
>
> (814–15)

We can see the effect of this rather mechanical transition if we compare it to the Squire's habits at similar moments (401–8 are an exception), for instance at the end of the first part of his tale:

> But thus I lete in lust and jolitee
> This Cambyuskan his lordes festeiynge,
> Til wel ny the day bigan to sprynge.
>
> (344–6)

The second part then opens with a 54-line description of the court going to sleep, and of Canacee waking up and deciding to go for a walk. This kind of transition seems to treat the characters as though, even while they are not present 'on stage', they continue to exist. 'Thus lete I Canacee hir hauk kepyng' (651) implies that Canacee lives on, whether or not we look at her. Perhaps an attempt to correct the Squire, the Franklin's transition focuses not on his characters' lives, but on his audience's. This becomes especially apparent at the end of the tale, when first Dorigen and then Aurelius must repeat the story of what happened when they met in the garden. When the Franklin suppresses the repetiton, in each case he refers to the audience's prior knowledge of the facts:

> 'Thus have I seyd,' quod she, 'thus have I sworn'—
> And toold hym al *as ye han herd bifore*;
> It *nedeth nat reheerce it yow namoore.*
>
> (1464–6; emphasis mine)

And again:

> Aurelius his tale anon began,
> And tolde hym al, *as ye had herd bifoore*;
> It *nedeth nat to yow reherce it moore.*
>
> (1592–4; emphasis mine)

Where the Squire tends to tell time by his characters, following the course of their lives with zealous naturalism even when they are sleeping (perhaps Andy Warhol learned something from the Squire), the Franklin tells time by his audience. His elaborate concern with the pacing of the story suppresses repetition to keep the pilgrims from being bored. It punctures the illusion that his characters are real by emphasising the process of creating them and interpreting them.

One of the striking features of the Franklin's Tale is that it does not include anything like Boccaccio's long 'coda' (Miller, 1977, pp. 129–34) in which the teller and the audience (especially the Queen) argue about the question posed at the end: Which of the three men was most generous? Boccaccio offers something of an answer in the form of the Queen's victory. Of course, this resolution must also be interpreted, but the Franklin's ending is even more open, for he ventures no answers at all to the questions he poses. His question is as open as the Knight's *demande d'amour*, open-ended and deferential to the judgement of the audience (see I[A], 1347–54).

In asking the pilgrims their opinions, the Franklin accomplishes several things, He compliments the Knight by echoing his *demande d'amour* (as Kee comments, 1975, p. 8), and he compliments the pilgrims by handing his tale to them. He calls them 'Lordynges' (1621), respectfully requesting their interpretations of his tale and his characters. He suppresses the fiction in favour of the reality of the pilgrims, as the plot of his tale and his various narrative techniques have attempted to do all along. He thus emphasises the interpretive community that surrounds his tale— the social context that gives it meaning. He protects us as much as he can from illusion by making us aware of our role as audience. He cannot break out of the hermeneutical circle, but he can highlight it to warn readers about it. Readers who are aware of the perils of interpretation are perhaps protected from illusion in a way that the unsuspecting Dorigen, who 'nevere erst hadde herd speke of apparence' (1602), is not.

This interpretation of the Franklin's Tale illustrates the hermeneutical principles I listed at the start of section I above (in the following list, the numbers are coordinated with those in section I):

1. The prejudgement that shapes Dorigen's response to Aurelius is her ignorance of appearance.
2. Dorigen's playful response to Aurelius is influenced by the context provided by the garden: gardens are places to play in. The garden may also be a source of Aurelius's expectation that Dorigen is approachable: Ladies who walk in gardens are available as lovers.

Later, Dorigen conforms herself to Aurelius's expectations, but what she is imitating is her own interpetation of Aurelius (as a man who deserves to be listened to about promises, for instance). At the end of the tale, the men all choose a significant aspect of the others to imitate (generosity). The process is circular.

3. Good faith is preferable to cynicism, as we learn when Aurelius wilfully interprets Dorigen as a woman who has promised.
4. The process by which people choose to be influenced by their contexts (as defined by the garden and by other people) means

that subject and object are not separate, but mutually influence each other. Echo is an emblem for this process.

5. This circle is not vicious. Aurelius finally learns enough about Dorigen's wishes to have the 'greet compassioun' and 'greet routhe' (1515, 1520) that enable him to release her from her supposed promise. He shows his empathy with her when, in telling his story to the magician, he empathises with her feelings (1598–602). The empathy is especially striking in contrast to his almost solipsistic preoccupation earlier in the tale. He is self-absorbed and asks for 'compassioun' for himself (1079–84). Aurelius's compassion (on which see Hamel, 1983, pp. 328–9; and Lane, 1984, pp. 120–1) seems to be prompted by his response to Dorigen's arrival to fulfill the so-called promise 'half as she were mad' (1511). The extremity of her emotions disturbs him: He 'gan wondren on this cas' (1514). His wonder allows him to abandon his self-interested interpretation of her as a woman who has made a promise for something much closer to her own view of herself as a wife who wishes to remain faithful to her husband. Wonder comes from the disjunction between the world and Aurelius's selfish expectations, and leads to new understanding. Dorigen, too, learns something from her uncomfortable collision with the world: She learns about appearance.

If the tale works as I have hypothesised, the other important example of those who have learned about appearance is the audience.[8]

Notes

1. E.g. Robins (1951), Colish (1968), Bursill-Hall (1971) and Henry (1984). For literary criticism that attempts to link medieval literature and medieval language theory, see Peck (1978) and Shoaf (1983).
2. See Lefebvre and Martin, (1976) pp. 15–28. Also see Janet Coleman's (1981) discussion of late fourteenth-century English literacy, including the development of an educated lay reading audience, the interest in learning outside the universities, the increasing opportunities for individuals to read the Bible and theological commentaries for themselves, and the Church's uneasiness about independent reading (esp. pp. 56, 123, 202–31).

Coleman notes (1981, p. 275) that in the *Book of the Duchess*, the *Parliament of Fowls*, and the *House of Fame*, Chaucer portrays himself as one of the solitary readers she describes.

3. All quotations from Chaucer are from Robinson's edition (1957).

4. The work of Glending Olson (1982) suggests that there were, in medieval writing about literature, justifications of fiction as recreation and entertainment. They did not, apparently, persuade the Franklin, who seems more engaged by the kind of theory of narrative described by Judson Allen (1982) in his work on medieval literary theory.

5. See, for instance, Dempster and Tatlock, 1958, p. 377; Donaldson, 1958, p. 1089; and Miller, 1977, p. 121.

6. Alan Gaylord (1964) argues that there should be no dilemma because the promises should not be honoured. Mary J. Carruthers (1981) comments that to take a woman's promise seriously is a kind of moral breakthrough. Elizabeth Kirk (1983) recently made a strong case for this point of view.

The reasons for Dorigen's seemingly automatic internalisation of Arveragus's view of her are obscure. According to Robert Lane (1984; see esp. p. 118), she lets Aurelius equate her speaking with swearing ('Thus have I seyd ... thus have I sworn', 1464) when she allows him to separate her words from the context in which they were spoken. He appeals to her 'truth to self'. But she has had less experience with personal integrity than with 'her truth to her sense of self as wife', and cannot independently reassert her original intentions. She is too used to letting herself be defined by a man. (On the part played by Dorigen's lack of self-knowledge in her marriage vows, her playful answer to Aurelius, and the resolution of the tale, see Mitchell, 1976.) In a similar vein, David Aers commented to me that Dorigen's inability to assert herself is the result of the strength of cultural stereotypes of male dominance and female passivity. For him, it is no accident that the garden is the product of the 'craft of mannes hand' (909). On the characters' reliance on 'traditional ideologies', see Aers, 1980, pp. 165–9.

7. On a similar parallel between Chaucer and the Pardoner, see Howard, 1976, p. 376.

8. I appreciate the helpful comments of David Aers, James Dean, Elizabeth D. Kirk, Robert Lane and John H. Smith.

References

Aers, David (1980) *Chaucer, Langland and the Creative Imagination* (London: Routledge & Kegan Paul).

Allen, Judson Boyce (1982) *The Ethical Poetic of the Later Middle Ages: A Decorum of Convenient Distinction* (Toronto: University of Toronto Press).

Augustine, St (1961) *Confessions*, trans. R.S. Pine-Coffin (Baltimore, Md: Penguin Books).

Berger, Harry, Jr (1966) 'The F-Fragment of the *Canterbury Tales*: Part II', *Chaucer Review*, 1, 135–56.

Bloomfield, Morton W. (1982) '*The Franklin's Tale*: A Story of Unanswered Questions', in *Acts of Interpretation: The Text in Its Contexts, 700–1600*, ed. Mary J. Carruthers and Elizabeth D. Kirk Norman, Oklahoma: Pilgrim Books:) pp. 189–98.

Bursill-Hall, G. L. (1971) *Speculative Grammars of the Middle Ages: The Doctrine of* Partes Orationis *of the Modistae*, Approaches to Semiotics, 11 (The Hague: Mouton).

Carruthers, Mary J. (1981) 'The *Gentilesse* of Chaucer's Franklin', *Criticism*, 23, 283–300.

Coleman, Janet (1981) *Medieval Readers and Writers: 1350–1400* (New York: Columbia University Press).

Colish, Marcia L. (1968) *The Mirror of Language: A Study in the Medieval Theory of Knowledge* (New Haven, Conn.: Yale University Press).

Dante Alighieri (1967) *The Divine Comedy: Inferno*, trans. John D. Sinclair (New York: Oxford University Press).

Dempster, Germaine and J. S. P. Tatlock (1958) 'The Franklin's Tale', in *Sources and Analogues of Chaucer's Canterbury Tales* (New York: Humanities Press).

Donaldson, E. Talbot (ed.) (1958) *Chaucer's Poetry* (New York: John Wiley and Sons; rpt. 1975).

Donaldson, E.T. (1970) *Speaking of Chaucer* (New York: W. W. Norton).

Ferster, Judith (1985) *Chaucer on Interpretation* (New York: Cambridge University Press).

Gadamer, Hans-Georg (1975) *Truth and Method* (New York: Seabury Press).

Gaylord, Alan (1964) 'The Promises in the "Franklin's Tale"', *English Literary History*, 31. 331–65.

Hamel, Mary (1983) 'The *Franklin's Tale* and Chrétien de Troyes', *Chaucer Review*, 17, 316–31.

Henry, Desmond Paul (1984) *That Most Subtle Question ('Quaestio*

Subtilissima'): *The Metaphysical Bearing of Medieval and Contemporary Linguistic Disciplines* (Manchester: Manchester University Press).

Howard, Donald R. (1976) *The Idea of the Canterbury Tales* (Berkeley: University of California Press).

Hugh of St Victor (1961) *The Didascalicon of Hugh of St. Victor: A Medieval Guide to the Arts*, trans. Jerome Taylor (New York: Columbia University Press).

Hume, Kathryn (1972) 'Why Chaucer Calls the *Franklin's Tale* a Breton Lai', *Philological Quarterly, 51*, 365–79.

Jauss, Hans Robert (1979) 'The Alterity and Modernity of Medieval Literature', *New Literary History*, 10, 181–229.

Jordan, Robert (1967) *The Shape of Creation: The Aesthetic Possibilities of Inorganic Structure* (Cambridge, Mass.: Harvard University Press).

Kee, Kenneth (1975) 'Illusion and Reality in Chaucer's Franklin's Tale', *English Studies in Canada*, 1, 1–12.

Kirk, Elizabeth D. (1983) 'Courtly Love in a World of Rocks, or, Did Arveragus Give His Wife an Order?', Paper read at the Medieval Institute, Western Michigan University, Kalamazoo, May.

Lane, Robert (1984) '*The Franklin's Tale*: Of Marriage and Meaning' in *Portraits of Marriage in Literature*, ed. Anne C. Hargrove and Maurine Magliocco (Macomb, Ill.: Western Illinois University Press) pp. 107–21.

Lefebvre, Lucien and Henri-Jean Martin (1976) *The Coming of the Book: The Impact of Printing, 1450–1800*, trans. David Gerard (London: New Left Books).

Magnus, Laury (1983) 'The Hem of Philosophy: Free and Bound Motifs in the *Franklin's Tale*', *Assays*, 2, 3—18.

Medieval Literature and Contemporary Theory (1979) constituting an entire issue (no. 2) of *New Literary History*, 10. It contains articles and comments by Hans Robert Jauss, Paul Zumthor, Rainer Warning, Eugene Vance, Maria Corti, Morton Bloomfield, and others.

Miller, Robert P. (ed.) (1977) *Chaucer: Sources and Backgrounds* (New York: Oxford University Press).

Mitchell, Susan (1976) 'Deception and Self-Deception in "The Franklin's Tale"', *Proceedings of the Patristic, Medieval and Renaissance Conference*, 1, 67–72.

Noakes, Susan (1983) 'The Double Misreading of Paolo and Francesca', *Philological Quarterly*, 62, 221–39.

Olson, Glending (1982) *Literature as Recreation in the Later Middle Ages* (Ithaca, N.Y.: Cornell University Press).

Ovid, (1955) *The Metamorphoses*, trans. Mary M. Innes (Baltimore, Md.: Penguin Books; rpt. 1983).

Ovid, (1977) *Metamorphoses* ed. William S. Anderson (Leipzig: B. G. Teubner).

Peck, Russell A. (1978) 'Chaucer and the Nominalist Questions', *Speculum*, 53, 745–69.

Ricoeur, Paul (1976) *Interpretation Theory: Discourse and the Surplus of Meaning* (Fort Worth: Texas Christian University Press).

Ridley, Florence (1981) 'Questions Without Answers—Yet or Ever? New Critical Modes and Chaucer', *Chaucer Review*, 16, 101–6.

Robertson, D. W. Jr (1962) *A Preface to Chaucer: Studies in Medieval Perspectives* (Princeton, N. J.: Princeton University Press).

Robertson, D. W. Jr (with Bernard F. Huppé) (1963) *Fruyt and Chaf* (Princeton, N. J.: Princeton University Press).

Robertson, D. W. Jr (1980) *Essays in Medieval Culture* (Princeton, N. J.: Princeton University Press).

Robins, R. H. (1951) *Ancient and Mediaeval Grammatical Theory in Europe with Particular Reference to Modern Linguistics* (London: G. Bell & Sons Ltd).

Robinson, F. N. (ed.) (1957) *The Works of Geoffrey Chaucer*, 2nd edn (Boston: Houghton Mifflin).

Shoaf, Richard Allen (1983) *Dante, Chaucer and the Currency of the Word: Money, Images, and Reference in Late Medieval Poetry* (Norman, Oklahoma: Pilgrim Books).

Schofield, William Henry (1901) 'Chaucer's *Franklin's Tale*', *PMLA*, 16, 405–49.

Yoder, Emily K. (1977) 'Chaucer and the "Breton" Lai', *Chaucer Review*, 12, 74–7.

9

Carnival and *The Canterbury Tales:* 'Only equals may laugh' (Herzen)

Jon Cook

I

It is characteristic of the fragmentary nature of *The Canterbury Tales* that they end abruptly with a Retraction and not a Conclusion. In the Retraction, Chaucer disclaims most of the work for which he is remembered including 'the tales of Canterbury, thilke that sownen into synne'. Given the pious and homiletic nature of a number of the stories, this may seem an odd judgement to modern readers and so 'thilke' is taken as a pronoun which discriminates amongst the tales, pointing to a division between the sinful and pious. The classification of Chaucer's work in the Retraction is significant in its crudity: whoever or whatever speaks in the text at this point, the first impulse is to include *The Canterbury Tales* amongst the sinful works. Even though there may be tales which tend to virtue in the collection, their presence is not sufficient to get the whole work classified with the translation of Boethius and 'othere bookes of legendes and omilies and moralitie and devocioun'. The language of the retraction is formal, ritualistic, modelled on the confession of sins at the point of death. What motivated the Retraction is difficult to decipher. Certainly, Chaucer was not the only medieval writer to write one, but the formulaic and impersonal character of the language cannot be taken as an argument for its insignificance. Pressed by the fear of hell, anxious about the un-Christian character of some of his writing, Chaucer engaged in an act of self-criticism which was simultaneously an attempt to sponsor a certain version of his work. He speaks in the language of the ecclesiastical

169

hierarchy in a way that provides a disquieting anticipation of the treatment meted out to writers in totalitarian states. At least, that is one hypothesis. But, whatever puzzles about voice and intention surround the retraction, an obvious question remains: Why should *The Canterbury Tales* be judged in the main as 'sownen into synne'? (*Canterbury Tales*, X (I), 1081–92).

An obvious question may seem to have an obvious answer. Teachers of sixth-form students will know the 'problem' of teaching Chaucer if the 'A' level set text is the *Miller's Tale*. The story is about illicit sex, about farting and pissing, about an arse branded with a hot iron. The atmosphere seems closer to a *Carry On* film than to the high seriousness we expect of great literature. Or, as another example, there is the Host's response to the manipulative conclusion of the Pardoner's tale:

> But, by the croys which that Saint Eleyne fond
> I wolde I hadde thy coillons in myn hond
> In stide of relikes or of seintuarie.
> Let kutte him of, I wol thee helpe hem carie;
> They shul be shryned in an hogges toord!
>
> (*Canterbury Tales*, VI (C), 951–5)

Confronted with this kind of language, modern criticism often looks the other way. Even when the comic force of such episodes is acknowledged, as in Alfred David's book, *The Strumpet Muse* (1976), it is done so in terms of an argument which subsumes comic profanity to some larger sacred purpose. In this way, the work's seriousness can be guaranteed and its claim to greatness assured. The modern critic can implicitly rebuff the charge in the retraction about the sinfulness of some of the tales. The strategy is to disregard or subsume what makes them sinful in the first place, their comedy. Modern criticism and official medieval piety are embarrassed by one and the same thing. As readers we are invited to laugh at adultery and other forms of deception, and instead of being reproved for this by a spiritually vigilant narrator, we find our laughter echoed back to us by the pilgrims themselves. At the end of *The Miller's Tale*, instead of a sermon on the sins of the flesh, we find this:

> When folk hadde laughen at this nyce cas
> Of Absalom and hende Nicholas

> Diverse folk diversely they seyde
> But for the moore part they loughe and pleyde.
> (*Canterbury Tales*, I (A), 3855-8)

The Reeve is the only exception to this general laughter and this is so not because he finds the story sinful, but because it insults his craft. The pilgrims' response to the Miller's Tale is just one example of the way they prove themselves a tolerant and worldly audience. Their disposition to laugh and play seems to go beyond those occasions when the narrator specifically refers to it. This is one effect of the link passages between the tales. Given their obvious functions—to effect a transition between one story and the next; to mark the passage of time—they also create a secular and contingent context for a response to particular stories, one that draws upon the model of comic debate, and absorbs the serious and homilectic intent of the most pious tales. Narrative authority is in constant circulation and this undermines the bids for power made by particular stories and by particular narrators. Laughter is an important condition of this mobility.

Mikhail Bakhtin's account of Carnival provides a context for understanding the importance of laughter in *The Canterbury Tales*. Carnival is an implicit and explicit reference-point throughout Bakhtin's work, but his book, *Rabelais and his World* (1968), provides the most sustained exposition of the meaning of carnival. (See too Chapter 5, above.) Rabelais's work is seen in terms of a history of laughter which seeks to restore a sense of the importance of comedy. According to Bakhtin, in the medieval and Renaissance world:

> Laughter has a deep philosophical meaning, it is one of the essential forms of truth concerning the world as a whole, concerning history and man; it is a peculiar point of view relative to the world; the world is seen anew ... (Bakhtin, 1968, p. 66)

But this relation to laughter changes from about the mid-seventeenth century onwards:

> It [laughter] can refer only to individual and individually typical phenomena of social life. That which is important and essential cannot be comical. ... The sphere of the comic is narrow and specific (private and social vices). ... Therefore the place of laughter in literature belongs

to the low genres …. Laughter is a light amusement or a form of salutary social punishment of corrupt and low persons. (ibid., p. 67)

Bakhtin's argument has various implications for a reading of *The Canterbury Tales*. One of these concerns our relation as reader to the work: namely, that we read it within a cultural perspective which no longer affords comedy the power that it had in medieval and Renaissance Europe. Bakhtin's work then offers an opportunity to recover this perspective by assessing the relevance of his account of carnival language, the medium of philosophic laughter, to *The Canterbury Tales*.

This is not the place for a detailed resumé of what Bakhtin means by carnival, but a schematic outline, at least, is important for what follows. Carnival is a form of great antiquity. Its origins pre-date the emergence of Christianity: carnivalesque elements can be found, for example, in Aristophanes' comedies. It is a popular language and it exists independently of written forms: in the market-place, in the feast, in the carnival procession. It is what Bakhtin describes as the 'culture of the loud word spoken in the open' (Bakhtin, 1968, p. 182). But the force of carnival is such that it affects written forms, and one purpose of Bakhtin's work is to write the history of the signs of carnival in medieval and renaissance writing, a history which, according to Bakhtin, finds its apogee in Rabelais's work. Carnival forms, then, occupy a strategic position in the interaction and division between oral and literate languages so central to the culture of medieval Europe. Then as now, forms of language were connected to particular institutions—learned, written Latin with the Church, French with the court, vernacular with the market-place and the inn—and these connections, in their turn, formed the basis for the social and political connotations coined by different linguistic forms. So, for Bakhtin, carnival language has an oppositional role *vis-à-vis* the official world view of the medieval church. Carnivalesque laughter provides an alternative to 'The very contents of medieval ideology—asceticism, sombre providentialism, sin, atonement, suffering, as well as the character of the feudal regime, with its oppression and intimidation' (Bakhtin, 1968, p. 73).

Bakhtin repeatedly refers to carnival as an 'alternative' or a 'second' world to institutional Christianity. It is nothing less than a rival metaphysic to Christianity, one grounded in popular institutions and experiences, working through devices of parody and inversion to counter and mitigate the various forces of authority in the medieval world.

II

The opening lines of *The Canterbury Tales* draw our attention to change and season renewal. These can be read as the first signs of carnivalesque values in the work. According to Bakhtin, carnival occasions are closely connected to seasonal change and give them a particular meaning:

> In this succession all that is new or renews, all that is about to draw nearer is emphasized as a positive element. And this element acquires a wider and deeper meaning: it expresses the people's hope of a happier future. (Bakhtin, 1968, p. 81)

Seasonal renewal, then, is given a popular utopian inflection. Again, the opening lines of the poem can be read in these terms. There is a utopian sense of release from the confinement and immobility of Lent and Winter, as though the struggle for survival had been momentarily suspended:

> Thanne longen folk to goon on pilgrimages
> And palmeres for to seken straunge strondes
> To ferne halwes, kowthe in sondry londes.
> (*Canterbury Tales*, I (A), 12–14)

These lines emphasise a collective and general movement born out of impulse. They stand in marked contrast to the motivation of either Langland's or Dante's narrative: the individual pursuit of salvation arising out of spiritual crisis, the passionate encounter with doctrine. In *The Canterbury Tales*, the reasons for pilgrimage are left vague, the result of longing or a curiosity for new experience and, given the context of the lines, these are the human equivalents to the renewal of activity in the natural world. In so far as the poem offers something more specific, we discover that the pilgrims do not go to Canterbury to prepare themselves for a holy death, but in order to give thanks for continuing life:

The hooly blisful martir for to seke,
That hem heth helpen whan that they were seeke.
(*Canterbury Tales*, I (A), 1117–18)

The beginning of the poem subtly assimilates a spiritual occasion, pilgrimage, to a secular context. This in itself is a typical manoeuvre of the carnival, a process whereby the spiritual and the ideal are converted 'downwards' to the carnal and the secular. Evidently, at this point in the poem, Chaucer does not employ the aggressive forms of carnival language—curses, oaths, parody, grotesque imagery—but the absence of these forms need not indicate the absence of carnivalesque attitudes. Bakhtin argues that carnival is a ubiquitous presence in medieval culture, focused on particular occasions and styles, but extending beyond these as a popular, alternative philosophy to the official doctrines of Church and Court. It is something more than a literary model which Chaucer might have drawn upon in his composition of the poem. If we think of carnival as a popular relation to power, Chaucer is indicating at the outset the affiliation of *The Canterbury Tales* to carnival, placing the work within the contending forces of medieval culture.

Stylistically, the beginning of the poem gives evidence of its affiliation as well. A number of critics have noticed the transition from the high, courtly style of the first eleven lines to the colloquial directness of what follows. This has been read as indicative of a purpose in the writer to root the dreamy universality of the poem's opening in the observed realities of late medieval England. But this mingling of styles can carry other connotations which renew the question of what is meant by Chaucer's realism. According to Bakhtin, linguistic diversity is a mark of the carnivalesque: 'The colloquial and artistic forms are sometimes so closely interwoven that it is difficult to trace a dividing line' (Bakhtin, 1968, p. 153).

The first 19 lines of the poem are an example of just such an interweaving of colloquial and artistic forms. As such, they can be taken as another indication to the poem's audience of its closeness to the carnival mode. They quietly anticipate what is to become thematically significant later on in the work, the particular cultural and ideological allegiances represented by different linguistic styles. Each of the tales tends to gravitate towards one of two models of discourse: those oriented towards the written, learned, 'foreign' modes or those oriented towards the oral, vernacular and 'native' mode. The relations here are particularly complex and derive from the close interaction of oral and written forms in the period. Latin had an established identity as a written language, but was itself spoken by a scholarly and ecclesiastical élite as well as being used in the customary rituals of the Church. Within the existing forms of written Latin, there was a distinction between serious and recreational forms. Moreover, Latin and French, the languages of the court, had their effects on the development of written and spoken English. But there was another kind of interaction at work, too, between the predominantly oral forms of the vernacular and the attempt to establish a literary, written identity for the vernacular. *The Canterbury Tales* emerge out of these diverse interactions and the work can be read as an inventory of the various elements that might make up a written English which could be a differently constituted but equal power to the élite languages of French and Latin. To take stock in this way was not a politically or culturally neutral act. It meant contesting an established hierarchy which gave authority to Latin and French, and to the forms of English modelled on Latin and French style, over the vernacular. It meant giving the status of written language to the vernacular and its associated forms of life, at the same time as writing began to model itself on the provisional and variable character of spoken language. In its character as a text *The Canterbury Tales* seems to hesitate amidst these various possibilities. On the one hand it is a work written to be spoken and it is part of the inherited cultural myth about *The Canterbury Tales* that it is a work of that sort. On the other hand, the narrator can address his audience as readers not listeners as in *The Miller's Prologue*. An amphibious text, then, itself very much in the process of becoming, and, as such, *The Canterbury Tales* is a fertile ground for the emergence of carnivalesque values with their emphasis on the relativity of different perspectives and styles and on the open-ended character of invention.

As the *General Prologue* develops the signs of carnival accumulate, noticeably in the language used to describe the appearance of the pilgrims. Carnival had a distinct sense of the physical body and its relation to the world. Bakhtin referred to this as the 'grotesque concept of the body':

The grotesque image reflects a phenomenon in transformation, an as yet unfinished metamorphosis of death and birth, growth and becoming.... The other indispensable trait is ambivalence. For in this image we find both poles of transformation, the old and the new, the dying and the procreating, the beginning and the end of metamorphosis. (Bakhtin, 1968, p. 24)

And:

The body discloses its essence as a principle of growth which exceeds its own limits only in copulation, pregnancy, child-birth, the throes of death, eating, drinking, or defecation. (ibid., p. 26)

The 'grotesque concept of the body' typically foregrounds certain physical features: the mouth, the nose, the genitals, warts, boils, whatever protrudes from the body or allows entrance to it. It is opposed to the classical concept of the body with its emphasis on the harmony, completion and independence of the physical form. Whatever the classical concept of the body finds disgusting the grotesque affirms and celebrates.

Scholars have done a considerable amount of work on the origins of Chaucer's description of the pilgrims in *The Canterbury Tales*. Some have claimed particular individuals as a model. Others have seen the Prologue as a development of systems of social classification current in medieval Europe. To these two explanations, a third needs to be added: the description of the pilgrims is motivated by a Carnivalesque account of the body. This can be a matter of the way in which particular physical details are selected and described, as in the case of the Miller:

> Upon the cop right of his nose he hade
> A werte, and thereon stood a toft of herys
> Reed as the brustles of a sowes erys
> His nosethirles blake were and wyde.
> A swerd and bokeler bar he by his syde.
> His mouth as greet was as a greet forneys.
> (*Canterbury Tales*, I (A), 554-9)

In this passage the Miller is made up of hyperboles, a typical rhetorical form of carnival. He becomes his nose and mouth, both cardinal features are subject to an extravagant verbal play, a comic revaluation. Excrescence grows out of excresence: the wart grows out of the Miller's nose, and hairs grow out of the wart. These in turn are subject to a fundamental grotesque device—the comparison of the human and the animal—which recall earlier parts of this same description when the Miller's beard is compared in its redness to that of a sow or a fox. The doubling 'greet' in the last line exaggerates the already fantastic comparison between the miller's mouth and a 'forneys' at the same time as it makes a comic image out of hell-fire, a transformation characteristic of carnival in that it takes a threatening emblem from the armoury of official Church culture and reviews it from the perspective of laughter.

The Miller is a carnivalesque figure—a fact more easily recognised by a medieval than a present-day audience. The problem is that that's not all he is. As Jill Mann has argued in her study of the *General Prologue*, Chaucer presents a novel kind of social realism in his description of the pilgrims: each is described as a professional, with a particular history of work or vocation. Each is offered in an interplay of perspectives, such that we see what might be reprehensible or praiseworthy about the pilgrims, but the simple activities of condemnation or approval are suspended because we also see how the pilgrims regard themselves, and more particularly how condemnation from one point of view can become praise from another. The Miller is presented in terms of his work. He gets on by cheating his customers:

> Wel koude he stelen corn and tollen thries;
> And yet he hadde a thombe of gold, pardee.
> (*Canterbury Tales*, I (A), 562-3)

Mann's point would be that this formulation leaves the audience divided between condemning his dishonesty and admiring his worldly success. And this is part of a more general effect:

> The baffling feature of the Prologue ... is how often it weakens our grasp of the truth about a character, even while suggesting that it is somehow at odds with the narrator's enthusiastic praise. (Mann, 1973, p. 195)

How would this kind of reading connect with the carnivalesque mode? One hypothesis is to see the realism that Mann describes as a 'carnival realism'. Weakening our grasp on truth is an effect of carnival in the sense that it opposes dogmatic judgement, the assumption that a person is to be known in terms of a fixed truth. The truths of carnival are the truths of becoming and process which are released in the unfixing of authoritarian judgement and in the overturning of the equation of seriousness with truth. The effect of description in the *General Prologue* creates a sense of the pilgrims as figures in time, moving from definite pasts into possible futures, all characterised by ambivalence: the Knight, *Miles Christianus*, and mercenary; the Prioress caught between religion as spiritual devotion and as genteel erotic romance; and so on. But this may assimilate the styles of carnival and realism too readily. The Miller changes before our eyes from a man who works into a carnival clown; he seems to alternate between the two. This improvised quality, switching from one style to another, indicates the closeness of the General Prologue to oral modes of composition, which do not obey the same laws of consistency and coherence that came to typify written discourse. But this proliferating structure in the *General Prologue* is not just indicative of the cultural origins of the work. It anticipates both the diversity of the stories told by the pilgrims and the question of what kind of relationship will prevail amongst them. Each pilgrim represents a form of life; each gravitates towards one domain or another of medieval culture: the courtly, the pious, the carnivalesque, or some admixture of these. These are so many styles, but not in an exclusively literary sense: we need to extend a sense of style to include allegiance to particular beliefs and an implicit conception of social relations. The narrator's apologies for his failure to observe 'degree' at line 744 of the *General Prologue* can be understood retrospectively: it refers to a pre-existing belief about the relations between the three estates in medieval social theory, and marks Chaucer's departure from a customary presentation of the estates according to degree. But it is also an anticipation of what is to come: the observance of degree is not necessarily going to prevail amongst the pilgrims. And this anticipation is re-inforced by the agreement amongst the pilgrims that they shall play a game. It is this fact rather than 'degree' which shall regulate their relations. The narrator's apologia and the pilgrims' agreement to the game are both indicative of the closeness of the *General Prologue* to the conventions of carnival when, typically, the observation of the customary hierarchy of social ranks is suspended, and replaced by the relative freedom of the game:

> games drew the players out of the bounds of everyday life, liberated them from the usual laws and regulations and replaced established conventions by other lighter conventionalities. (Bakhtin, 1968, p. 235)

Within carnival, Bakhtin argues, the game has the status of a philosophic emblem: 'The images of games were seen as a condensed formula of life and historic process: fortune and misfortune, gain and loss, crowning and uncrowning' (ibid.). And the prize proposed by the Host for the winner of the game is drawn from the provenance of carnival: neither a courtly favour nor a spiritual vision but 'a soper at oure aller cost', the material pleasures of food and drink.

There are further signs of carnival in the *General Prologue* which can only be briefly noted here. The Miller is not the only pilgrim marked out in carnivalesque terms. In her analysis of the *General Prologue*, Jill Mann has described the uniqueness of the Wife of Bath: 'although she has certain traits in common with the vetulae Chaucer presents her as attractive' (Mann, 1973, p. 126). The combination of signs of age and youth in the Wife may point to her individuality. But she is also recognisably a figure from carnival, both in the public boldness of her speech ('laughe and carpe'), and in her appearance which accords with the typical ambivalent features of the grotesque image. Similarly, Chaucer's description of the Monk, 'an outridere, that loved venerie', is informed by the perspective of carnival in this case the importance of banquet imagery to the carnival lexicon:

> In Latin recreational literature of the twelfth and thirteenth centuries, banquet images as well as those linked with procreative force are usually centred around the figure of a monk, portrayed as a drunkard, glutton and lecher. The character of the monk is either complex or intermittent. First, as a devotee of the material bodily life, he sharply contradicts the ascetic ideal he serves. Second, his gluttony represents the parasitism of a sluggard. But third, he also expresses the positive 'shrove' principles of food, drink, procreative force and merriment. The author offer these three aspects concurrently, and it is difficult to say where praise ends and condemnation begins. (Bakhtin, 1968, p. 294)

The devotion to the 'material bodily life', the contradiction of the 'ascetic ideal', the expression of 'the positive shrove principles', the difficulty of knowing where 'praise ends and condemnation begins'; these are all important features of Chaucer's description of the Monk. As with the Miller, not everything can be accounted for in these terms: 'the parasitism of the sluggard' does not seem particularly emphasised in Chaucer's portrait, although it may be, as with other complex cultural forms, that to refer to some aspects of it would bring to mind the whole. But the carnival image is not simply in the background of the Monk's portrait, it is there in the idiom of Chaucer's language, whether in his version of the monk's own comic defiance of the Augustinian monastic ideal—'Let Austyn have his swynk to hym reserved'—or in the fantastical, hyperbolic descriptions of the monk's body, anticipating the subsequent depiction of the Miller:

> His eyen stepe, and rollynge in his heed
> That stemed as a forneys of the leed.
> (*Canterbury Tales* I (A), 201–2)

Puzzling details become explicable once the importance of carnival to the *General Prologue* is acknowledged. Why, for example, does the Summoner have a 'bokeleer' made of 'a cake'? Bakhtin argues that a main feature of carnival logic is its transformation and revaluation of already existing signs (in this context, artefacts have a signifying function). Carnival converts the world into its own terms and it does so by debasing what is lofty, idealistic or threatening into what is comic, festive and carnal. A shield of bread is just such a debasement: the original connotations of the object—with the ideals of war and combat—are mocked, rendered harmless, and revalued by turning a weapon into food. If we add the enormous garland the Summoner wears, the 'bokeler' made of 'a cake' may indicate that he intends to treat the pilgrimage as a carnival. But it should be clear by now that this kind of detail is not remarkable in the *General Prologue*. Taken with the other evidence—and this would include the sounds Chaucer associates with the pilgrims, both the way they speak, but also the sounds of bells, pipes and comic song that attend their gathering—it is clear that the pilgrims converge as much in a spirit of carnival as of other worldly devotion. Certain figures stand out by virtue of their contrast to this context—the silent

Clerk, for example—but it is precisely to the point that they do stand out in this way. At the very least, the carnivalesque potential of the pilgrimage is clearly signalled, whatever other cultural forces may be in play.

How is this potential developed in what follows? Again the evidence is not of a single kind. We can begin with the Miller's drunken intervention after the knight has told his tale:

> The Millere, that for dronken was al pale
> So that unnethe upon his hors he sat
> He nolde avalen neither hood ne hat
> Ne abyde no man for his curteisie,
> But in Pilates voys he gan to crie,
> And swoor, 'By armes, and by blood and bones
> I kan a noble tale for the nones,
> With which I wol now quite the Knyghtes tale.'
>
> (*Canterbury Tales*, I (A), 3120–7)

In his discussion, Alfred David has noted the Miller's refusal of the claims of social hierarchy, and, invoking Bakhtin, commented on the carnivalesque connotations of this moment in *The Canterbury Tales*:

> The Miller in pushing himself to the fore is, therefore, claiming no more than the privilege of the Boy Bishop, the Master of the Feast of Fools, and the Lord of Misrule. By challenging the Knight, the figure of authority, he follows the pattern of medieval comedy. His tale will be outrageous in the same way that the holiday revels were outrageous. Just as in his rudeness, aggressiveness and profanity we can see an inversion of the qualities of the Knight, so the Miller's Tale can be looked at as a burlesque romance inverting the traditional values of feudal society. (David, 1976, pp. 94–5)

This description puts a certain emphasis on the Miller's refusal to recognise his place in the social hierarchy. He is claiming 'no more than the privilege of the Boy Bishop'; the Miller is 'following the pattern of medieval comedy'; his story 'can be looked at as a burlesque romance'. These judgements make the Miller's intervention predictable, part of a pattern in which the rituals of carnival act as a 'safety-valve'. The ruling values of medieval society are strengthened and sustained precisely because they can withstand a temporary inversion. This view of carnival was advanced by writers in the late medieval world, as in the case of a group of French clerics defending the Feast of Fools:

> We do these things in jest and not in earnest, as the ancient custom is, so that once a year the foolishness innate in us can come out and evaporate. Don't wine skins and barrels burst very often if the air-hole is not opened from time to time? We too are old barrels. (Burke, 1978, p. 202)

But the Miller's challenge to the Knight is not simply of this kind. The occasion is not manifestly ritualistic but profane and contingent. As the 'gentels everichoon' are taking particular pleasure in their pleasure at *The Knight's Tale*, the Miller reasserts his identification of the pilgrimage as a time of carnivalesque freedom, and he announces his intention with one of carnival's characteristic speech acts, the blasphemous oath. Social comedy not ritual order predominates as the Host unsuccessfully tries to assert the claims of 'degree'. The Miller ruffles feathers, causes embarrassment, like a fart at a polite dinner-party. After the elaborate, idealised and violent fore-play of the Knight's Tale we are rapidly brought into a carnal world where desire is to be gratified rather than restrained. Again the carnivalesque echoes in the Miller's language are strong as he levels the distinctions between spiritual and profane meanings:

> As housbande shal not been inquisityf
> Of Goddes pryvetee, nor of his wyf.
> (*Canterbury Tales*, I (A), 3163–4)

Alfred David's assertion that the Miller's Tale deploys burlesque romance to invert the 'traditional values of medieval society' begs the question about what are to count as traditional values: those based in the popular, carnivalesque idiom which, as Bakhtin reminds us, have roots in the pre-Christian history of Europe, or those of the feudal hierarchy, the values of Church and Court.

The Miller's Prologue foreshadows other occasions in the *Canterbury Tales* when the pressures of feudal hierarchy are resisted or displaced by carnivalesque values. The Hosts's response to the Pardoner, already quoted in this essay, draws upon the resources of carnival language (*Canterbury Tales*, VI (C), 946–55). The corruption of official Church culture frankly represented by the Pardoner is confronted by a different kind of comic corruption, the representation of sacred symbols in terms of base matter and the body. Three motifs of carnival inform the Hosts's speech: arse-kissing—the substitution of the buttocks for the face, as in *The Miller's Tale*; rending the human body—the Host's threat to castrate the Pardoner's narcissistic and isolate body; and debasement, according to Bakhtin 'the fundamental artistic principle of grotesque realism; all that is sacred and exalted is rethought on the level of the material bodily stratum or else combined and mixed with its images.' (Bakhtin, 1968, pp. 370–1). In this case the sacred relics which the Pardoner sells are debased by the Host into a new carnivalesque form: the Pardoner's testicles become parody relics, 'shryned in an hogges toord'.

The Host's speech reduces the Pardoner to silence. Given the Pardoner's pride in his rhetorical skills, this may be seen as a triumph for the carnivalesque idiom and a refutation of the form of life represented by the Pardoner: narcissistic detachment, the manipulation of beliefs which do not regulate his own actions, and, in particular, the exploitative use of the fear of damnation. The conventional moral gloss on the Pardoner's Tale would have it that we witness the spectacle of a man warning others of damnation who is himself damned. But that is not the Host's response. He does not resist the Pardoner's power by pointing up his spiritual corruption. The Pardoner, both by his presence and by his story, infuses the pilgrimage with the fear of death and damnation. It may, indeed, be that the Host's speech is fuelled by the suspicious fear that the Pardoner is the devil incarnate. However corrupt in himself, his discourse draws upon the authority of the medieval Church and, in order to defend himself against that authority, the Host falls back on the language of carnival.

The carnivalesque framing of the Pardoner's Tale is elaborated by what follows the quarrel between the Host and the Pardoner. The narrative persepctive drifts and we become aware of the quarrel itself as a comic spectacle, when the Knight intervenes:

> But right anon the worthy Knyght bigan
> When that he saugh that al the peple lough
> Namore of this, for it is right ynough
> . . .
> And, as we diden, let us laughe and pleye.
> (*Canterbury Tales*, VI (C), 960–2, 967)

The formula, 'laughe and pleye', echoes the pilgrims' earlier reaction to the Miller's Tale, and points up a tendency in the *Canterbury Tales* to absorb moments of ideological and personal antagonism into collective laughter. The combination of the Host's abuse and the pilgrims' laughter effectively carnivalise both the Pardoner and his Tale.

A parallel process is at work in the case of the Clerk. In the General Prologue he is described in terms which recall the symbolic antithesis of the carnival spirit:

> A CLERK ther was of Oxenford also,
> That unto logyk hadde long ygo.
> As leene was his hors as is a rake
> And he was not right fat, I undertake
> But looked holwe and thereto sobrely.
>
> (*Canterbury Tales*, I (A), 285-9)

As with the other pilgrims, the Clerk cannot be reduced to the terms of a single discourse, but the language here resonates with the associations of the Lenten figure in the carnival procession. The opposition between carnival and Lent was a structural principle of the carnival world, indicating, as it did, the struggle between the popular and official cultures of medieval Europe:

> According to the law of the Church, Lent was a time of fasting and abstinence—of abstinence not only from meat but from eggs, sex, play-going and other recreations. Hence it was natural to represent Lent as emaciated (the very word 'Lent' means 'lean-time'), as a kill-joy, associated with the cold-blooded creations of the Lenten diet. (Burke, 1978, p. 188)

These preliminary associations of the Clerk with the figure of Lent are developed in the ensuing description: we are told about his books and learning—the fact that he owns books at all makes him a remarkable, even exotic, figure—and the narrator intimates that the Clerk uses his religious authority instrumentally, as a means of funding his scholarship. He is verbally reticent in contrast to the carnivalesque culture 'of the loud word spoken in the open' and when he does speak his language is 'short and quyk and ful of hy sentence'. The Clerk's speech is noteworthy because, in its formality and concentration, it reflects his immersion in a culture of the written word. In this case the writing was in Latin and the implications of this kind of relation to language have been analysed by W. J. Ong:

> It would appear likely that a textualized, chirographically controlled language such as learned Latin aided greatly in establishing the distance between observer and observed, between the knower and the known that science and especially modern science required. No longer a mother tongue, learned Latin left all its users free of the rich, emotional unconscious but often confusingly subjective involvements of a language learned orally from infancy. (Ong, 1984, p. 9)

The Clerk bears all the ambivalent character traits of such a learnedness. The prestige attached to his ownerhip of books, the distinctiveness of his restrained and formal speech, make him at the same time an orphan, distanced from the resources of his mother-tongue: his status is bound up with his relation to language and this relation sets him apart from the popular and vernacular forces at work in the pilgrimage.

The Clerk's tale sustains his initial presentation as a figure opposed to carnival. This is true whether we read it as a covert form of preaching about the relationship between Christians and their God or about the proper role of women in marriage. The story carries messages about the importance of submission and suffering which were characteristic of the official teaching of the medieval Church. But the opposition to carnival is more than doctrinal. It consists, as well, in the story as a form of imagination and with the conceptions of the world embedded in that form. There is, for example, an erotic fascination with suffering, encoded in the repeated motif of the stripping and dressing of Griselda. She becomes the vehicle for imaginary humiliations even greater than those she undergoes in the events of the story:

> The remenant of your jueles redy be
> Inwith your chambre, dar I saufly sayn.
> 'Naked out of my fadres hous,' quod she,
> 'I cam and naked moot I turne agayn.
> Al youre plesance wod I folwen fayn;
> But yet I hope it be not youre entente
> That I smoklees out of youre paleys wente.

> Ye koude not doon so dishonest a thyng,

That thilke wombe in which youre children leye,
Sholde inform the peple, in my walkyng,
Be seyn al bare; wherefore I yow preye,
Let me not lyk a worm go by the weye.
(*Canterbury Tales*, 4 (E). 869–80)

The spectacle of the victim negotiating the terms of her degradation no doubt intensifies the pleasure. The passage is a classic instance of the logic of negation, entertaining the very circumstance it purports to deny: Griselda repeatedly presents the possibility of her nakedness in order to remain clothed.

This is an other-worldly sensuality, the eroticism of Christianity, which is permitted but hardly explained by the virtuous recourse to an allegorical interpretation of the story. It reminds us that the cultural power of Christianity resides in the forms of pleasure that it offers as well as in its claim to truth. Carnival offers a contrasting version of both. Griselda's humiliations are visited upon her by a higher authority; her erotic pathos anticipates, if it is not already identical with, the structures of sadistic sexuality. Carnival enjoys humiliation too, as we have seen in the Host's response to the Pardoner. But what is humiliated is established authority, or the claim to possess it. Pleasure derives from what Bakhtin calls a comic 'uncrowning' of authority, not from an intensification of the sufferings of the victim.

This difference is connected to others. In the *Canterbury Tales*, carnivalesque humiliation is directed towards men: John in *The Miller's Tale*, Symkyn in *The Reeve's Tale*, January in *The Merchant's Tale*, Peter in *The Shipman's Tale*—all are variants of a familiar carnival figure, the cuckold or the senex, and they also point to the critical role played by women in carnival:

Womanhood is shown in contrast to the limitations of her partner; she is foil to his avarice, jealousy, stupidity, hypocrisy, bigotry, sterile senility, false heroism and abstract idealism.... She represents in person the undoing of pretentiousness, of all that is finished, completed, and exhausted. (Bakhtin, 1968, p. 240)

In *The Clerk's Tale*, by contrast, it is the woman who suffers and, whatever latent sympathy there may be for Griselda, she does not represent 'in person' a critical foil to Walter's masculine authority. In *The Second Nun's Tale*, there is a parallel fascination with the suffering of women at the hands of men and with its transcendent justification. The lengthy description of St Cecile's martyrdom provides the relevant evidence (*Canterbury Tales*, 8 (G), 519–53). Given the whole context of *The Canterbury Tales* and the running opposition within it between the carnival culture and the official culture of Christianity, *The Clerk's Tale* and *The Second Nun's Tale* represent the official discourse in which speech and gesture are characterised by 'the pitifully serious tones of supplication, lament, humility and piousness' as well as 'the menacingly serious tones of intimidation, threats, prohibition' (Bakhtin, 1968, p. 38). Implicit in these tones is the simultaneous hatred and idealisation of woman.

The Clerk's Tale is a paradigm of the official culture in another crucial respect. A hint is given by the narrator when he refers in the *General Prologue* to the Clerk's 'Twenty bookes, clad in blak or reed, of Aristotle and his philosophy'. I have argued that this information about the Clerk's culture can be connected to the restrained and formal character of his speech, but his devotion to Aristotle points to another feature of the Clerk's relation to language. Aristotelean philosophy was on one side of a long-standing debate about the relation between language and reality:

An important assumption of both Platonic and Aristoltelian positions ... was that ideas represented by signs were eternal, while the spoken utterances by which we know them were bound by time. For the philosophers such ideas always stood in purely logical relationship to each other, no matter how imprecise were the forces of expression used to describe them. For the rhetoricians, on the other hand, life, or rather life informed by texts, was always providing the raw material for new interpretations; and it was experience, rather than presuppositions, to which language was ultimately referred. ... As a consequence in the rhetorical strategy, the actual was not invariably understood in terms of the ideal; instead, the acting out, in speech, gesture, or concrete action, gave meaning to the present. (Stock, 1984, p. 28).

The narrator's presentation of the Clerk in the *General Prologue* indicates that he is on the Aristotelean and Platonic side of the debate about the relation between language and reality. He is an other-worldly presence communing with the unchanging truths of eternity and empowered to do so by a technique of interpretation, allegorical reading, which was very much the preserve but not the exclusive domain of the learned clergy. Allegorical reading is the technique which can reveal the eternal truths through the time-bound and fluctuating forms of language. Unsurprisingly the Clerk tells a story which can be interpreted in exactly this way: the marriage of Walter and Griselde figures an eternal truth about the proper relations between Christians and their God. But, as I have already suggested, this reading through the time-bound contexts of the story is also a means of reading away from other meanings in the story: its compulsive misogyny and sadistic sexuality. And the general question of the meaning of *The Clerk's Tale* becomes a part of the comic drama of its conclusion. The Clerk supplies a contorted interpretation of his tale which at first seeks to deflect the accusation of misogyny:

> This storie is seyd, nat for that wyves sholde
> Folowen Grisilde as in humylitee.
> (*Canterbury Tales*, 4 (E), 1142–3)

He then turns to a broad allegorical interpretation which subordinates the implication of gender: men and women alike should behave as Griselde because this is the path of the true Christian. But the Clerk cannot let go of that part of his traditional authority which consists in castigating women as especially sinful and failing in their duty. The point is made nostalgically:

> It were ful hard to fynde now-a-dayes
> In al a toun Grisildis thre or two,
> (*Canterbury Tales*, 4 (E), 1164–5).

But in the end he is obliged to concede that the authority of his story resides as much in the way it is understood by his audience as in its appeal to any eternal truths of Christian doctrine. He moves away from what Stock (1984) describes as the philosophical view toward a more fluid, social and rhetorical conception of language. He does this first by acknowledging the authority of the Wife of Bath, and then by breaking into song (*Canterbury Tales* 4 (E), 1169–76). In choosing to 'stynte of ernestful matere' the Clerk has, however provisionally, moved some way from his initial identification with 'hy sentence'. His song is an extravagant praise of women and concedes their authority. But in making this sudden transition from the misogynistic implication of his story to the praise of women in his song the Clerk joined the carnival world which he initially opposed. The transition from praise to abuse, abuse to praise, is described by Bakhtin as central to the logic and rhythm of carnival, one of the means by which it unfixes static judgements and counterposes them to the truths of relativity and becoming. The Clerk is carnivalised by the pilgrimage and, in the process, he moves from one discursive world to another.

III

As with other canonical works, critical interpretation of *The Canterbury Tales* is fuelled by nostalgia. Amongst some critics the tales are read as Christian art, committed to the celebration of transcendent and unchanging forms and showing the emergence of these truths through the skilful orchestration of various forms of medieval narrative. Or, as in the criticism of Jill Mann (1973) and Gabriel Josipovici (1971), Chaucer is presented as a sceptical intellectual testing the representational adequacy of the conventions at his disposal. One consequence of the fragmentary nature of *The Canterbury Tales* is their peculiar openness to critical rewriting. My own discussion is no doubt similarly motivated, but the nostalgia has a different goal, for a popular and materialist radicalism which can redescribe the world through the powers of democratic comedy. I have sketched some of the evidence for this view. A great deal more could be added, including, for example, an analysis of the narrator which would show how the passive narrator of Chaucer's early dream poems is changed in *The Canterbury Tales* into a carnivalesque figure, a prototype of the popular narrator who 'is one with the crowd; he does not present himself as its opponent, nor does he teach, accuse or intimidate it' (Bakhtin, 1968, p. 167). Reading *The Canterbury Tales* as carnival enables us to see the interaction between stylistic and formal features of the text and social practice. We are given a sustained literary realisation of voices largely unheard in medieval literature before *The Canterbury Tales*. These voices come not from the Church or the Court but from the unofficial worlds of medieval culture, from the market-place, from the tavern, from domestic life. In the special world of the pilgrimage these voices interact freely with the established authorities of medieval culture. Those authorities are interrupted, defied and questioned by the forces of popular comedy. Of course, we cannot know what the outcome of this interaction might have been, because of the fragmentary nature of the tales. Equally there are sustained examples of official discourse within the work: notably in *The Parson's Tale*, that long slab of homily whose doctrinal intentions are defeated by the greater power of sheer tedium. To read such a work as the significant conclusion to *The Canterbury Tales* is to mistake an act of suppression for an act of resolution. What is suppressed are the voices of carnival. What is also suppressed is the emergent project of *The Canterbury Tales*. In writing about Rabelais, Bakhtin notes that:

> By the end of the Middle Ages a gradual disappearance of the dividing line between humour and great literature can be observed. The lower genres begin to penetrate the higher levels of literature ... official seriousness and fear could be abandoned even in everyday life. (Bakhtin, 1968, p. 97)

A parallel process is at work in *The Canterbury Tales*. Lodged in a world which was ostensibly attached to hierarchy and its manifold religious and social rituals, *The Canterbury Tales* develops a contrary set of values based upon an individual and collective freedom of speech. For the first time in the history of English writing we find a work which offers a model of secular, social freedom, one that is of continuing value.

References

All references to *The Canterbury Tales* are taken from *The Works of Geoffrey Chaucer*, ed. F. N. Robinson (Oxford University Press, 2nd edn 1957).

Critical and Historical Texts

Bakhtin, M. (1968) *Rabelais and his World*, tr. H. Iswolsky (Cambridge, Mass.: MIT Press).

Burke, P. (1978) *Popular Culture in Early Modern Europe* (London: Temple Smith).

David, A. (1976) *The Strumpet Muse* (Bloomington: Indiana University Press).

Josipovici, G. (1971) *The World and the Book* (London: Macmillan).
Mann, J. (1973) *Chaucer and Medieval Estates Satire* (Cambridge: Cambridge University Press).
Ong, W. J. (1984) 'Orality, Literacy and Medieval Textualization', *New Literary History*, vol. 16, Autumn pp. 1–11.
Stock, B. (1984) 'Medieval Literacy, Linguistic Theory, and Social Organization', *New Literary History*, vol. 16, Autumn pp. 13–29.

10

John Skelton: Finding a Voice—
Notes after Bakhtin

Bernard Sharratt

Alexander Pope in 1737 glossed 'Skelton' thus: 'Poet Laureat to Hen. 8. a Volume of whose Verses has been lately reprinted, consisting almost wholly of Ribaldry, Obscenity, and Billingsgate Language'.[1] If, in a changed cultural climate, Pope's acid summary might actually induce curious readers to sample the recent Penguin edition of *The Complete English Poems*[2] of John Skelton, they might indeed alight upon some Billingsgate language:

> Now Garnyche, garde thy gummys;
> My serpentins and my gunnys
> Agenst ye now I bynde;
> Thy selfe therfore defende.
> Thou tode, thow scorpyon,
> Thow bawdy babyone,
> Thow bere, thow brystlyd bore,
> Thou Moryshe mantycore,
> Thou rammysche, stynkyng gote
> Thou fowle, chorlyshe parote,
> Thou gresly gargone glaymy ...
> (*Agenst Garnesche*, p. 128)

But are just as likely to encounter, say,

> *Moderata juvant* but *toto* dothe exede;
> Dyscrecion ys modyr of nobyll vertues all;
> *Myden agan* in Grekys tonge we rede,
> But reason and wytte wantythe theyr provynciall,
> When wylfulnes ys vicar generall.

'*Hec res acu tangitur*, Parrott, *par ma foye—*'
'*Tycez-vous*, Parrott, *tenes-vous coye*.'
(*Speke Parott*, p. 232)

And a preliminary flip through the substantial volume will reveal 150 pages of densely elucidatory notes, 50 pages of 'Select Glossary', and—even more off-putting—the regular inclusion of French, Latin and Greek passages within the 'English' poems themselves. Since, moreover, Skelton falls into a peculiar critical abyss—a poet of uncertain status awkwardly straddling convenient periodisations—the initial problem, it might seem, is not to encourage any fashionable *re*-reading of Skelton but simply to get him read at all.

Yet it may be that the initially deterrent effect of multilingualism itself suggests a framework within which we can approach this unfamiliar writer, finding in his work a considerable overlap with some contemporary critical concerns.

Languages in Crisis

In the mid-thirteenth century Roger Bacon assumed that an educated Englishman should speak English, French and Latin '*sicut maternum in qua natus est*'. Two centuries later, the proto-Puritan, William Turner, sourly complained that some contemporary writers 'writ so french Englishe and so latine that no man except he be both a latin man, a french man and also an englishe man shalbe able to vnderstande their writinge'.[3] Whereas in the fourteenth century Gower's three major works are each written in a different language (*Confessio Amantis* in English; *Vox Clamantis* in Latin; *Speculum Meditantis* in French), by the late sixteenth century 'English' had been consolidated as the obvious medium of English poets, however extensively later poets were still to write also in Latin (Donne, Jonson, Marvell, Milton). Yet 'English' long remains a problematic term: in 1490, England's first printer, William Caxton, in his Preface to his own translation of a French translation of the *Aeneid*, noted not only that 'comyn englysshe that is spoken in one shyre varyeth from another', but that in seeking 'to vse olde and homely termes' in his translations, the 'englysshe' in the 'olde bokes' he consulted was 'so rude and brood that I coude not wele vnderstande it', 'it was more lyke to dutche than englysshe' (Aurner, 1965, pp. 286–7).

In that same Preface by Caxton we find the first public mention of Skelton:

> But I praye mayster John Skelton late created poete laureate in the vnyuersite of oxenforde to ouersee and correcte this sayd booke. ... For hym I knowe for suffycyent to expowne and englysshe euery dyffyculte that is therin/ For he hath late translated the epystlys of Tulle/ and the boke of dyodorus syculus. and diuerse other werkes oute of latyn in to englysshe not in rude and olde langage. but in polysshed and ornate termes craftely.

Skelton's translation of Cicero's *Familiar Letters* is lost, and his version of Diodorus Siculus (not directly from Greek but from the Italian Poggio's Latin translation) remained in manuscript until 1950, when its editors remarked that the translation employs '816 words ... he there used fifty, seventy-five, one hundred, and even three hundred years before the first use of these words ... recorded in the *OED*', in addition to the 640 'first' instances already credited to him. Skelton's impressive total of perhaps 1500 'first' usages is, in part, a matter of his coinciding with what the *OED* regards as the 'normalisation' of English in the sixteenth century, and in particular the consolidation of 'London' English as a national standard, at least for literary purposes, displacing the previous situation of comparative parity, and of formidable diversity of vocabulary, grammar and spelling systems, as between, say, Langland, the *Gawain* poet and Chaucer.[4] Skelton's work comes at the very beginning of recognisably 'modern' English, as it takes its place in that privileged London literary—linguistic 'line' from Chaucer to Shakespeare; while at the same time it straddles and deliberately juxtaposes a variety of other classical and colloquial registers.

It is Mikhail Bakhtin's work which may enable us to understand more precisely this historical location and condition of Skelton's work, and to recognise more fully the peculiar nature of his achievement, though this essay can only provide mere pointers to a Bakhtinian 're-reading'.[5]

Aspects of Bakhtin

Trilingualism fascinated Bakhtin. He constantly returns to the emergence of 'Latin' literature itself in the work of

> all the translator-stylisers who had come to Rome from lower Italy, where the boundaries of three languages and cultures intersected with one another—Greek, Oscan and Roman.... This literature was born in the interanimation of three languages—one that was indigenously its own, and two that were other but that were *experienced* as indigenous.' (p. 63)

This initiating confluence is indeed, for Bakhtin, a special case of the general condition of all language; the intimate interanimation of 'languages', of *polyglossia* and *heteroglossia*. What concerns Bakhtin is not only Greek Oscan Roman (or Latin French English) but 'the language of the cadet, the high-school student, the trade-school student; 'every age group has its own language, its own vocabulary, its own particular accentual system'; 'even languages of the day exist: today's and yesterday's socio-ideological and political "day" do not, in a certain sense, share the same language: every day represents another socio-ideological semantic "state of affairs."'

> At any given moment of its historical existence, language is heteroglot from top to bottom: it represents the co-existence of socio-ideological contradictions between the present and the past, between differing epochs of the past, between different socio-ideological groups in the present, between tendencies, schools, circles and so forth, all given a bodily form. (p. 291)

Bakhtin's emphasis allows him to assert afresh an insight of Ferdinand Bruno, the historian of the French language:

> the very attempt of the Renaissance to establish the Latin language in all its classical purity inevitably transformed it into a dead language. It was impossible to sustain the classical Ciceronian purity of language while using it in the course of everyday life.... The re-establishment of a classically pure Latin restricted its area of application to essentially the sphere of stylization alone.... At the same time classical Latin illuminated the face of medieval Latin. This face, as it tured out, was hideous; but this face could only be seen in the light of classical Latin. (p. 80)

It is through this double disqualification that a contemporary 'vernacular' can assume an independent stature. For Bakhtin the

Renaissance moment of transition to national *vernacular* standards is one crucial instance of the repeated, permanent 'struggle between two tendencies in the languages of European peoples: one a centralizing (unifying) tendency, the other a decentralizing tendency (that is, one that stratifies languages)' (p. 67). Out of that moment, the modern 'novel' emerges:

> The literary-artistic consciousness of the modern novel, sensing itself on the border between two languages, one literary, the other extra-literary, each of which now knows heteroglossia, also senses itself on the border of time: it is extraordinarily sensitive to time in language (p. 67)

One thinks of Skelton's 1500 'new' words.

What characterises the 'novel' (for Bakhtin a much wider term than in normal usage) is polyphony, double-voicedness, the dialogical use of 'languages': 'every novel is a dialogized system made up of the images of "languages", styles and consciousnesses that are concrete and inseparable from language' (p. 49).

> Heteroglossia, once incorporated into the novel (whatever the form of its incorporation), is *another speech in another's language*, serving to express authorial intentions but in a refracted way. It serves two speakers at the same time and expresses simultaneously two different intentions: the direct intention of the character who is speaking, and the refracted intention of the author. In such discourse there are two voices, two meanings, and two expressions. And all the while these two voices are dialogically related; ... it is as if they actually hold a conversation with each other. Double-voiced discourse is always internally dialogized. (p. 324)

It is time to return to Skelton. A detailed Bakhtinian reading of his whole *oeuvre* is beyond the scope of this essay, but by juxtaposing these and other passages from Bakhtin with some introductory comments on Skelton's poems, I hope to suggest fruitful ways of 'reading' this body of work produced on the very brink of the English 'Renaissance'.

Skelton at Court

Skelton was born about 1460, probably graduated from Cambridge in 1480, and in 1488 received the title of 'Laureate' (indicating qualifications in Rhetoric) from Oxford. The same year he entered royal service at the Court of the recently victorious Henry VII, and throughout the 1490s was apparently tutor to Prince Arthur and Prince Henry. In that capacity he wrote a brief handbook of advice for princes (*Speculum Principis*; first published in 1934) and several pedagogical works (now lost), including a Grammar. But by 1502 Arthur was dead, and Skelton seems to have been retired as tutor, becoming Rector of Diss, a country parish near Norwich. Despite pleading overtures when Henry VIII succeeded to the throne in 1509, Skelton did not return to Court office until 1513, when he assumed the title Orator Regius. His contemporaries and acquaintances included More, Erasmus, Wyatt and Surrey as well as such figures as Stephen Hawes, Alexander Barclay and Dunbar. He died in 1529, just as the issue of the King's divorce broke surface and with it the beginnings of the Henrican Reformation.[6]

Thus, after his academic years of scholarship and translating, Skelton spent two periods at Court, with a spell as a country vicar between, and some of his poems can clearly be linked to these different social environments. The Court poems from both periods include some obviously 'official' pieces, in Latin and English, celebrating military victories, lamenting royal deaths and castigating national enemies. He also wrote a competent and substantial Morality play, *Magnyfycence*,[7] for the court's edification and, for the King's amusement, contributed scathing diatribes to a number of 'flytings', *Against Dundas* and *Agenst Garnesche* (quoted earlier)—the Billingsgate language of each outburst against Garnesche is concluded with 'By the kyngys most noble commaundemennt'. But the most intriguing of his Court poems is itself a critique of court life, bringing together, and freshly enlivening, a number of long-conventional satiric devices.

*The Bouge of Court** was written *c.* 1498, at Henry VII's court. Skelton uses the dream convention to dramatise a nightmare of court intrigue. The dreamer, and victim, is a persona but one not easily distinguished from Skelton: a man of learning, a scholar, somewhat marginal to the court, neither lord nor administrator, neither soldier nor prelate; his position makes him both vulnerable and, perhaps, potentially powerful. He is aboard the

*Bouge; rations or reward.

Ship of Court (and of fools?) and his name is significant: Drede—dread, fear, uncertainty, unsureness. Yet at first there is nothing specific to be afraid of; on the contrary, the other courtiers seem only too friendly. But if their names, and their number—seven: Favell (flattery), Suspycyon, Hervy Hafter (swindler), Disdayne, Ryote, Dyssymulation and Disceyte—do not warn us, what they say should. First, Flavell to Drede:

> Ye be an apte man, as ony can be founde
> To dwell with us and serve my ladyes grace.
> Ye be to her, yea, worth a thousande pounde.
> I herde her speke of you within shorte space,
> Whan there were dyverse that sore dyde you manace.
> And, though I say it, I was myselfe your frende,
> For here be dyverse to you that be unkynde.
> …
> Farewell tyll soone. But no word that I sayde:
>
> (155–61, 175)

But then Drede overhears this same Favell speaking with Suspycyon:

> 'In fayth,' quod Suspecte, 'spake Drede no worde of me?'
> 'Why? What than? Wylte thou lete men to speke?
> He sayth he can not well accorde with the.'
> 'Twyst,' quod Suspecte, 'goo playe; hym I ne reke!'
> 'By Cryste,' quod Favell, 'Drede is soleyne freke!
> What, lete us holde him up, man, for a whyle.'
> 'Ye, soo,' quod Suspecte, 'he may us bothe begyle.'
>
> (183–9)

Yet Suspycyon's first words to Drede are:

> 'Ye remembre the gentylman ryghte nowe
> That commaunde with you, me thought, a praty space?
> Beware of him, for I make God avowe,
> He wyll begyle you and speke fayre to your face.
> Ye never dwelte in suche an other place,
> For here is none that dare well other truste;
> But I wolde telle you a thynge, and I durste.
>
> Spake he, a fayth, no worde to you of me?
> I wote, and he dyde, he wolde me telle.
>
> (197–205)

After this Hervy Hafter sidles up, with some even more intricate advice, before going off for a whispered conversation with Disdayne, who then comes over to Drede and angrily accuses him:

> 'Remembresthou what thou sayd yesternyght?
> Wylt thou abyde by the wordes agayne?
>
> (323–4)

Although Disdayne and Drede have not met before, Disdayne is claiming that Drede said something to him (or to someone else) the previous night and that Disdayne knows about it and resents it; but what it is that Drede is alleged to have said neither he nor the reader ever discovers. Dyssymulation further increases this sense of paranoid backstairs whispering and tale-bearing, while (of course) deploring it to Drede. The climax comes when Disceyte slinks up to Drede with yet more obscure messages, rumours and reports, culminating in a veiled warning that Drede is in great danger (512–25). At this Drede finally loses whatever courage he has left:

> And as he rounded thus in myne ere
> Of false collusyon confetryd by assente,
> Me thoughte I see lewde felawes here and there
> Came for to slee me of mortall entente.
> And as they came, the shypborde faste I hente
> And thoughte to lepe; and even with that woke,
> Caught penne and ynke, and wroth this lytell boke.
>
> (526–32)

What Skelton is presenting, dramatising, in the poem is the complex and threatening atmosphere of a court in which the main weapon against others is language itself, a bewildering cross-current of speech and alleged speech, rumour and accusation, calumny and lying. Caught at the centre of these whirlpools of half-understood whisperings and overheard plottings, Drede's nerve finally cracks. By the end of the poem he is no longer sure of what has been said about him, or to whom, or even what he has said himself. Any move he makes may be misinterpreted; any ally he finds might be betraying him behind his back; any advice he trusts may be a device to ensare him. He opts out. He simply leaps over the side, in an act of suicide—and thereby wakes up.

But the leap is a curious one: he jumps out of his dream, but only to awaken, presumably, in the same kind of court situation that the poem has depicted. The poet, like Drede, is a courtier too. And the final stanza makes it clear that in the real court of Henry VII language is similarly open to interpretation and misinterpretation; words remain weapons, and the poem itself may be used against him.

> I wolde therwith no man were myscontente;
> Besechynge you that shall it see or rede,
> In every poynte to be indyfferente,
> Syth all in substaunce of slumbrynge doth procede.
> I wyll not saye it is mater in dede,
> But yet oftyme suche dremes be founde trewe.
> Now constrewe ye what is the resydewe.

> (533–9)

Skelton here is beginning to explore what will become a central problem for him: how, as a poet, he can use words to tell the truth in a situation where words are dangerous weapons, even for their user. And he has done so in a form which closely matches Bakhtin's notion of the dialogic novel. Not only is much of the poem constructed in actual dialogues, but the interanimation of distinct 'voices' creates a double structure: at one level, a conspiracy of courtiers converging upon a central protagonist, Drede; at another, a decentred series of implicit relations between the seven deadly courtiers themselves, in which each is both practitioner and victim of his own and others' characteristic courtly vices. The resulting narrative is genuinely 'novelistic', in Bakhtin's extended sense.

Three 'Love' Poems

In his study of humanism and poetry at the court of Henry VIII, H. A. Mason offers a comparison between 'the delicacy of Wyatt's poise' and the 'ludicrous attempt' in Skelton's 'The auncient acquaintance, madam, betwen us twayn', 'to preserve a courtly tone of politeness' (Mason, 1959, p. 189). Yet if we read the poem (p. 42), in a Bakhtinian rather than Leavisite frame of mind, it is certainly not an 'attempt to preserve a courtly tone of politeness' on the poet's part that will strike us, but rather the sharp and deliberately humorous clash between the 'refined' Latinate vocabulary and over-polite tones of the first two stanzas and the colloquial, sexually-charged 'horsey' (or whore-sy?) terms and rhythms of the succeeding stanzas. It is the very excess of involvement with 'madam's' sexual energies, registered in the language, that retrospectively turns the satire against the speaker. It is curdled jealousy and wounded lust, not moral indignation or sympathy for an abused husband, that really speaks: the 'I' has also been 'your old, trew, loving knyght' (another horseman) in that 'former dalyaunce', and we find ourselves registering the ornate compliments of the opening as barely concealed inducements to join in the imagined orgies to come, while the violence of the 'jentyll' husband disposes us to side with the pleasure-seeking wife and finally to concur with the advise to her, not to abstain from but simply to conceal more effectively ('warke more secretly') her affairs. The opening and closing tones of the poem are destabilised and subverted by the explosion of a quite 'other' language at the centre of the poem, yet, noticeably, that language is itself another 'language' of the 'I' in which is imagined the lusty cries of 'madam' and her lovers. In the relation between these two languages there is even an echo of today's officers' mess: that revealing combination of, and sudden slide between, refinement and rectitude, chauvinist crudity and brutality, which perhaps always shadows the overt codes of 'knightly' chivalry.

In 'Manerly Margery Mylk and Ale' (p. 35), as Stanley Fish has argued (1965, 11. 42–6), we need to insert quotation marks at various points to establish the contributions of two speakers, in a dialogue of a traditional kind between 'serving maid' and 'clerk'. But in order to distribute the lines confidently we probably need a finer aural discrimination between fifteenth-century social languages than present knowledge allows. Or, quite plausibly, Skelton has deliberately constructed a poem which allows a variety of possible dialogical performances, a variable orchestrating not only of overt sexual responses but also of male—female power relations. (Some medieval poems can be punctuated variously to yield either a social 'complaint' or a utopian celebration.) But certainly the play of the poem is the effect of a constant relay between 'languages' which gives 'bodily shape' to the relations between two interacting social representatives in a dramatic present, while the refrain may well add a third 'voice', in a coarsely earthy idiom which can be appropriated by either speaker or by the narrating poet.

'My darlyng dere' (p. 41) offers a more complex play between languages and attitudes, since the opening refrain,

> With 'lullay, lullay,' lyke a chylde,
> Thou slepyst to long, thou art begylde!

deploys a register of affectionate gentleness that the poem initially sustains in the lovers' dialogue, only to undermine it, remorselessly ending with an explicit address by the narrating voice that wholly punctures the superficially sympathetic tones of the rest:

> What dremyst thou, drunchard, drousy pate?
> Thy lust and lykyng is from the gone;
> Thou blynkerd blowboll, thou wakyst to late;
> Behold, thou lyeste, luggard, alone! ...
> I wys, powle hachet, she bleryd thyne I!

In their use of distinctly 'low' language and vivid ventriloquism, these poems may be linked with 'Womanhod, wanton, ye want' (p. 40), addressed to 'Mastres Anne' who lived at 'The Key' in Thames Street (an inn? a brothel?), and the marvellously rumbustious and rightly famous 'the Tunnyng of Elynour Rummynge' (p. 214). To move from these to, say, the ornate elegance of 'Knowledge, aquayntance, resort, favour, with grace' (p. 43) or the finely poised tributes to the ladies of the Howard family, in 'The Garlande of Laurell' (pp. 335–43), is to realise the range of social languages Skelton could deploy within his verse, the potential for linguistic interanimation available to him.

Church poems

One crucial social language was that of the Church, and a number of the poems after Skelton's ordination, in 1498, are relatively straightforward in their parodic and goliardic use of ecclesiastical Latin and liturgical phrasing. The 'Devoute Trentale for old John Clarke, sometyme the holy patriarke of Dis' (p. 106) records, for example, that:

In parochia de dis	In the parish of Diss
Non erat sibi similis	Was no one like this
In malicia vir insignis	A man renowned for malice
Duplex corde et bilinguis	Fork-tongued and treacherous
Senio confectus	Consumed by senility
Omnibus suspectus	Mistrusted by everybody
Nemini dilectus.	Beloved by nobody
Sepultus est amonge the wedes	Buried he is among the weeds
God forgeve hym his mysdedes.	God forgive him his misdeeds.

And so on, for 90 lines! Adam Uddersale, 'the holy bailiff of Dis', is given a similarly 'devout' epitaph. But the interplay between liturgy and satire is less easy to decipher in two major poems 'Philip Sparrow' and 'Ware the Hawk'.

The ostensible situation in 'Ware the Hawk' is simple enough: a 'lewde curate, A parson benyfyced' has been discovered by Skelton exercising his hunting hawks within the church at Diss and the poem is (apparently) an all-out attack on this dastardly sacrilege. A picture of sheer mayhem is conjured up: one hawk devours a pigeon on the altar itself; a second perches on the rood loft, is enticed down with meat and bludgeoned into insensibility; the parson threatens to bring his hounds in and chase foxes through the sanctuary; he overturns

>   my offerynge box,
> Boke, bell and candyll,
> All that he myght handyll;
> Cros, staffe, lectryne and banner,
> Fell downe on thys manner.
>
>   (111–15)

A slanging-match follows in which the parson

>   wysshed withall
> That the dowves donge downe myght fall
> Into my chalys at mas,
> When consecrated was
> The blessyd sacrament
>
>   (182–6)

Skelton finally takes it upon himself to castigate this polluter of holy places, in an extraordinary rhetorical diatribe:

> Of no tyrand I rede,
> That so far dyd excede;
> Neither yet Dyoclesyan,
> Nor yet Domysyan;
> Nother crokyd Cacus,
> Nor yet dronken Bacus
> Nother Olybryus,
> Nor Dyonysyus;
> Nother Phalary,
> Rehersyd in Valery,
> Nor Sardanapall,
> Unhappyest of all;
> Nor Nero the worst,
> Nor Clawdyus the curst;

and so on, ending with:

>   nor the Turke,
> Wrought never such a worke,
> For to let their hawkys fly
> In the church of Saynt Sophy;
> With moch matter more
> That I kepe in store.
>
>   (190–221)

Given that Skelton must have known of the actual plundering of St Sophia when the Turks took Constantinople in 1453, this final assertion that at least they didn't fly hawks in the place (they merely slaughtered several thousand Christians) is the last straw in this crazy catalogue of comparative (and often madly inappropriate) outrage.

By this stage our composite image of Skelton spluttering and fulminating amidst the wreckage of his church, with bloodied hawks flying around, foxes leaping for cover, pigeons shitting in the chalice, is surely irresistibly funny. And the final section of the poem takes the absurdities even further, with a ludicrous Latin cryptogram (which defied decipherment till 1896) which the parson (and the baffled reader?) is ridiculed for not understanding! The culminating accusation might well be turned against Skelton himself:

> This dowtless ye ravyd
> Dys church ye thus depravyd; ...

Quare? Quia evangelia	Why? Because the holy gospels
Concha et conchelia	The vestments and the vessels
Accipiter et sonalia	The hunter and its bells
Et bruta animalia	And senseless animals
Cetera quoque talia	And everything else too
Tibi sunt equalia.	Are all the same to you.

(307–16)

The effect of this extraordinary organisation of rhetorical ploys is to make us laugh at the exaggerated inappropriateness and extravagance of Skelton's cantankerous reaction—all this because a hawk was exercised in his church! And yet, precisely within the framework of a deeply-held conviction of the real presence of Christ Himself within the sacramental celebration, such desecration is truly more horrendous than any offence within the purely human range, is in a different category of sin altogether. Nevertheless, the interplay of endorsement and implicit mockery of this belief, of serious outrage and irreverent fun, produces in the poem as a whole an ambivalence of attitude beyond mere parody; precisely a sense of 'an unconcluded dialogue between ideological attitudes' (Bakhtin) which the *reader* has to resolve. As Bakhtin remarked: 'The author participates in the novel (he is omnipresent in it) with almost no direct language of his own. The language of the novel is a *system* of languages that mutually and ideologically interanimate each other' (p. 47).

The same comment applies even more to 'Philip Sparrow', a marvellous 1400-line poem which falls clearly but intriguingly into two main sections and 'voices'. In the first 800 lines a young girl, Jane, laments her dead sparrow, killed by a convent cat. This first half has been generally praised for the vivid picturing of the bird itself; the structural device of linking its various sections according to patterned Latin phrases from the liturgical office for the dead; the magnificent curse upon cats uttered by Jane; the delightful idea, pursued in detail, of all the other birds performing the various liturgical roles in a mass for the dead sparrow. But, above all, readers have warmed to the persona of Jane herself, her näivety, her innocence, her adolescent half-learning, her genuine sorrow. By a delicate interweaving of naive emotional response and solemn liturgical resonance, a vivid presence is created, an audible voice, a palpable presence:

It had a velvet cap,
And wold syt upon my lap,
And seke after small wormes,
And somtyme white bred crommes;
And many tymes and ofte
Betwene my brestes softe
It wolde lye and rest—
It was propre and prest.
  Somtyme he wolde gaspe
Whan he sawe a waspe;
A fly, or a gnat,
He wolde flye at that;
And prytely he wolde pant
Whan he saw an ant;
Lord, how he wolde pry
After the butterfly!
Lorde, how he wolde hop
After the gressop!
And when I sayd, 'Phyp, Phyp,'
Than he wold lepe and skyp,
And take me by the lyp.
Alas, it wyll me slo,
That Phillyp is gone me fro!

Si in i qui ta tes
Alas, I was evyll at ease!
De pro fun dis cla ma vi,
Whan I sawe my sparowe dye!

(120–46)

The whole first part seems a gently sympathetic portrayal of the
young girl, touched lightly with humour and psychological insight.
The verse is simple, open, moving.

But a change comes in the second part. Jane finally tries to
compose an epitaph for her sparrow, not in 'Myne Englyssh halfe-
abused' but in 'Latyne playne and lyght', at which point a second
voice intervenes and takes over, that of 'laureate poet Skelton':

Flos volucrum formose, vale!	Flower of birds most beautiful, farewell!
Philippe, sub isto	Philip, beneath that
Marmore iam recubas,	Marble now you rest
Qui mihi carus eras.	Who to me was dear.
Semper erunt nitido	Always there will be
Radiantia sydera celo;	Radiant stars in the bright sky;

206

John Skelton

Impressusque meo	Always you will be
Pectore semper eris.	Imprinted on my heart.
Per me laurigerum	Through this laureated one
Britanum Skeltonida vatem	Brittanic Poet Skelton
Hec cecinisse licet	These made-up songs could sing
Ficta sub imagine texta.	By my imagining:
Cuius eris volucris,	She whose bird you were
Prestanti corpore virgo:	Is a maiden past compare:
Candida Nais erat,	Nympho was fair,
Formosior ista Joanna est:	This Jane's a stunner!
Docta Corinna fuit,	Corinna was clever,
Sed magis ista sapit.	But Jane's an all round winner!
Bien men souvient.	How well I remember:

(826–44)

The effect of these lines is to set up a whirligig of levels of reality: 'Jane' laments the dead bird while Skelton lauds the live girl. But the Jane who laments is a fiction of Skelton's (even if there *was* a real Jane) so the Jane he drools over is (for us at least) the product of his own imagination—as indeed is the sparrow so persuasively created for the reader in the fictional Jane's sorrow. By acknowledging the constructed character of the first part, the status of the second part is also thrown into question, since what follows is an apparently blasphemous appropriation of liturgical praise of the Virgin Mary to celebrate Skelton's patently lustful regard for the girl, And yet that persona is also signalled as playfully deliberate:

> Lorde, how I was payned!
> Unneth I me refrayned,
> How she me had reclaymed,
> And me to her retayned,
> Enbrasynge therewithall
> Her goodly myddell small
> With sydes longe and streyte;
> To tell you what conceyte
> I had than in a tryce,
> The matter were to nyse,
> And yet there was no vyce,
> Nor yet no vyllany,
> But only fantasy.

(1123–35)

> Her kertell so goodly lased,
> And under that is brased
> Such pleasures that I may
> Neyther wryte nor say;
> Yet though I wryte not with ynke,
> No man can let me thynke,
> For thought hath lyberte,
> Thought is franke and fre.
>
> (1194–1201)[8]

We are unavoidably drawn back to *apparently* naive and coyly innocent moments in Jane's own words, and recognise 'Skelton's leer behind them:

> For it wold come and go,
> And fly so to and fro;
> And on me it wolde lepe
> Whan I was aslepe,
> And his fethers shake,
> Wherewith he wolde make
> Me often for to wake
> And for to take him in
> Upon my nakyd skyn.
> God wot, we thought no syn—
> What though he crept so lowe?
> ... Phyllyp, though he were nyse,
> In him it was no vyse;
> ... Phyllyp myght be bolde
> And do what he wolde
>
> (159–78)

We can sense running through the poem an implicit wish-fulfilling identification of 'Skelton' with 'Philip' and a far from innocent knowingness both attributed to and denied of Jane. And when the whole poem ends with an 'addicyon' ostensibly rebutting 'Jane's own complaints about the bad taste of the poem, we recognise that this too may be a further manipulation of personae.

The double- (or triple)-voiced character of 'Philip Sparrow' should be apparent. Not only are different registers of language deployed (liturgical, rhetorical, erotic, elegaic) but the 'voice' that speaks the whole poem is that of a Skelton who superbly constructs a 'Skelton' who imagines a 'Jane' who conjures up a 'Philip' who is a substitute for 'Skelton' and each of these layers of persona has its appropriate tone, vocabulary and voice. And at work in it overall, as in 'Ware the Hawk', is a contradictory relation to religious attitudes, practices and norms, registered in the complex dialogisation of languages. Bakhtin again:

> Double-voiced discourse is always internally dialogized. Examples of this would be comic, ironic or parodic discourse, the refracting discourse of a narrator, refracting discourse in the language of a character and finally the discourse of a whole incorporated genre. . . . A potential dialogue is embedded . . ., one as yet unfolded, a concentrated dialogue of two voices, two world views, two languages. (p. 324)

Against Wolsey

Arguably, Skelton's most complex and brilliant poem is 'Speak, Parrot' which almost defies brief commentary and even defeats quotation. One stanza has already been quoted. Another sample:

> *Ic dien* serveth for the estrych fether,
> *Ic dien* is the language of the land of Beme;
> In Affryc tongue *byrsa* is a thonge of lether;
> In Palestina there is Jerusalem.
> *Collustrum* now for Parot, whyte bred and swete creme!
> Our Thomasen she doth trip, our Jenet she doth shayle;
> Parot hath a blacke beard and a fayre grene tayle.
> (78–84)

Much of the first third of the poem is writen like this. Some things, at least, are clear: the main speaker, being a parrot, chatters and chatters in various languages (since parrots have no linguistic nationality, or national loyalty). A parrot, of course, *merely* chatters; he doesn't *mean* anything of what he says, and he chatters in unconnected fragments, a kind of nonsense. But a parrot, in myth, is also a bird of paradise, speaking with the tongues of angels as well as speaking in tongues: he prophesies, speaks the real truth in veiled fashion. He is also immortal, so his historical memory is a long one: he can draw parallels with the present from even the more obscure of olden times. But he is also a ladies' pet, so he chatters for reward, for food, delicacies and affection, and the reward may mean more to him than the chatter—if the chatter means anything at all.

Yet every line of the quoted stanza does indeed make sense, and very specific sense. As various scholars have shown,[9] the poem constitutes a critical comment on Cardinal Wolsey's negotiations at the Calais conference in 1521. Wolsey was at this point Henry's most powerful minister and a major figure on the European scene, but his father had allegedly been a butcher, hence the references to 'colostrum' (the milk got at first calving) and 'leather'. 'Ich dien', 'I serve', was the royal motto, as the ostrich plume was the royal emblem, but (the poem suggests) the royal ostrich has put its head in the sand, not realising that the motto is becoming literally true: the King himself is serving, being manipulated by, the King's servant, Wolsey, who may well be serving the interests of Charles V, Emperor of 'Beme' (Bohemia), instead. 'In Affryc tongue *byrsa* is a thonge of lether': it is (in Renaissance lexicons) but in English usage 'burse', 'purse', means treasury; the 'Affryc' Queen, Dido, used the trick of measuring out land using a square yard of leather cut into narrow strips and laid end to end to claim more than was bargained for; Wolsey is milking the treasury by similarly dubious devices. And in 1518 he had negotiated yet another abortive treaty, committing England, France and Spain to a new crusade—but Jerusalem was still in the hands of the Turks.

Of course, this use of language *obscures* the attack embedded in it; it is almost indecipherable. Contemporary readers may have found it slightly clearer but I doubt whether *any* reader ever found this part of the poem lucid. And that is part of the point. The Parrot *wants* to speak (it is a regular refrain in the poem) but only if he can get away with it. And the temptation is not to speak at all, to retreat into a pampered security: paring his toenails and enjoying his own mythic virility:

> Parrot, Parrot, Parrot, praty popigay!
> With my beke I can pyke my lyttel praty too;
> My delyght is solas, pleasure, dysporte and pley;
> Lyke a wanton, whan I wyll, I rele to and froo.
> (106–9)

Yet the movement of the poem denies these options: eventually Parrot is forced to speak out. The middle part of the poem is a complex dialogue between Parrot and Galathea (the name, incidentally, of Pygmalion's statue which finally found its human voice). Each exchange is given a specific date within the poem

which apparently refers to the detailed stages of Wolsey's
negotiations between August and November,—and which remind
us of Bakhtin's remark that 'even languages of the day exist'. At
last, Galathea, by referring (still obscurely) to Wolsey's alleged
plan to make himself Pope, finally persuades Parrot:

> Nowe, Parott, my swete byrde, speke owte yet ons agayn,
> Sette asyde all sophysms, and speke now trew and playne.

There then follows, in a total shift of gear, a long, perfectly clear
and direct general satire on every aspect of the contemporary
scene:

> So many morall maters, and so lytell usyd;
> So myche newe makyng, and so madd tyme spente;
> So myche translacion into Englyshe confused;
> So myche nobyll prechyng, and so lytell amendment;
> So myche consultacion, almoste to none entente;
> So myche provision, and so lytell wytte at nede—
> Syns Dewcalyons flodde there can no clerkes rede.
>   (449–55)

Parrot has at last found courage to *speak*. After ten similar stanzas
the poem ends triumphantly:

> *Dixit*, quod Parrot
> *Crescet in immensem me vivo Psitacus iste.*
> *Hinc mea dicetur Skeltonidis inclita fama.*
>   *Quod Skelton Lawryat*
>   *Orator Regius*

But it is not quite as simple as that. The diatribe that ends the
poem is clear, lucid, intelligible, critical, angry—but it is general, a
traditional lament for the times, a well-written, forceful example
of an old genre. It therefore lacks all the specificity, the detailed
allusions to Wolsey, and to precise political manipulations and
occasions, that the first part included but obscured. As with 'Philip
Sparrow', we have to take both parts together, as indicating now
not just a deliberate ambivalence but a desperate problem. To
speak out 'plainly' against Wolsey at the very height of his
power—Cardinal Legate, Archbishop of York, Lord Chancellor,
intermediary between Kings, Emperors and Popes—would be

suicidal, and we are all partly cowards. Skelton will speak out against Wolsey and he will speak out plainly, but not both at the same time. And this is partly because it seems that his resources as a poet, the conventions available to him, can hardly allow him to. The 'general complaint' is a recognised genre; the obscure prophetic saying is an old political safety device. But how can he find a mode that combines the virtues of both, what *language* can he use?

Skelton's next poem, 'Collyn Clout', begins, in effect, with these problems:

> What can it avayle ...
> To ryme or to rayle,
> To wryte or to indyte,
> Other for delyte
> Or elles for despyte?
> Or bokes to compyle
> Of dyvers maner style,
> Vyce to revyle
> And synne to exyle? ...
> Or yf he speke playne,
> Than he lacketh brayne:
> 'He is but a foole,
> Let hym go to scole!'
> (1–29)

'Colin Clout' finally adopts a far simpler and more direct language and style than the first part of 'Speke, Parrot', while being more detailed and specific than the second part. It depicts the various failings of the different social classes or 'degrees': the lack of learning, piety and responsibility in the clergy, the lack of authority in the nobility, the abdication of responsibility by the King. But where the style is simple, the structure of the poem and its political tactics are relatively sophisticated. Again, there is a persona, Colin Clout, lowly but honest, almost a peasant, one of a long line of spokesmen for the common man. Skelton uses Colin precisely as a *reporter* of other men's complaints. Colin endlessly reports 'what men say',—what the clergy say about the laity, what the laity say about the clergy, what they both say about the general state of society, for which the King is ultimately responsible. It is a useful tactic, since each kind of critic can be used to belabour someone else, but is in turn criticised: his opinions are endorsed, implicitly, but his own actions judged, while Colin himself can escape censure since he offers himself as merely relating these criticisms in order for them to be refuted. But, of course, the device is also a transparent one, and since so many of these 1300 lines of barbed and bitter 'reportage' could certainly have a particular application to Wolsey himself, Skelton could have been under no illusion as to the possible reaction—and he boldly includes that reaction within the poem itself, in the very tones of Wolsey's alleged behaviour in Star Chamber proceedings:

> 'How darest thou, daucocke, mell?
> Howe darest thou, losell,
> Allygate the gospell
> Agaynst us of the counsell?
> Avaunt to the devyll of hell!
>
> Take him, wardeyn of the Flete,
> Set hym fast by the fete!
> I say, lieutenaunt of the Toure,
> Make this lurdeyne for to loure;
> Lodge hym in Lytell Ease,
> Fede hym with beanes and pease!
> The Kynges Benche or Marshalsy,
> Have hym thyder by and by!
> The vyllayne preceth openly
> And declareth our vyllany.'
>   (1160–74)

The poem ends on a note of sad defiance:

> *Ah, pudet! Ah, miseret! Vetor hic ego pandere plura*
> *Pro gemitu et lacrimis; prestet peto premia pena.*
> [It's shameful! It's deplorable! I have to desist from disclosing more now Because of my groans and my tears; I pray the prize will outweigh the penalty.]

With astonishing courage, Skelton did not stop there. In another lengthy attack he abandoned all personae and simply launched himself on Wolsey. 'Why Come Ye Nat to Courte?' maintains at first a play of voices. The question in the title is repeated and ambiguously addressed (to the poet; to the nobles appealed to in the opening lines; to the reader), and various responses, excuses and explanations are given. The questioning voice seeks out gossip about Court figures who are ducking their responsibilities, and news about contemporary events and scandals. But finally, the responding voice bursts out of this framework of prevarication and procrastination:

> Ones yet agayne
> Of you I wolde frayne
> Why come ye nat to court?
>
> To whyche court?
> To the kynges courte?
> Or to Hampton Court*
>
> Nay, to the kynges court!
> The kynges courte
> Shulde have the excellence;
> But Hampton Court
> Hath the preemynence!
> And Yorkes Place,
> With, 'My lordes grace',
> To whose magnifycence
> Is all the conflewence,
> Sutys, and supplycacyons,
> Embassades of all nacyons.
> Strawe for lawe canon,
> Or for lawe common,
> Or for lawe cyvyll;
> It shall be as he wyll.
>
> (399–419)

Almost as if he were conducting another 'flyting' and Wolsey merely another greasy Garnesche—but this time in deadly and dangerous earnest—Skelton piles up accusations for nearly 1000 lines. A sample:

> So he dothe undermynde
> And suche sleyghtes dothe fynde,
> That the kynges mynde
> By him is subverted
>
> (437–40)

*Wolsey's palace since 1515

To tell the trouth playnly,
He is so ambicyous,
So shamles and so vicyous,
And so supersticyous,
And so moche oblivyous
From whens that he came,
That he falleth into *Acidiam*,
Whiche truly to expresse,
Is a forgetfulnesse,
Or wylfull blyndnesse,
Wherwith the Sodomites
Lost theyr inward syghtes.
                              (460–71)

                    now the same
Cardynall is promoted,
Yet with lewde condicyons cotyd
As herafter ben notyd:
Presumcyon and vayne glory,
Envy, wrath, and lechery,
Covetys and glotony;
Slouthfull to do good,
Now frantick, now starke wode!
Shulde this man of suche mode
Rule the swerde of myght?
                              (570–80)

Yet whan he toke first his hat,
He said he knew what was what.
All justyce he pretended:
All thynges sholde be amended,
All wronges he wolde redresse,
All injuris he wolde represse,
All perjuris he wolde oppresse.
And yet, this gracelesse elfe,
He is perjured himselfe.
                              (1108–16)

The poem concludes with an 'Apostrophe to the citizens of London':

Excitat, en, asinus mulum, mirabile visu,
Calcibus! O vestro cives occurite asselo
Qui regnum regemque regit, qui vestra gubernat

215

Predia, divitias, nummos, gasas, spoliando!
[Look! the ass arouses the mule—a marvel to see—
With his heels! Citizens! rise against your little ass
Who rules kingdom and king, who lords it over
Your lands, your wealth, your cash, your treasures
—by sheer plunder!]

Skelton was eventually reconciled with Wolsey, and they found a common enemy in the emergent Lutheran heresies—'A Replycacion' is humbly dedicated to the Cardinal—but it is not surprising that Skelton was long reputed to have spent his final years in sanctuary.

Bakhtin, Stalin and Skelton

This essay has been partly shaped by reference to Bakhtin's notion of the dialogic 'novel', but Skelton's work could, obviously, be approached within several other frameworks. The elucidatory tools and preoccupations of traditional literary scholarship provide an indispensable aid to the comprehension of much of his work, as well as the necessary clarification of his biography, the canon of his poetry, and the generic conventions he utilised.[10] From a quite different perspective, it is relatively easy to imagine a 'deconstructionist' reading of at least some of his work. An intriguing temptation along such lines would be provided by the enigmatic marginal glosses (of deliciously uncertain authorial status) found alongside some poems, and reproduced in Dyce's 1843 edition. An important context in which to locate Skelton would be the transition from a manuscript culture to a print culture, as Caxton's tribute indicates.[11] It would be possible to incorporate such a context within a more extended 'Bakhtinian' reading, elaborating also Skelton's relation to rhetoric, to the tension between aureate and plain diction, to the 'New Learning' and the Grammarians' War (important concerns in 'Speke, Parrot'). A rather different Bakhtinian reading might be developed, indebted more to his book on Rabelais and exploring Skelton's possible relation to a popular cultural ethos: the grotesque realism of 'Elynour Rummynge' or even the tradition of 'Merry Tales' strongly associated with Skelton (which bedevilled earlier biographers) might be central here. Yet this essay has not sought to impose or elaborate any tightly systematic application of Bakhtin. Why, then, for an essay in this volume, the deliberate choice of Bakhtin as a partner in dialogue with Skelton? An answer might begin with Bakhtin's own insistence upon considering actual utterances in social situations (cf. p. 292). For it is surely obvious that Bakhtin's own work has a hidden agenda, legible in the light of events in the Soviet Union in the late 1920s and 1930s. Bakhtin's emphasis upon the diversity and fruitful interanimation of national and cultural languages opposes the drive towards Great Russian hegemony; his recognition of ramified social complexity, of the multitude of coexistent 'socio-ideological groups' and their variable contradictions, problematises any easily reductive and prematurely schematic class analysis; his own polyphonic personae (as himself, as 'Volosinov', as 'Medvedev') and the double-focused intent of his cultural analyses are, at one level, a tactical response to the difficulties and dangers of 'living in a time of translation'. It is worth recalling that Stalin joined the first Soviet government as Commissar for Nationalities in 1918 (and quickly abandoned the principles of his own 1913 pamphlet *Marxism and the Nationalities*) while almost his last substantial publication was *Concerning Marxism in Linguistics* (1950), in which he anticipated a single world language. For Bakhtin, perhaps, all the emphases of his analyses—from the tensions of trilingualism to the conflict between carnival and centralisation—were unified by an 'impulse' against Stalinism, and his own tactics of survival reproduced some of the devices he charted. Meanwhile, his great literary contemporary, Mandelstam, died in a labour camp for directly addressing Stalin as a 'murderer' in an unpublished poem.

If, now, we think of Skelton, one contrast is clear enough. Whatever the truth of Skelton's depiction of Wolsey, he obviously saw himself confronting an overweening centralisation of all power in one man, an illegitimate absolutism on an awesome scale,[12] and, finally, abandoning the protection of veiled, allusive, cryptic 'double-voiced' criticism, he attacked in the plainest possible terms. It is worth, in conclusion, comparing two quotations. Bakhtin wrote, in 1934–35:

In Rabelais ... a parodic attitude toward almost all forms of ideological discourse—philosophical, moral, scholarly, rhetorical, poetic and in particular the pathos-charged forms of discourse (in Rabelais, pathos almost always is equivalent to lie)—was intensified to the point where it became a parody of the very act of conceptualising anything in language ... Rabelais taunts the deceptive human word by a parodic destruction of syntactic structures, thereby reducing to absurdity some of the logical and expressively accented aspects of words (for example, predication, explanations, and so forth). Turning away from language (by means of language, of course), discrediting any direct or unmediated intentionality and expressive excess (any "weighty" seriousness) ... presuming that all language is conventional and false, maliciously inadequate to reality—all this achieves in Rabelais almost the maximum purity in prose. But the truth that might oppose such falsity receives almost no direct intentional and verbal expression in Rabelais, it does not receive its *own* word—it reverberates only in the parodic and unmasking accents in which the lie is present. (p. 309)

The passage, characteristically, hovers between praise and critique. Bakhtin's descriptions of dialogical polyphony invariably appear to imply an evaluative endorsement—and, in his own context, perhaps rightly so. But much of today's depoliticised concern with polyphonic, elliptical, allusive, multilayered textuality, with instant deconstruction of all attempts at predication and explanation, runs the risk of undervaluing and even dismissing other priorities and, sometimes, necessities. A re-reading of Skelton which simply, and enjoyably, rediscovers 'Speke, Parrot' as an admirable precursor of *The Waste Land* or *Finnegans Wake* may easily ignore 'Why Come Ye Nat to Courte?' and the affirmation of a writer's responsibility which underpins it. Skelton's own poetic credo is formulated in theological terms we need not subscribe to, but the 'impulse' of his impassioned declaration ought at least to (re-)enter the current dialogue:

> We are kyndled in suche facyon
> With hete of the Holy Gost,
> Which is God of myghtes most,
> That he our penne dothe lede,
> And maketh in us suche spede
> That forthwith we must nede
> With penne and ynke procede,
> Somtyme for affection,
> Sometyme for sadde dyrection,
> Somtyme for correction,

John Skelton

Somtyme under protection
Of pacient sufferance,
With sobre cyrcumstance,
Our myndes to avaunce
To no mannes anoyance.
Therfore no grevance,
I pray you, for to take,
In this that I do make
Agaynst these frenetykes,
Agaynst these lunatykes,
Agaynst these sysmatykes,
Agaynst these heretykes,
Now of late abjured,
Most unhappely ured;
For be ye wele assured,
That frensy nor jelousy
Nor heresy wyll never dye.
Sunt infiniti, sunt innumerique sophiste,
Sunt infiniti, sunt innumerique logiste,
Innumeri sunt philosophi, sunt theologique,
Sunt infiniti doctores, suntque magistri
Innumeri; sed sunt pauci rarique poete.
(*A Replycacion*, 382 ff.)

'But poets are few and rare.' Milton and Marvell, for example, would have agreed—both plain-speaking 'Puritans' who could also practise a veiled allusiveness when it seemed necessary. In our own context, of course, the heresies and dogmatism, the frenzies and fanaticism, the centralising tendencies of arrogant power and blind wilfulness, may all be different from those Skelton or Bakhtin confronted; but faced with a modern Wolsey we might be glad of another Skelton.

Perhaps, though, we should give the final word—as if on Skelton, but also in simultaneous homage—to Bakhtin:

The word, breaking through to its own meaning and its own expression across an environment full of alien words and variously evaluating accents, harmonizing with some of the elements in this environment and striking a dissonance with others, is able, in this dialogized process, to shape its own stylistic profile and tone. (p. 277)

Notes

1. In a note to his 'Imitations of Horace', included in Edwards (1981), p. 75.
2. Edited by John Scattergood (1983). All quotations from Skelton's poems are from this edition, following Scattergood's text, except for my own translations from Latin. There is a modernised edition of the poems by Philip Henderson (revd edn, 1948); the first modern edition was that of Alexander Dyce in 1843.
3. Cf. Roger Bacon, *Compendium studii philosophiae*, quoted in Salter (1983), pp. 26, 186; and William Turner, *The Sum of Divinitie* ... (1548), quoted in Jones (1953), p. 99.
4. For Skelton's 'first' usages, cf. Skelton (1957), vol II., pp. xxxii-xxxiii; and Salter (1946), pp. 119-217. For the general history cf. e.g. Leith (1983), chs 1 and 2.
5. Bakhtin's main works available in translation are *Problems of Dostoievsky's Poetics* (1929; 1963); *Rabelais and his World* (1965); and *The Dialogical Imagination*, essays edited by Michael Holquist. Quotations from Bakhtin in this essay are taken from *The Dialogical Imagination*, to which page references are given. Cf. Todorov (1984) and Clark and Holquist (1984) for the debate on Bakhtin's possible authorship of works published under the names Voloshinov and Medvedev.
6. For biographical information on Skelton, cf. Nelson (1939); Gordon (1943); Edwards (1949); Pollet (1971).
7. The play is included in Happé (1979), and there is a critical edition by Neuss (1980). Cf. also Harris (1965).
8. A nice instance of Skelton's playing with the rhetorical tradition; his model and target here is Geoffrey de Vinsauf's *Poetria Nova* (*c.*1210).
9. Cf. works cited in note 6 above, and Brownlow (1971).
10. Cf. e.g. Fishman (1971), for a recent survey; Kinsman and Yonge (1967); Heiserman (1961).
11. For the general context, see. e.g. Chaytor (1945); Febvre and Martin (1958); Blake (1969); Eisenstein (1979). It would, obviously, be interesting to investigate the mode of distribution and extent of circulation of Skelton's anti-Wolsey writings.
12. For Wolsey, cf. e.g. Cavendish (1558); Pollard (1929); and Ferguson (1958). Also relevant are Russell (1969); Guy (1977); Green (1980).

John Skelton

References.

Aurner, N.S. (1965) *Caxton: Mirror of Fifteenth-Century Letters* (New York: Russell & Russell).

Bakhtin, M. M. (1981) *The Dialogical Imagination: Four Essays*, ed. Michael Holquist (Austin: University of Texas Press).

Blake, N. F. (1969) *Caxton and his World* (London: André Deutsch).

Brownlow, F. M. (1971) 'The Book compiled by Maister Skelton, Poet Laureate, called *Speake, Parrot'*, *English Literary Renaissance*, I, pp. 3–26.

Cavendish, George (1558) *The Life and Death of Cardinal Wolsey*, in *Two Early Tudor Lives*, ed. R. S. Sylvester and D. P. Harding (New Haven: Yale University Press; reprt. 1962).

Chaytor, H. J. (1945) *From Script to Print* (London: Sidgwick and Jackson; reprt. 1966).

Clark, K. and Holquist, M. (1984) *Mikhail Bakhtin* (Cambridge, Mass.: Harvard University Press).

Edwards, A. S .G. (ed.) (1981) *Skelton: The Critical Heritage* (London: Routledge & Kegan Paul).

Edwards, H. L. R. (1949) *Skelton: The Life and Times of an Early Tudor Poet* (London: Jonathan Cape).

Eisenstein, E. (1979) *The Printing Press as Agent of Change* (Cambridge: Cambridge University Press).

Febvre, L. and Martin, H.-J. (1958) *The Coming of the Book* (London: New Left Books: reprt. 1976).

Ferguson, C. W. (1958) *Naked to Mine Enemies* (Toronto: Little, Brown).

Fish S. E. (1965) *John Skelton's Poetry* (New Haven: Yale University Press).

Fishman, B. (1971) 'Recent Studies in Skelton', *English Literary Renaissance*, I, pp. 89–96.

Gordon, I. A. (1943) *John Skelton: Poet Laureate* (Melbourne University Press).

Green, R. F. (1980) *Poets and Princepleasers* (Toronto: University of Toronto Press).

Guy, J. A. (1977) *The Cardinal's Court* (Brighton: Harvester).

Happé, P. (ed.) (1979) *Four Morality Plays* (Harmondsworth: Penguin Books).

Harris, W. O. (1965) *Skelton's Magnyfycence and the Cardinal Virtue Tradition* (Chapel Hill: University of North Carolina Press).

Heiserman, A. R. (1961) *Skelton and Satire* (Chicago: University of Chicago Press).

Jones R. F. (1953) *The Triumph of the English Language* (Stanford University Press).

221

Kamin, L. (1974) *The Science and Politics of I.Q.* (Hillsdale: Erlbaum)

Kinsman, R. S. and Yonge, T. (1967) *John Skelton: Canon and Census* (Renaissance Society of America, Bibliographies and Indexes no. 4).

Leith R. (1983) *A Social History of English*. (London: Routledge & Kegan Paul).

Mason, H. A. (1959) *Humanism and Poetry in the Early Tudor Period* (London: Routledge & Kegan Paul).

Nelson, W. (1939) *John Skelton, Laureate* (rprt. New York: Russell & Russell, 1964).

Neuss, P. (ed.) (1980) *John Skelton: Magnificence* (Manchester: Manchester University Press).

Pollet, M. (1962) *John Skelton: Poet of Tudor England* (London: Dent; rprt. 1971).

Russell, J. G. (1969) *The Field of Cloth of Gold* (London: Routledge & Kegan Paul).

Salter, E. (1983) *Fourteenth-Century English Poetry* (London: Oxford University Press).

Salter, F. M. (1946) 'Skelton's Contribution to the English Language', *Transactions of the Royal Society of Canada*, XXXIX, section 2, pp. 119–217.

Skelton, J. (1957) *The Bibliotheca Historica of Diodorus Siculus translated by John Skelton*, ed. F. M. Salter and H. L. R. Edwards (Early English Text Society, Oxford University Press).

Skelton, J. (1983) *The Complete English Poems*, ed. J. Scattergood (Harmondsworth: Penguin Books).

Todorov, T. (1984 *Mikhail Bakhtin: The Dialogical Principle* (Manchester: Manchester University Press).

Index